Lecture Notes in Computer Scie

T0238327

Commenced Publication in 1973
Founding and Former Series Editors:
Gerhard Goos, Juris Hartmanis, and Jan van Leeuwen

Nicolas Guelfi   Didier Buchs (Eds.)

Rapid Integration of Software Engineering Techniques

Third International Workshop, RISE 2006
Geneva, Switzerland, September 13-15, 2006
Revised Selected Papers

 Springer

Volume Editors

Nicolas Guelfi
University of Luxembourg
6, rue Richard Coudenhove-Kalergi
1359 Luxembourg, Luxembourg
E-mail: nicolas.guelfi@uni.lu

Didier Buchs
University of Geneva
Computer Science Department
24, rue du Général-Dufour
1211 Geneva 4, Switzerland
E-mail: didier.buchs@cui.unige.ch

Library of Congress Control Number: 2007923956

CR Subject Classification (1998): D.2, F.3, K.6.1, K.6.3

LNCS Sublibrary: SL 2 – Programming and Software Engineering

ISSN   0302-9743
ISBN-10   3-540-71875-3 Springer Berlin Heidelberg New York
ISBN-13   978-3-540-71875-8 Springer Berlin Heidelberg New York

Springer is a part of Springer Science+Business Media

springer.com

© Springer-Verlag Berlin Heidelberg 2007
Printed in Germany

Typesetting: Camera-ready by author, data conversion by Scientific Publishing Services, Chennai, India
Printed on acid-free paper   SPIN: 12045778   06/3180   5 4 3 2 1 0

Preface

RISE 2006 constituted an international forum for researchers and practitioners interested in the advancement and rapid application of novel, integrated, or practical software engineering approaches, being part of a methodological framework, that apply to the development of either new or evolving applications and systems. It provided a good opportunity to present and discuss the latest research results and ideas in the rapid and effective integration of software engineering techniques. The ERCIM (European Research Consortium for Informatics and Mathematics) RISE working group selected application areas such as the Web, mobility, high availability, and embedded and user-interface software in specific industry sectors comprising finance, telecommunications, transportation (avionics, automotive) and eGovernment. The research issues covered stemmed from the following software engineering domains:

- software and system architectures
- software reuse
- software testing
- software model checking
- model driven design and testing techniques
- model transformation
- requirements engineering
- lightweight or practice-oriented formal methods
- software processes and software metrics
- automated software engineering
- software patterns
- design by contract
- defensive programming
- software entropy and software re-factoring
- extreme programming
- agile software development
- programming languages
- software dependability and trustworthiness

All papers submitted to this workshop were reviewed by at least two members of the International Program Committee. Acceptance was based primarily on originality and contribution. We have selected, for these proceedings, 10 papers amongst 30 submitted and an invited paper. The organization of such a workshop requires a lot of work. We would like to acknowledge the efforts of the Program Committee members, the additional referees, the organization committee members, the scientific and technical staff of the University of Geneva, including the Centre Universitaire d'Informatique, and of the University of Luxembourg, Faculty of Science, Technology and Communication department.

RISE 2006 was supported by ERCIM, European Research Consortium for Informatics and Mathematics, the "Ministère de l'enseignement supérieur et de la recherche" and by the "Fond National pour la Recherche au Luxembourg".

September 2006   Nicolas Guelfi and Didier Buchs

Organization

RISE 2006 was organized by the University of Geneva, Software Modeling and Verification Group.

Program Chairs

Guelfi, Nicolas   University of Luxembourg, Luxembourg
Buchs, Didier   University of Geneva, Switzerland

International Program Committee

Arve Aagesen, Finn   NTNU, Norway
Avgeriou, Paris   University of Groningen, The Netherlands
Bertolino, Antonia   CNR-ISTI, Italy
Bicarregui, Juan   CCLRC, uk
Bolognesi, Tommaso   CNR-ISTI, Italy
Born, Marc   Fraunhofer FOKUS, Germany
Buchs, Didier   SARIT, University of Geneva, Switzerland
Carrez, Cyril   NTNU, Norway
Dony, Christophe   LIRMM, University of Montpellier, France
Dubois, Eric   CRP Henri-Tudor, Luxembourg
Guelfi, Nicolas   FNR, University of Luxembourg, Luxembourg
Haajanen, Jyrki   VTT, Finland
Issarny, Valérie   INRIA, France
Klint, Paul   CWI, The Netherlands
Moeller, Eckhard   Fraunhofer FOKUS, Germany
Mistrik, Ivan   Fraunhofer IPSI IM, Germany
Monostori, Laszlo   SZTAKI, Hungary
Nawrocki, Jerzy   Poznan University of Technology, Poland
Pimentel, Ernesto   SpaRCIM, University of Malaga, Spain
Romanovsky, Alexander   DCS, University of Newcastle, UK
Reggio Gianna, ISI   Genoa, Italy
Savidis, Anthony   FORTH, Greece
Schieferdecker, Ina   Fraunhofer FOKUS, Germany

Organizing Committee

Buchs, Didier   University of Geneva
Pedro, Luis   University of Geneva
Bertossa, Catia   University of Geneva
Gusthiot, Germaine   University of Geneva

Sponsoring Institutions

  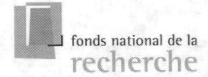

This workshop was supported by the ERCIM, the "Ministère de l'enseignement supérieur et de la recherche" and by the "Fond National pour la Recherche au Luxembourg".

Table of Contents

Invited Paper

Graphical Composition of Grid Services

Kenneth J. Turner and Koon Leai Larry Tan

Computing Science and Mathematics, University of Stirling, Scotland FK9 4LA
kjt@cs.stir.ac.uk, klt@cs.stir.ac.uk

Abstract. Grid services and web services have similarities but also significant differences. Although conceived for web services, it is seen how BPEL (Business Process Execution Logic) can be used to orchestrate a collection of grid services. It is explained how CRESS (Chisel Representation Employing Systematic Specification) has been extended to describe grid service composition. The CRESS descriptions are automatically converted into BPEL/WSDL code for practical realisation of the composed services. This achieves orchestration of grid services deployed using the widely used Globus Toolkit and ActiveBPEL interpreter. The same CRESS descriptions are automatically translated into LOTOS, allowing systematic checks for interoperability and logical errors prior to implementation.

1 Introduction

1.1 Motivation

This paper presents a unique blend of ideas from different technical areas: distributed computing, software engineering, service-oriented architecture, and formal methods. Grid computing has emerged as a leading form of distributed computing. However, grid computing has largely focused on the development of isolated applications. Service-oriented architecture provides a framework for combining grid services into new ones.

The emphasis of this paper is on integrating software engineering techniques (visual programming, formal methods) into an evolving application area of considerable importance (grid computing). The aim has been to achieve immediate and practical benefits from advanced software techniques. Grid computing is a comparatively new field that has so far focused mainly on pragmatic, programmatic aspects. The work presented here offers a number of advantages:

- As with component-based approaches, grid services are combined into new composite services using BPEL as an emerging standard for web services.
- Grid service composition is described graphically, making it comprehensible to less technical users. Compared to the automatically generated code, the approach is compact and much more attractive than writing the raw XML that underlies it.
- A sound technique has been defined, benefiting from formal methods behind the scenes yet supporting automated implementation.

The approach is therefore application-driven (orchestrating grid services), novel (combining practice and theory), practical (automated implementation and validation), and integrated (complementing existing grid practice).

N. Guelfi and D. Buchs (Eds.): RISE 2006, LNCS 4401, pp. 1–17, 2007.

1.2 Background to Grid Computing

Grid computing is named by analogy with the electrical power grid. Just as power stations are linked into a universal electrical supply, so computational resources can be linked into a computing grid. Distributed computing is hardly a new area. But the architecture and software technologies behind the grid have captured the attention of those who perform large-scale computing, e.g. in the sciences. Grid computing offers a number of distinctive advantages that include:

- support for virtual organisations that transcend conventional boundaries, and may come together only for a particular task
- portals that provide ready access to grid-enabled resources
- single sign-on, whereby an authenticated user can make use of distributed resources such as data repositories or computational servers
- security, including flexible mechanisms for delegating credentials to third parties to act on behalf of the user
- distributed and parallel computing.

Grid computing is governed by OGSA (Open Grid Services Architecture [8]). Open standards for the grid are being created by the GGF (Global Grid Forum). Grid applications often make themselves available via services that are comparable to web services – another area of vigorous development. For a time, grid services and web services did not share compatible standards. The major issue was the need for stateful services that have persistent state. A grid-specific solution to this was developed. However, this was clearly something that web services could also benefit from.

A harmonised solution was defined in the form of WSRF (Web Services Resource Framework [10]). This is a collection of interrelated standards such as WS-Resource and WS-ResourceProperties. WSRF is implemented by various toolsets for grid computing such as GT4 (Globus Toolkit version 4, *www.globus.org*).

1.3 Background to Service Orchestration

This paper emphasises the *composition* of grid services, not the description of *isolated* grid services. Composing services has attracted considerable industrial interest. This is achieved by defining a *business process* that captures the logic of how the individual services are combined. The term *orchestration* is also used for this. A nice feature of the approach is that a composed service acts as a service in its own right.

Competing solutions were originally developed for orchestrating web services. A major advance was the multi-company specification for BPEL4WS (Business Process Execution Language for Web Services [1]), which is being standardised as WS-BPEL (Web Services Business Process Execution Language [2]). BPEL is now relatively well established as the way of composing web services. However, its use for composing grid services has received only limited attention. The work reported in this paper has used ActiveBPEL (an open-source BPEL interpreter, *www.activebpel.org*).

1.4 Background to CRESS

CRESS (Communication Representation Employing Structured Specification) was developed as a general-purpose graphical notation for services. Essentially, CRESS describes the flow of actions in a service. It thus lends itself to describing flows that combine grid services.

CRESS has been used to specify and analyse voice services from the Intelligent Network, Internet Telephony, and Interactive Voice Response. It has also been used to orchestrate web services [19]. In the new work reported here, CRESS has been extended to the composition of grid services. The present paper discusses how the same approach can be used for practical but formally-assisted development of grid services. Formally-based investigation of composite grid services will be reported in a future paper.

The work reported in this paper has been undertaken in the context of the GEODE project (Grid Enabled Occupational Data Environment, *www.geode.stir.ac.uk*). This project is researching the use of grid computing in social science, specifically grid services for occupational data analysis. The authors have investigated how services from this domain can be composed, formalised and rigorously analysed.

Service descriptions in CRESS are graphical and accessible to non-specialists. A major gain is that descriptions are automatically translated into implementation languages for deployment, and also into formal languages for analysis. CRESS offers benefits of comprehensibility, portability, automated implementation and rigorous analysis.

CRESS is extensible, with plug-in modules for application domains and target languages. Although web service support had already been developed for CRESS, it has been necessary to extend this significantly for use with grid services. In addition, grid services have specialised characteristics that require corresponding support in CRESS.

CRESS is intended as part of a formally-based method for developing services. In the context of grid computing, the steps are as follows:

- The desired composition of grid services is first described using CRESS. This gives a high-level overview of the service interrelationships. Because the description is graphical, it is relatively accessible even to non-specialists.
- The CRESS descriptions are then automatically translated into a formal language. CRESS supports standardised formal languages such as LOTOS (Language Of Temporal Ordering Specification [11]) and SDL (Specification and Description Language [12]), though this paper uses only LOTOS. Obtaining a formal specification of a composite service is useful in its own right: it gives precise meaning to the services and their combination.
- Although CRESS creates an outline formal specification for each of the partner services being combined, it defines just their basic functionality. This is sufficient to check basic properties such as interoperability. However for a fuller check of composite functionality, a more realistic specification is required of each partner. This allows a rigorous analysis to be performed prior to implementation.
- A competent designer can be expected to produce a satisfactory service implementation. However, combining services often leads to unexpected problems. The services may not have been designed to work together, and may not interoperate properly. The issues may range from the coarse (e.g. a disagreement over the interface) to the subtle (e.g. interference due to resource competition). This is akin to the feature interaction problem in telephony, whereby independently designed features may conflict with each other. CRESS supports the rigorous evaluation of composite services. Problems may need to be corrected in either the CRESS descriptions or in

the partner specifications. Several iterations may be required before the designer is satisfied that the composite grid service meets its requirements.
- The CRESS descriptions are then automatically translated into an implementation language. The interface to each service is defined by the generated WSDL (Web Services Description Language [22]). The orchestration of the services is defined by the generated BPEL. The partner implementations must be created independently, hopefully using the formal specifications already written. However, CRESS can generate outline code that is then completed by the implementer. This avoids simple causes of errors such as failing to respect the service interface.

1.5   Relationship to Other Work

As noted already, orchestration of web services has been well received in industry. Scientific workflow modelling has been studied by a number of projects. The MyGrid project has given an overview of these (*http://phoebus.cs.man.ac.uk/twiki/bin/view/Mygrid*). Only some of the better known workflow languages are mentioned below.

JOpera [16] was conceived mainly for orchestrating web services, though its applicability for grid services has also been investigated. JOpera claims greater flexibility and convenience than BPEL. Taverna [15] was also developed for web services, particularly for coordinating workflows in bioinformatics research. The underlying language SCUFL (Simple Conceptual Unified Flow Language) is intended to be multi-purpose, including applications in grid computing.

CRESS is designed for modelling composite services, but was not conceived as a workflow language. CRESS serves this role only when orchestrating grid or web services; its use in other domains is rather different. An important point is that CRESS focuses on generating code in standard languages. For service orchestration, this means BPEL/WSDL. This allows CRESS to exploit industrially relevant developments.

Several researchers have used BPEL to compose grid services. [5] describes a graphical plug-in for Eclipse that allows BPEL service compositions to be generated automatically. This work is notable for dealing with large-scale scientific applications. [3] discusses programmatic ways in which BPEL can support grid computing. [18] examines how extensibility mechanisms in BPEL can be used to orchestrate grid services. However, the focus of such work is pragmatic. For example, grid services may be given a web service wrapping for compatibility. (Semi-)automated methods of composing grid services have been investigated, e.g. work on adapting ideas from the semantic web [14].

An important advantage of CRESS is that practical development is combined with a formal underpinning. Specifically, the same CRESS descriptions are used to derive implementations as well as formal specifications. The formalisation permits rigorous analysis through verification and validation. A number of approaches have been developed by others for formalising *web* services. However, the authors are unaware of any published work on formal methods for composing *grid* services.

As an example of finite state methods for web services, LTSA-WS (Labelled Transition System Analyzer for Web Services [7]) allows composed web services to be described in a BPEL-like manner. Service compositions and workflow descriptions are automatically checked for safety and liveness properties. WSAT (Web Service Analysis Tool [9]) models the interactions of composite web services in terms of the global sequences of message they exchange. For verification, these models are translated into Promela and verified with SPIN. The ORC (Orchestration) language has also been used to model the orchestration of web services. [17] discusses its translation into coloured Petri nets. Both this and the alternative translation into Promela support formal analysis of composed web services. CRESS, however, is a multi-purpose approach that works with many kinds of services and with many target languages.

As an example of process algebraic methods for web services, automated translation between BPEL and LOTOS has been developed [4,6]. This has been used to specify, analyse and implement a stock management system and a negotiation service. CRESS differs from this work in using more abstract descriptions that are translated *into* BPEL and LOTOS; there is no interconversion among these representations. CRESS descriptions are language-independent, and can thus be used to create specifications in other formal languages (e.g. SDL). CRESS also offers a graphical notation that is more comprehensible to the non-specialist. This is important since service development often involves non-computer scientists as well as technical experts.

The CRESS notation has been previously been described in other papers. More recently, [19] has shown how web services can be modelled by CRESS. Since grid services are similar, but certainly not the same, this paper focuses on the advances that have been necessary to model and analyse the composition of grid services.

2   Describing Composite Grid Services with CRESS

CRESS is a general-purpose notation for describing services. Figure 1 shows the subset of constructs needed in this paper for grid services; CRESS supports more than this.

2.1   CRESS Notation for Grid Services

External services are considered to be *partners*. They offer their services at *ports* where *operations* may be performed. Invoking a service may give rise to a *fault*.

A CRESS diagram shows the flow among activities, drawn as ellipses. Look ahead to figures 2 and 3 for examples of CRESS diagrams. Each activity has a number, an action and some parameters. Arcs between ellipses shown the flow of behaviour. Note that CRESS defines flows and not a state machine; state is implicit.

Normally a branch means an alternative, but following a **Fork** activity it means a parallel path. An arc may be labelled with a value guard or an event guard to control whether it is traversed. If a value guard holds, behaviour may follow that path. An event guard defines a possible path that is enabled only once the corresponding event occurs.

In CRESS, operation names have the form *partner.port.operation*. Fault names have the form *fault.variable*, the fault name or variable being optional.

A CRESS rule-box, drawn as a rounded rectangle, defines variables and subsidiary diagrams (among other things). Simple variables have types like **Float** *f* or **String** *s*. CRESS also supports grid computing types such as **Certificate** (a digital security certificate), **Name** (a qualified name) and **Reference** (an endpoint reference that characterises a service instance and its associated resources).

CRESS	Meaning
/ *variable* <− *value*	assignment associated with a node or an arc
Catch *fault*	A handler for the specified fault. A fault with name and value requires a matching **Catch** name and variable type. A fault with only a value requires a matching **Catch** variable type. A fault is considered by the current scope and progressively higher-level scopes until a matching handler is found.
Compensate *scope*?	Called after a fault to undo work. Giving no scope means compensation handlers execute in reverse order of being enabled.
Compensation	A handler that defines how to undo work after a fault. A compensation handler is enabled only once the corresponding activity completes successfully. When executed, it expects to see the same process state as when it was enabled.
Fork *strictness*?	Used to introduce parallel paths; further forks may be nested to any depth. Normally, failure to complete parallel paths as expected leads to a fault. This is strict parallelism (**strict**, the default). Matched by **Join**.
Join *condition*?	Ends parallel paths. An explicit join condition may be defined over the termination status of parallel activities. This gives the node numbers of immediately prior activities, e.g. '1 && 2' means these (and the prior ones) must succeed.
Invoke *operation output* (*input faults**)?	An asynchronous (one-way) invocation for output only, or a synchronous (two-way) invocation for output-input with a partner service. Potential faults are declared statically, though their occurrence is dynamic.
Receive *operation input*	Typically used at the start to receive a request for service. An initial **Receive** creates a new process instance. Usually matched by a **Reply** for the same operation.
Reply *operation output* | *fault*	Typically used at the end to provide an output response. Alternatively, a fault may be thrown.
Terminate	Ends a process abruptly.

Fig. 1. CRESS Notation (using BNF)

Structured types are defined using '[...]' for arrays and '{...}' for records. For example, the following defines the variable *scores*. This is a record with fields: float *length* and string array *frequency*. A typical value would be the string *scores.frequency[2]*.

{ **Float** length [**String** word] frequency } scores

2.2   Content Analysis Using Grid Services

The examples in this paper are drawn from the field of document content analysis (e.g. [13]). This is used for many purposes such as investigating disputed authorship of a document, analysing different versions of a document to identify likely antecedents, or comparing two documents for plagiarism. This is a rich field, so only a simplified version is described in order to illustrate how orchestrated grid services can be used.

In the example of this paper, documents are compared for similarity using the following two metrics that lie in the range [0, 1]. For both of these, identical documents have a 'distance' of 0. Documents with a 'distance' of 1 are maximally different.

Clause Length: The average number of words per clause is computed for each document. Suppose the numbers are 6 and 8. The 'distance' between the documents is the difference between these divided by the larger value: $\frac{8-6}{8}$, i.e. 0.25.

Word Frequency: the instances of each word are counted (disregarding common words) and the words are placed in order of decreasing frequency. This gives an ordered list of words for each document (truncated to some practical limit such as 50 words). The 'distance' between the two word lists is then computed from the relative positions of each word in the two lists (counting the first as 0). Suppose 'grid' is the second most frequent word in one list (i.e. position 1) but the fourth most frequent in the other (i.e. position 3). The distance for this word is the difference between their positions: $3 - 1$, i.e. 2. If a word does not appear in the other list, its position there is notionally the length of that list. Thus if 'grid' did not appear in the second list (of size 50), the distance would be $50 - 1$ or 49. This ensures that if a more frequent word is missing, it has a greater distance. The total distance between two word vectors is the sum of the distances for all the individual words, normalised to yield a value between 0 and 1.

The content analysis example makes use of two external partner grid services that could exist already or should be developed separately because they are generally useful:

Counter: This calculates various measures over a document. The *clause* operation computes the average clause length. The *word* operation determines the words in decreasing frequency. The *distance* operation computes the metrics explained above from the raw clause and word information.

Parser: This handles word lists for a document. The *parse* operation takes a document as a string of text and splits it up into words (consecutive letters and possibly digits), disregarding white space. Consecutive punctuation marks (e.g. ':-') are also grouped as 'words'. Like many grid services, the parser holds its results in persistent storage and just returns an endpoint reference for the word list. This reference can be used by other services to perform further analyses. The *delete* operation removes a stored word list.

2.3   CRESS Description of the Scorer Service

The scorer is an auxiliary service that supports the main content analysis application. Its CRESS description appears in figure 2. The rule-box to the bottom right of the figure defines types and variables. The raw data is *words* – a reference to the word list being analysed. The result is *scores* – the average clause length and word frequency list.

Initially the scorer receives a request to perform a *score* operation on the words list (node 1). Since calculating the two distance metrics may be time-consuming, each is computed concurrently (node 2). In one parallel branch, the counter service is invoked to calculate the average clause length (node 3). In another parallel branch, a different

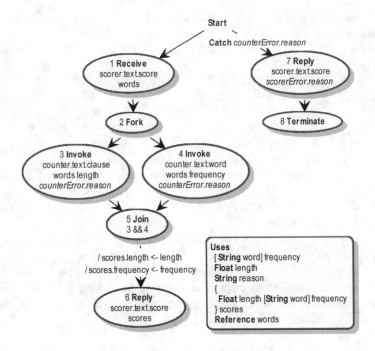

Fig. 2. CRESS Description of The Scorer Service

instance of the counter service is invoked to determine words in decreasing order of frequency (node 4). Where both paths converge at node 5, they must have produced a successful result ('3 && 4'). The two metrics are combined into one record (arc leading to node 6). Finally, the scores are returned by the scorer to its caller (node 6).

The scorer must allow for the counter process faulting. For example, the word list may be empty or may contain only punctuation. Both invocations of the counter statically declare that a *counterError* may occur (node 3 and 4). If this happens, the fault is caught (arc leading to node 7). The scorer then returns the fault reason to its caller (node 7) and terminates (node 8).

2.4   CRESS Description of the Matcher Service

The matcher offers the primary content analysis service to the user. Its CRESS description appears in figure 3. The rule-box at the bottom right again defines types and variables. The raw data is *texts* – text strings containing the two documents. The analysis yields *metrics* – the clause length and word frequency distances. The final entry in the rule-box '/ SCORER' indicates that the matcher depends on the scorer service.

Initially the matcher receives a request to perform the *match* operation on the texts (node 1). Since the documents are independent and may be large, their metrics are computed separately on two parallel paths (node 2). Each starts by setting the relevant text (*text1/text2* on the arc leading to node 3/4). The parser is invoked to create a word list from a document (node 3/4). The word lists are held by the parser, and returned

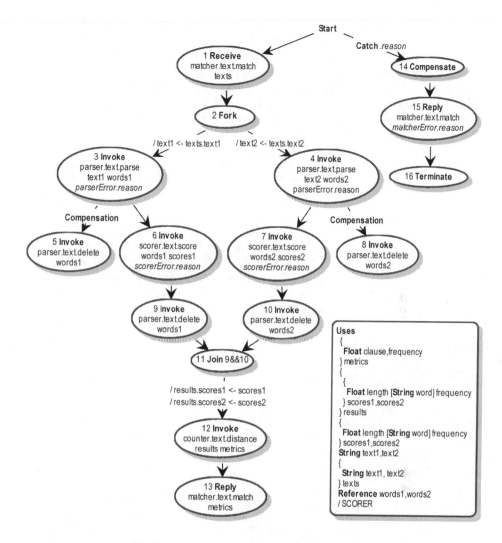

Fig. 3. CRESS Description of The Matcher service

as endpoint references (*words1/words2*). The scorer is then invoked to compute the metrics (*scores1/scores2* in node 6/7). The word lists have now served their purpose and are deleted (node 9/10). The converging paths must both be successful ('9 && 10' in node 11). The separately computed scores are combined (arc leading to node 12) and passed the counter to compute distances (node 12). The matcher returns the resulting metrics to its caller (node 13).

The matcher allows for faults in the services it calls: either of two invocations of the parser or the scorer may fail. Any such fault is caught (arc leading to node 14). The use of a fault variable (*reason*) without a fault name means that only a fault value is required: either *parserError* or *scorerError* is caught. Compensation is invoked by the fault handler to undo any actions that have been taken (node 14). The matcher returns the fault to its caller (node 15) and terminates (node 16).

Compensation may be needed after invoking an external partner, since this is often where work needs to be undone after a fault. The parser invocations to store data (node 3/4) make permanent changes and so have associated compensation: the corresponding word list is deleted (node 5/8). A compensation handler is enabled once its associated activity completes. If compensation is invoked without an explicit scope (node 14), compensation handlers are invoked in reverse order (most recent first). If one parser invocation succeeds but the other fails, only the former will be compensated.

As has been seen, the matcher service orchestrates the actions of two external partner services (counter and parser) as well as the scorer service (figure 2). In turn, the scorer service orchestrates further operations of the counter partner. Although four services now have to cooperate, the user of the matcher service sees it as a whole. This is a major advantage, because the detailed design of the service is then hidden.

The major issue is whether the services work together smoothly, or whether there are interoperability problems. Even though this is a comparatively small example, it will be appreciated that there are many possibilities for error. It is very easy to make a mistake when calling a service, for example supplying an integer where a float is expected. Deadlocks are also a risk. Many more subtle problems can arise from semantic incompatibilities among the services. For these reasons, it is highly desirable to embed grid service development within a rigorous methodology.

2.5   The CRESS Service Configuration

Now that the various services have been introduced, the CRESS configuration diagram can be shown. Figure 4 shows how the services here are described. The **Deploys** clause lists the tool options and, following '/', the services to be deployed. Although only *MATCHER* is named, this implicitly includes all of the other services because of the inferred dependencies. The parameters of each service then follow in the configuration diagram. All services, such as *COUNTER*, have a namespace prefix ('cntr'), a namespace URI (Uniform Resource Name, 'CounterPoint'), and a base URI where they are deployed ('localhost:8880/wsrf'). As can be seen, in this case the services were deployed on the local computer. However, they can be deployed anywhere in the network.

Grid services (counter, parser here) may have resources, declared after the other parameters. The counter has no resources (shown as '-'). The parser has a resource: the word list it stores, identified by *textName*. Every instance of the parser has a unique resource value, identified by its *resource key* in grid terminology. A composite service

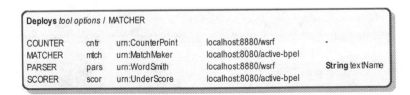

Fig. 4. CRESS Description of The Service Configuration

may also have resources. For example, if the matcher service were stateful then it too would have resource declarations.

2.6 Translation of the CRESS Diagrams

Translating the CRESS representation of *web* services has been described previously for BPEL [20]. However, the work reported in this paper has considerably extended and specialised this to handle *grid* services:

- A wider range of data types is now supported, including arrays and arbitrarily nested structured types. Specialised types have been added for dealing with grid services, such as certificates and endpoint references.
- Additional orchestration constructs have been added to match BPEL better.
- Support has been introduced for external partners shared amongst a number of services. Special treatment is needed to merge such descriptions in different diagrams.
- Grid service resources are now handled.

The CRESS diagrams (scorer, matcher, configuration) hold all that is needed to automatically generate a BPEL implementation and a LOTOS specification. Figure 5 compares translations of the content analysis example in figures 2 to 4:

- The fixed code is the framework common to all grid applications. This is substantial in the case of LOTOS because it contains many complex data types.
- The automatically generated code is shown for data types and behaviour. The BPEL translation yields many files: one BPEL file per service, one WSDL file per service/partner, and several deployment files. In addition, the WSDL files are automatically converted into Java. The LOTOS translation is a single file.
- The code for the external partners (counter, parser) has to be written manually. The Java coding conventions for grid services require several files per partner.

Target	Fixed Code	Generated Code			Partner Code		Total
		Files	Types	Behaviour	Files	Behaviour	
BPEL	20	51	14570	1640	10	2830	**19060**
LOTOS	840	1	530	400	2	290	**2060**

Fig. 5. Comparison of BPEL and LOTOS Translations *(lines of code except for Files columns)*

The BPEL implementation is substantially larger than the LOTOS specification, despite the fact that the LOTOS has a significant common overhead in data types. LOTOS has to explicitly specify functions on numbers, strings, etc. that would be expected in an implementation language. With larger examples, LOTOS is even more compact compared to BPEL. The most striking difference is in the large number of files required to support BPEL.

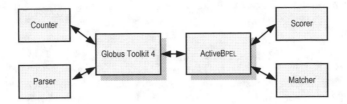

Fig. 6. Content Analysis Service Deployment

3   Translating Web Services to BPEL

Once the CRESS service diagrams have been created, their translation into BPEL/WSDL is automatic. The principles behind translating *web* services are outlined in [20]. Only a high-level description is given here, particularly covering where *grid* services differ.

3.1   Service Creation

Orchestrating grid services require a considerable amount of XML that is generated automatically by CRESS. Translation and deployment of a CRESS diagram is entirely automated, except for the one-off implementation of partner grid services. Partner services are automatically deployed using GT4 (Globus Toolkit version 4), while the orchestrating process is automatically deployed using ActiveBPEL.

The most important generated code is the BPEL that describes the orchestration. A WSDL definition is created for this process since it is a grid service in its own right. A WSDL file is also created for message and type definitions that are common to the process and its partners.

The translation from CRESS to BPEL is complex, partly because BPEL needs to be defined in a particular order, and partly because a lot of information has to be inferred.

3.2   Service Deployment

The deployment architecture is shown in figure 6. The grid services (counter, parser) are executed with GT4. Their orchestration (matcher, scorer) is handled by ActiveBPEL 2.0. Both GT4 and ActiveBPEL deploy services within a container that uses AXIS (the Apache SOAP engine). In principle, GT4 and ActiveBPEL could be executed within the same Apache Tomcat container. In practice, this is not feasible with the current versions. GT4 presently uses an older version of AXIS that is incompatible with ActiveBPEL; an updated version of GT4 is required before this can be resolved. For now, GT4 and ActiveBPEL are run in separate containers. Actually, this is reasonable since BPEL can coordinate grid services running on completely different computers. This would be quite likely in a realistic deployment of the content analysis example described in this paper.

GT4 currently imposes another limitation on the orchestration of grid services. The most desirable form of security is the so-called WS-SecureConversation that allows *credential delegation* in grid terminology. Unfortunately the current implementation of GT4 requires all services to use the same container for delegation to work. The authors have developed a solution combining GT4 and ActiveBPEL, but the current AXIS incompatibilities mean this cannot be used yet. A newer version of GT4 will allow credential delegation to be realised.

Current limitations of ActiveBPEL mean resources have to be treated transparently. It is intended to make resources directly available to the orchestrating process. Endpoint references cannot be used directly by ActiveBPEL. It is planned to make BPEL processes behave more like grid services and less like web services.

3.3 Service Flow

BPEL may use a variety of constructs to describe the flow: conditions (*if, switch*), sequences (*sequence*), loops (*while*), arbitrary parallel flows (*flow*), and several kinds of handlers (event, fault, compensation, correlation). CRESS simplifies this to conditions (expression guards), arbitrary flows, and one kind of handler (event guard). A number of constructs used by BPEL are intentionally hidden by CRESS. For example scopes are implicit, and specialised constructs such as *onMessage* as opposed to *receive* are used implicitly by CRESS as required.

CRESS automatically determines and declares the links among activities, which are then chained using BPEL *source* and *target* elements. The BPEL function *getLinkStatus* is used with **Join** to check whether a linked activity has terminated successfully.

A CRESS handler is translated into the corresponding type of BPEL handler. For example, **Catch** and **CatchAll** introduce a fault handler, while **Compensation** introduces a compensation handler. In principle, handlers may be defined in any scope including the global one. In fact, WS-BPEL does not allow global compensation handlers. CRESS regularises this situation by allowing handlers at two levels. Global handlers are translated as part of the top-level flow. The other place where CRESS allows handlers is in association with **Invoke**. Although this is a restriction compared to BPEL, it is where a handler is mostly likely to be required anyway.

3.4 Supporting Orchestration

Data types in CRESS are either simple ones defined by XML schemas (e.g. float, string) or are arbitrarily nested structures of records and arrays. Built-in types are used for the former, while complex types are generated for the latter. CRESS automatically handles the rather different ways in which BPEL uses variables: as message variables (input, output) or as data variables (assignment, expression).

BPEL processes orchestrate external partner services. In fact these may be web services or grid services (more precisely, stateless or stateful). The WSDL for partners is automatically generated from the CRESS diagrams, along with service deployment descriptors. If a partner service already exists, it can be used directly. The CRESS view is likely to be a subset of the partner WSDL, since an orchestrating process is likely to use only certain ports and operations of an already defined partner. If a partner web service does not already exist, its WSDL is translated into Java using the GT4 tool *wsdl2java*. The skeleton partner service must then be implemented manually.

3.5   Compatibility of ActiveBPEL and GT4

Resource addressing is a key issue for grid services. State information is handled separately from the service itself. A WS-Resource pair (service plus state) is encoded in an endpoint reference, as defined by the WS-Addressing schema. GT4 handles this implicitly, meaning that the ports used by clients are bound to a service and resource. To use another resource with the same service, a separate endpoint reference is created with the relevant resource key.

However, ActiveBPEL is not able to handle such a resource implicitly. Endpoint references thus have to be passed explicitly as parameters to grid service partners, allowing them to infer resource pairs. This requires compatibility of the WS-Addressing used by GT4 and ActiveBPEL. Unfortunately, the endpoint references generated by GT4 do not currently conform to the usual schema. Instead a variant schema with a *ReferenceParameters* element is used, leading to incompatibility. By altering the schemas in use, it is possible share endpoint references consistently. However, work remains to allow ActiveBPEL to use resources directly.

Grid services supported by GT4 require a *document/literal* SOAP binding. This is one of the binding styles that complies with the WS-Interoperability standard. However, this binding does not convey the operation name. Instead, the structure of the SOAP message body must be used implicitly to identify the operation being invoked. This causes ambiguity when a service has several operations with the same input signature, forcing use of distinct message parts even though they are not logically necessary.

4   Translating Grid Services to LOTOS

CRESS also translates grid services in LOTOS. Only the rigorous analysis this permits is discussed here. LOTOS was originally standardised for specifying and analysing communications standards (Open Systems Interconnection). However, LOTOS is a general-purpose language that supports precise specification of both behaviour and data: it is a process algebra supplemented by algebraic data types.

A LOTOS specification is automatically generated from the *same* CRESS diagrams that are translated into BPEL/WSDL. A default specification is provided for external partner services, though this just respects their operation interfaces. For more detailed analysis, the partners are specified manually.

Because CRESS is graphical, it is more understandable and compact than the corresponding code. Although this paper is focused on practical development of composite grid services, the use of a formal method is an important first step in their design. Apart from giving a precise definition of what orchestration means, it allows rigorous analysis of services prior to implementation. The use of formal methods is thus integrated into more conventional development techniques.

In practice, grid services are manually debugged. The generated LOTOS can, of course, be manually simulated as well. However, an important benefit of the formalisation is that it supports a wide variety of automated analyses.

An important issue in orchestrating grid services is to ensure their interoperability. Problems arise from simple misinterpretation of interfaces or from more subtle semantic incompatibility. Such problems often lead to deadlock in LOTOS terms, as determined by automated behaviour exploration or through model checking.

Service properties can also be model checked. Safety and liveness properties of grid services can be formulated in ACTL (Action-based Computational Temporal Logic). For example, the matcher service must not fault (safety), and an invocation of it must eventually receive a response (liveness). Unfortunately the complex data types and infinite data sorts make model checking somewhat impractical. For this reason, the authors favour the use of rigorous validation instead of verification.

MUSTARD (Multiple-Use Scenario Test and Refusal Description [21]) has been developed as a language-independent and tool-independent approach for expressing use case scenarios. These scenarios are automatically translated into the chosen language (here, LOTOS) for automatic validation against the specification. This is useful for initial validation of a specification, and also for later 'regression testing' following a change in the service description. Scenario-based validation is also good for checking interference among supposedly independent services – the so-called feature interaction problem. Interactions may arise for technical reasons (e.g. conflicting services activated by the same input) or for resource reasons (e.g. services sharing a resource or external partner).

A major advantage of MUSTARD is that the use of an underlying formal method is entirely hidden from the user. An automated procedure translates CRESS and MUSTARD into LOTOS, validates the scenarios, and reports the analysis in language-independent terms. In other words, the use of LOTOS (or any other formal language) is invisible. In fact, the tool user merely draws diagrams and clicks a button to check their integrity.

Grid services are formally validated by MUSTARD scenarios that check critical aspects of their behaviour. It is possible to check services in isolation as well as in combination. This can effectively and efficiently detect service interactions, though failure to find interactions does not mean the services are interaction-free. MUSTARD supports scenarios with sequences, alternatives, non-determinism, concurrency and service dependencies. In addition, both acceptance tests and refusal tests may be formulated.

5   Conclusions

It has been seen how CRESS has been adapted to support orchestration of grid services. This offers the advantage that new composite services can be constructed from existing ones. As a realistic example, document content analysis has been used to explain how grid services can be orchestrated.

CRESS descriptions of composite grid services are translated into BPEL/WSDL for implementation. The orchestration is performed by ActiveBPEL, while the partner grid services are executed by GT4. The same CRESS descriptions are also translated into LOTOS for rigorous validation and verification. The whole development process is highly automated. The use of advanced software engineering techniques (visual programming, formal methods) has thus been integrated into the current grid computing practice.

Content analysis has been used as an example of how orchestration can be useful in grid computing. This is a realistic problem, although the illustration is a small one. The authors have also researched the use of grid computing in social science, specifically grid services for occupational data analysis. Services from this domain are much more complex, and yet can be formalised and analysed rigorously using CRESS.

It has hopefully been demonstrated that CRESS is valuable in orchestrating grid services, implementing and analysing them.

Acknowledgements

Larry Tan's work was supported by the UK Economic and Social Research Council under grant RES-149-25-1015. The authors are grateful for the collaboration with their GEODE colleagues, particularly Paul Lambert (University of Stirling) and Richard Sinnott (University of Glasgow).

References

1. T. Andrews, F. Curbera, H. Dholakia, Y. Goland, J. Klein, F. Leymann, K. Liu, D. Roller, D. Smith, S. Thatte, I. Trickovic, and S. Weerawarana, editors. *Business Process Execution Language for Web Services*. Version 1.1. BEA, IBM, Microsoft, SAP, Siebel, May 2003.
2. A. Arkin, S. Askary, B. Bloch, F. Curbera, Y. Goland, N. Kartha, C. K. Lie, S. Thatte, P. Yendluri, and A. Yiu, editors. *Web Services Business Process Execution Language*. Version 2.0 (Draft). Organization for The Advancement of Structured Information Standards, Billerica, Massachusetts, USA, Dec. 2005.
3. K.-M. Chao, M. Younas, N. Griffiths, I. Awan, R. Anane, and C.-F. Tsai. Analysis of grid service composition with BPEL4WS. In Y. Shibata and J. Ma, editors, *Proc. 18th. Advanced Information Networking and Applications*, volume 1, pages 284–289. Institution of Electrical and Electronic Engineers Press, New York, USA, 2004.
4. A. Chirichiello and G. Salaün. Encoding abstract descriptions into executable web services: Towards A formal development. In *Proc. Web Intelligence 2005*. Institution of Electrical and Electronic Engineers Press, New York, USA, Dec. 2005.
5. W. Emmerich, B. Butchart, L. Chen, B. Wassermann, and S. L. Price. Grid service orchestration using the business process execution language (BPEL). *Grid Computing*, 3(3-4): 283–304, Sept. 2005.
6. A. Ferrara. Web services: A process algebra approach. In *Proc. 2nd. International Conference on Service-Oriented Computing*, pages 242–251. ACM Press, New York, USA, Nov. 2004.
7. H. Foster, S. Uchitel, J. Kramer, and J. Magee. Compatibility verification for web service choreography. In M. Aiello, editor, *Proc. 2nd. International Conference on Service-Oriented Computing*, New York, USA, Nov. 2004. ACM Press.
8. I. Foster, C. Kesselman, J. M. Nick, and S. Tuecke. Grid services for distributed system integration. *Supercomputer Applications*, 35(6), 2002.
9. X. Fu, T. Bultan, and J. Su. Analysis of interacting BPEL web services. In *Proc. 13th. International World Wide Web Conference*, pages 621–630. ACM Press, New York, USA, May 2004.
10. S. Graham, A. Marmakar, J. Mischinsky, I. Robinson, and I. Sedukhin, editors. *Web Services Resource*. Version 1.2. Organization for The Advancement of Structured Information Standards, Billerica, Massachusetts, USA, Apr. 2006.
11. ISO/IEC. *Information Processing Systems – Open Systems Interconnection – LOTOS – A Formal Description Technique based on the Temporal Ordering of Observational Behaviour*. ISO/IEC 8807. International Organization for Standardization, Geneva, Switzerland, 1989.

12. ITU. *Specification and Description Language*. ITU-T Z.100. International Telecommunications Union, Geneva, Switzerland, 2000.
13. K. Krippendorff. *Content Analysis: An Introduction to Its Methodology*. Sage, Thousand Oaks, California, USA, 2004.
14. S. Majithia, D. W. Walker, and W. A. Gray. Automated composition of semantic grid services. In *Proc. 3rd. UK e-Science All Hands Meeting*. University of Nottingham, UK, Aug. 2004.
15. T. Oinn, M. Addis, J. Ferris, D. Marvin, M. Senger, M. Greenwood, T. Carver, K. Glover, M. R. Pocock, A. Wipat, and P. Li. Taverna: A tool for the composition and enactment of bioinformatics workflows. *Bioinformatics*, 20(17):3045–3054, 2004.
16. C. Pautasso. JOpera: An agile environment for web service composition with visual unit testing and refactoring. In *Proc. IEEE Symposium on Visual Languages and Human Centric Computing*. Institution of Electrical and Electronic Engineers Press, New York, USA, Nov. 2005.
17. S. Rosario, A. Benveniste, S. Haar, and C. Jard. Net systems semantics of web services orchestrations modeled in ORC. Technical Report PI 1780, IRISA, Rennes, France, Jan. 2006.
18. A. Slomiski. On using BPEL extensibility to implement OGSI and WSRF grid workflows. In *Proc. Global Grid Forum 10*, Berlin, Germany, Mar. 2005. Humboldt University.
19. K. J. Turner. Formalising web services. In F. Wang, editor, *Proc. Formal Techniques for Networked and Distributed Systems (FORTE XVIII)*, number 3731 in Lecture Notes in Computer Science, pages 473–488. Springer, Berlin, Germany, Oct. 2005.
20. K. J. Turner. Representing and analysing web services. *Network and Computer Applications*, Mar. 2006. In press.
21. K. J. Turner. Validating feature-based specifications. *Software Practice and Experience*, 36(10):999–1027, Aug. 2006.
22. World Wide Web Consortium. *Web Services Description Language (WSDL)*. Version 1.1. World Wide Web Consortium, Geneva, Switzerland, Mar. 2001.

A UML 2.0 Profile for Architecting B3G Applications

Mauro Caporuscio and Valerie Issarny

INRIA-Rocquencourt
Domaine de Voluceau
78153 Le Chesnay, France
{mauro.caporuscio, valerie.issarny}@inria.fr

Abstract. B3G is an emerging network technology which conceives the convergence of telecommunication and IP-based networks for providing enhanced services able to transfer both voice and non-voice data through wired and wireless networks. Moreover, B3G networks can be no longer considered as "*passive*" entities which only transport data between endpoints, but they must be considered as "*active*" parties that have their own behavior and provide services. This creates a completely new application domain where applying current software engineering design tools, such as software architectures, fails. In fact, dealing with B3G networks requires to explicit low-level details usually abstracted by the architectural descriptions.

To this extent, we present an ongoing work on investigating B3G-oriented application modeling. In particular, we propose an enhanced UML profile to define and analyze software architectures that explicitly exploit the B3G domain properties.

1 Introduction

Beyond Third-Generation (B3G) [30] network is an emerging technology which conceives the convergence of telecommunication networks with IP based networks. Services associated with B3G provide the ability to transfer both voice data (i.e., a telephone call) and non-voice data (i.e., downloading information, exchanging email, and instant messaging) through different types of network, either wired or wireless. This opens to a new world where distributed applications can not only interact with each other over plenty of different networks, but they can also interact with non-software entities (i.e., humans), by exploiting services offered by telecommunication networks.

Such a vision breaks some assumptions posed so far by the software engineering community and requires for adapting/revising the software life-cycle, and the related tools, since the early activities. In particular, the *software design* is the first process activity to be affected by the B3G application domain. The *software design* aims to build the first description, both behavioral and structural, of the entire system under development. Consequently, since the *architectural design* is described by means of Software Architecture (SA) modeling [5][25], also this one should be adapted/revised accordingly.

N. Guelfi and D. Buchs (Eds.): RISE 2006, LNCS 4401, pp. 18–34, 2007.

SA has been largely accepted as a well suited tool to achieve a better software quality while reducing the time-to-market. This results in a proliferation of different Architectural Description Languages (ADLs), defined by both the academia and the industry [20].

The use of SA descriptions allows software engineers to model large, complex applications by using suitable abstractions of the system components and their interactions. This forces the separation of architectural concerns from other design ones, thus abstracting away many details. On the other hand, SA descriptions allow for analysis and verification of architectural choices, both qualitative and quantitative, since the early stages of the software life-cycle [6].

However, the use of SA fails when specifying B3G-oriented applications. In fact, dealing with B3G networks requires to explicit those low-level details usually abstracted by SA specifications. To this extent, we argue networks involved in B3G scenarios can be no longer considered as *"passive"* entities which only transport data between end-points, but they must be considered as *"active"* parties that have their own behavior and provide services. Hence, since they actively affect the overall system's performance and behavior, they cannot be taken apart but must be considered, along with all their characteristics, within the design process. According to this and due to the high degree of network heterogeneity inherent to the B3G application domain, it is important to raise up some characteristics such as *network type, quality of service, security, network services*, etc.

This paper presents an ongoing work on investigating B3G-oriented application modeling. In particular, we show how, starting from a small survey of the networks involved in B3G scenarios, it has been elicited a set of properties that characterizes B3G-oriented applications and, then we present an enhanced UML profile [24] for explicitly defining and analyzing SAs that take into account these properties of interest.

The paper is organized as follows: Section 2 first describes the different networks available in the B3G application domain and then presents the sets of properties elicited. Section 3 presents the B3G-oriented UML profile we designed while Section 4 discusses the analysis aspects related to the B3G application domain. Finally, Section 5 concludes and discuss future work.

2   B3G Network Properties Elicitation

B3G network technology indicates the convergence of telecommunication networks with IP based networks. Services associated with B3G provide the ability to transfer both voice data and non-voice data through different types of network, either wired or wireless. In this setting, wireless networks are categorized into three groups based on their coverage range: (*i*) Wireless Wide Area Networks (WWAN) that includes wide coverage area technologies such as 3G cellular (UMTS), Global System for Mobile Communications (GSM), General Packet Radio Service (GPRS), i-Mode, etc. . . , (*ii*) Wireless Local Area Networks (WLAN) that includes 802.11, HiperLAN, and several others, and (*iii*) Wireless

Personal Area Networks (WPAN) that represents wireless personal area network technologies such as Bluetooth and IrDA.

In this section we discuss the networks state-of-the-art by eliciting the properties of interest needed to architect B3G applications.

2.1   Networks in B3G

The widely accepted way to achieve interworking between heterogeneous network is the use of TCP/IP protocol suite. Figure 1 shows how the protocol stacks, implemented by (some) networks involved in B3G scenarios, relate to TCP/IP standard. In the following, we give a high-level description of such networks and their properties[1], namely Quality of Service (QoS), security, etc. . .

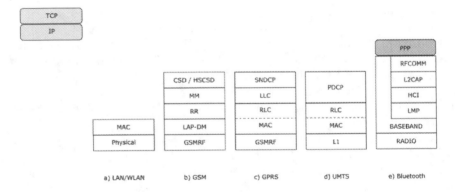

Fig. 1. Network protocol stacks underlying TCP/IP

Ethernet (IEEE 802.3) – Nowadays, the prominent technology for providing wired LANs is Ethernet [16]. Based on the shared-bus concept, it operates different data transfer rates (ranging from 10Mbps to 1Gbps) but it does not provide any support for QoS management neither any other type of service. As shown in Figure 1.a, using TCP/IP over this network does not require any additional effort.

WiFi (IEEE 802.11) – The WiFi 802.11 standard [15] (afterward enhanced by other task groups) defines the MAC and Physical levels in order to create Wireless LANs. It is worth noticing that WiFi network may operate in two different modes: (*i*) *infrastructure mode* and (*ii*) *ad-hoc*. While *infrastructure mode* defines a controlled network composed of a number of managed fixed nodes that provides access points to wireless clients, *ad-hoc mode* defines a self-managed network where wireless clients directly communicate each other without any control. Also in this case, using TCP/IP over this network does not require any additional effort (see Figure 1.a).

---

[1] For any further detail, please refer to the relative citations.

Global System for Mobile Communications (GSM) – The Global System for Mobile Communications standard [22] specifies infrastructures and services for digital cellular networks. GSM is based on circuit-switched protocol, where a traffic channel is allocated to a user for the entire duration of a call and it is simply unused if there is no data to be transmitted during the call. This limits both the data rates and the number of users that can be supported. Moreover, GSM specifies two circuit-switched protocols to tunnel and convoy data throughout the network. Thus, GSM clients can use TCP/IP directly on top of them (see Figure 1.b).

General Packet Radio Service (GPRS) – General Packet Radio Service (GPRS) [1] is a mobile communication standard based on packet-switched radio transmission. The main advantage over circuit-switched radio technologies is its handling of the radio resources. GPRS is structured as a GSM overlay, although it does require some changes to a few of the basic GSM network elements. GPRS provides an architecture for integrating external packet-data networks (e.g., the Internet backbone wired network) and mobile stations (i.e., cell phones, PDAs, and other such mobile devices). Thus, mobile stations are enabled to use TCP/IP based protocols directly on top of GPRS (see Figure 1.c).

Universal Mobile Telecommunication System (UMTS) – The Universal Mobile Telecommunication System (UMTS) [2] is part of the 3G Network family which defines both the circuit-switched and the packet-switched transmission for voice and data communications relatively. Also in this case, clients can use TCP/IP based protocols directly on top of UMTS (see Figure 1.d). Moreover, important characteristics of UMTS are (i) the high data transfer rate (up to 2Mbps) and (ii) the ability to negotiate/manage different fixed classes of QoS [3].

Bluetooth – The Bluetooth [8] technology is the de-facto standard for achieving short-range WPANs. In particular, Bluetooth allows users to set up wireless ad-hoc networks that achieve real-time voice and data exchange between limited-resources devices. However, Bluetooth does not directly support TCP/IP protocols and then the use of PPP protocol [23] is required (as shown in Figure 1.e).

2.2   QoS–Related Properties of Interest

This section describes the characteristics of the networks introduced above by summarizing their properties of interest. In particular, we firstly presents common QoS attributes that apply to all the B3G networks and, then we describe a set of enhanced QoS attributes that are specific of telecommunication networks such as GSM, GPRS, UMTS.

General QoS Properties – The set of general QoS properties is composed of few attributes that identify the basic metrics needed for describing the performance of a network. In particular, they relates to the *bandwidth, transmission time, packet ordering* and *error ratio* provided by the network under analysis:

- `Max Bitrate`: identifies the maximal data transfer rate that can be sustained between two end-points.
- `Transfer delay`: measures the time elapsed for delivering a packet from a sender, trough the network, to a receiver.
- `Jitter`: is calculated as the variation of the `transfer delay` attribute from one packet to the next packet within the same packet stream/flow.
- `Delivery order`: indicates whether the network shall provide in–sequence packets delivery or not.
- `Packet Error Ratio`: is the fraction of packets lost or detected as corrupted or erroneous.

Advanced QoS Properties – In order to fully describe B3G-related QoS properties we need to extend the set described above by adding some attributes specifically related to the GSM, GPRS, UMTS telecommunication networks. In fact, due to the inherent complexity of such networks, in terms of infrastructures and provided services, the general QoS properties set is not sufficient to describe all possible QoS purposes.

To this extent, UMTS QoS specification [3] defines four different classes of QoS related to the services provided by the network: (*i*) *Conversational* defines the QoS needed for real-time video/audio conversations (bidirectional), (*ii*) *Streaming* defines the QoS needed for real-time video/audio streaming (unidirectional), (*iii*) *Interactive* defines the QoS needed for achieving data communication used for request/response patterns (i.e., HTTP interactions) and, (*iv*) *Background* defines the QoS needed for providing background traffic (i.e., email, SMS/MMS messaging). Such classes are defined basing on both the general attributes detailed above and the following list of advanced attributes[2]:

- `Traffic Class`: is a string which identifies the class membership (i.e., "Conversational", "Streaming", "Interactive", "Background").
- `Guaranteed Bitrate`: defines the guaranteed number of bits delivered within a period of time, divided by the duration of the period.
- `Max. SDU size`: is the maximum size (number of octets) for which the network shall satisfy the QoS negotiated.
- `SDU format info`: is a list of possible exact size of SDU. This allows the up-layer application to specify the SDU size in order to let the bearer to be less expensive.
- `Residual bit error ratio`: is the undetected bit error ratio in the delivered SDU.
- `Delivery of erroneous SDUs`: specifies whether SDUs detected as erroneous shall be delivered or discarded.
- `Traffic handling priority`: represents the relative importance for handling of all SDUs belonging to the UMTS bearer.

---

[2] The following QoS attributes defined by UMTS cannot be directly applied to GSM and GPRS networks. However, the UMTS QoS Specification [3] defines how to map QoS attributes from UMTS to GSM/GPRS in order to achieve interworking.

- `Allocation/Retention priority`: is the relative importance for alloca-tion/retention of UMTS bearer.
- `Source Statistic descriptor`: may be either "speech" or "unknown" and defines the characteristics of the of SDU's source.
- `Signaling Indication`: indicates if the SDU is for signaling or not.

2.3 Network Services

As introduced above, in our vision B3G networks are no longer *"passive"* entities, but they are *"active"* parties that have their own behavior and provide services to the end-users. Hence, in this section, we briefly describe some of these services.

IEEE 802.3 and 802.11 – While Ethernet does not provide any service, WiFi offers some basic security services such as identification, encryption and authen-tication.

- Service Set Identifier (SSID) is a 32 alphanumeric characters code attached to all packets transmitted on a WiFi network to identify each packet as part of that network. In order to communicate each other, all the clients accessing the network must share the same SSID.
- Wi-Fi Protected Access (WPA and WPA2) is a encryption protocol designed to secure wireless networks. In order to access the network every clients must be provided with a pre-shared key that is used to encrypt/decrypt network packets.

Global System for Mobile Communications (GSM) – Services provided by the GSM network are:

- Basic voice call services (i.e., incoming and outgoing call management) and optional enhanced voice call services (i.e., Call Forwarding, Call Hold, Call Waiting, Barring of Outgoing/Incoming Calls, ...)
- A circuit-switched data transfer service which allows users to send/receive data streams. In particular, GSM defines two distinct circuit-switched data protocols: (*i*) the Circuit Switched Data (CSD) and the (*ii*) High-Speed Circuit-Switched Data (HSCSD). Due to a fixed amount of bandwidth is dedicated to connections over CSD and HSCSD (9.6Kbps and 14.4Kbps re-spectively), they are charged on a per-second basis, regardless of the amount of data sent over the link.
- Short Message Service (SMS) which allows users to send/receive textual messages.
- mobility management service which manage the client mobility by support-ing handover and network interoperability (aka global roaming).
- the GSM network provides a secure access mechanism based on personal information stored on the Subscriber Identity Module (SIM) card. In par-ticular, the communications between the subscriber and the base station is encrypted by using a crypt variable stored on the SIM.

General Packet Radio Service (GPRS) – As introduced above, GPRS is an extension of GSM which aims to upgrade the GSM data transfer services. In particular, services provided by GPRS are:

- Packet-switched data transmission protocol where bandwidth is used only when there is actually data to transmit. Hence, the billing policy for this type of connection is by the kilobyte instead of by the second.
- Short Message Service (SMS) which allows users to send/receive textual messages.
- Since GPRS is based on existing GSM networks, they share the same secure access mechanism and encryption facility.

Universal Mobile Telecommunication System (UMTS) – UMTS services are grouped into three classes: (*i*) *teleservices* which support the same teleservices handled by GSM (i.e., speech, SMS), (*ii*) *facsimile services* which provide the ability to send and receive fax, and (*iii*) *bearer services* which provide the capability for data transfer between end-points. In particular, the *bearer services* are:

- *Circuit switched data services* and *real-time data services* which allow for interworking with the GSM network.
- *Packet switched data services* which allow for interworking with packet networks such as IP-networks and LANs. This service provide also mechanisms for ensuring packet based handover between GSM and UMTS.

Bluetooth – Bluetooth provides services for transmitting both voice and data, and for service discovery:

- Asynchronous Connectionless (ACL) provides a packet switched service for data transmission.
- Synchronous Connection Oriented (SCO) service provides a circuit switched data service for audio/voice transmission.
- Service Discovery Protocol (SDP) allows for discovery of services on Bluetooth enabled devices.

3   An UML Profile for B3G Software Architectures

In previous section, we presented the common networks involved in B3G scenarios by eliciting their main properties of interest. In particular, we discussed their QoS properties and the services they offer to the end-user. As previously remarked, while designing B3G-oriented application these characteristics should not be abstracted away by SA descriptions, but rather they should be considered and analyzed since the early stages of the software life-cycle.

To this extent, in this section, we describe a UML 2.0 Profile for specifying B3G-oriented SAs which take into account all the discussed properties. In particular, we exploit the DUALLY approach [17][13] by extending it with the features needed to describe B3G SAs.

3.1   Background: The DUALLY Profile for Software Architectures

Even though UML is considered a well known standard-de-facto notation for specifying and modeling software systems, it does not obey the Architectural Description Languages (ADLs) [20] peculiarities and lacks some relevant aspects. To this extent, many approaches have been proposed to fill this gap and allow for SA specification in UML [19][27][18].

Among them, a relevant contribution is provided by DUALLY. DUALLY is a UML profile which provides a minimal core set of architectural concepts along with the ability to extend it in order to fit any specific need. Furthermore, the use of DUALLY allows engineers to carry on different types of analysis (i.e., Model checking, Testing, Performance, ...) on the defined SA. Figure 2 presents the DUALLY profile and describes how the common UML elements [24] have been extended in order to meet the requirements posed by SA specifications.

SA-Component – UML 2.0 defines a component as *"a subtype of Class which provides for a Component having attributes and operations, and being able to participate in Associations and Generalizations"*. Moreover, *"Component may optionally have an internal structure and own a set of Ports that formalize its interaction points"*. Hence, DUALLY simply maps SA-Components directly into UML components.

SA-Connectors – UML 2.0 introduces, for the first time, the concept of connector in UML. In particular, it defines two types of connector: (*i*) *assembly*, which represents a binding between an output port and an input port, and (*ii*) *delegation*, which binds an external component port with its internal implementation. However, both the *assembly* and the *delegation* connector definitions lack expressiveness and do not fulfill the requirements needed to specify an SA according to [25][14]. Different solutions have been proposed to fill this gap [18]. DUALLY represents an SA-Connector by means of a stereotyped UML component which embodies both functional and non-functional properties of the connectors.

SA-Channels – In UML 2.0: *"An assembly connector is a connector between two components that defines that one component provides the services that another component requires. An assembly connector is a connector that is defined from a required interface or port to a provided interface or port"*. In DUALLY, the SA-Channel stereotype is mapped into the UML assembly connector (see Figure 2).

SA-Relationships – While modeling SAs, a key issue is to analyze and keep trace of the relationships that occur among components [28][29]. In UML, *"a dependency is a relationship that signifies that a single or a set of model elements requires other model elements for their specification or implementation. This means that the complete semantics of the depending elements is either semantically or structurally dependent on the definition of the supplier element(s)"*. Hence, DUALLY implements the SA-Relationship by using the UML Dependency core element.

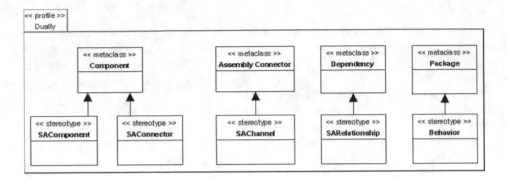

Fig. 2. DUALLY UML Profile

SA-Behavior – In order to carry on SA analysis DUALLY needs some additional information about the system dynamics by means of components internal behavior and components interactions. To this extent, DUALLY makes use of the UML State Machine for modeling components behavior and Sequence Diagrams for specifying components interactions.

3.2   Extending SA-Channels for B3G

The DUALLY profile described above fulfills the gap between ADLs and UML 2.0 in specifying SAs. However, it does not cope the needs posed by B3G-oriented SA specification. In fact, notwithstanding the SA-Connector is able to specify complex relationships between SA-Components, it cannot be used to describe networks properties (i.e. network type, QoS, security, network services, etc) which characterize the communication channels in B3G scenarios.

Hence, starting from the SA-Channel defined above, we extend it by creating a stereotyped class hierarchy, which exploits the characteristics of the different networks involved in B3G scenarios.

Referring to Figure 3, an SA-Channel can be specialized into a *Local Channel* (`CLocal`) which refers to local component interactions, or into a *Networked Channel* (`CNet`) which provides remote networked communications. Furthermore, `CNet` is specialized into the `CN_Wired` and `CN_Wireless` subtypes which provide *Wired Network Channel* and *Wireless Network Channel* respectively. While `CN_Wired` is not further specialized, `CN_Wireless` has `CNW_WWAN`, `CNW_WLAN` and `CNW_WPAN` as subtypes. `CNW_WWAN` defines *Wireless Wide Area Networks Channel*, `CNW_WLAN` represent *Wireless Local Area Networks Channel* and `CNW_WPAN` is *Wireless Personal Area Networks Channel*. Finally, while `CNW_WWAN` is specialized into `WWAN_GSM`, `WWAN_GPRS` and `WWAN_UMTS` which represent a possible set of formal telecommunication networks, `CNW_WLAN` is specialized into `WiFi_Structured` and `WiFi_Ad-Hoc` which represent two different types of wireless IP network.

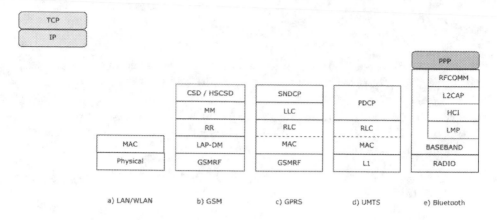

Fig. 3. SAChannel Hierarchy Tree

SAChannel – It represents the root of our hierarchy and provides the `Name` attribute which allows us to uniquely identify the instantiated channel within the SA under definition. It also defines the following naive services :

1. void **send**(*pkt, dest*): provides the service for sending a data packet *pkt* to a given destination *dest*.
2. pkt **receive**(): provides the service for receiving a data packet *pkt* from the network.

It is worth noticing that these services might be overridden/overloaded by the subclasses in order to meet the requirements specified by the different network they implement. For example, given a network specification which defines a packet-switched data transfer, both **send** and **receive** services must be implemented accordingly.

CLocal – `CLocal` refers to local communication channels used by processes, tasks and components residing on the same machine. CLocal overrides the services defined in `SAChannel` and defines an additional attribute, named `Type`, which indicates the type of communication implemented by the channel: i.e. pipe, shared memory, etc. . .

CNet – On the other side, `CNet` refers to remote communication channels used by components to interact with each other across a network. It extends `SAChannel` by defining a minimal set of QoS attributes according to the General QoS Properties discussed in Section 2.2.

CN_Wired – This class concerns the communication achieved by using a wired network (i.e. Ethernet, ATM, USB, . . .). It overrides the services defined by its ancestors and instantiates the QoS attributes.

CN_Wireless – This class identifies a communication channel implemented by means of a wireless link. `CN_Wireless` defines some additional services:

1. ack **connect**(*ID*): provides the service for joining the wireless network. It requires to provide an *ID* which uniquely identifies the client within the network.
2. void **disconnect**(*ID*): provides the service for disconnecting from the network. The *ID* is used to clean up the network clients table.

CNW_WLAN – This class defines a communication channel implemented by means of a WLAN. It instantiates the inherited QoS attributes and defines some additional services:

1. void **enableWPA**(*pwd*): enables the WPA service by providing the required password.

WiFi_Structured – Structured WiFi channel instantiates the inherited attributes and define the following service:

– [ID] **getSSID**(): provides the service for retrieving the SSIDs of the networks in range. [ID] represents an array containing all the SSIDs retrieved.

WiFi_Ad-Hoc – Operating in ad-hoc mode requires devices within range of each other to discover and communicate in peer-to-peer fashion without involving central access points. Hence, the Ad-Hoc WiFi channel instantiates the inherited attributes and define the following service:

– [ID] **peerDiscovery**(): provides the service for retrieving the ID of the peers in range. [ID] represents an array containing all the IDs retrieved.

CNW_WWAN – This class identifies a communication channel implemented by means of a wireless telecommunication network. In particular, it extends the set of attributes according to the advanced QoS properties discussed in Section 2.2, appropriately overrides inherited methods, and provide the following common services:

– void **mobilityManagement**(*ID*): provides the service for managing mobility issues, such as handover and roaming.
– void **billing**(): provides the service for managing services billing.
– void **sendSMS**(*MSG*): provides the service for sending Short Messages.
– MSG **getSMS**(): provides the service for receiving Short Messages.

WWAN_GSM – The GSM Class instantiates all the attributes defined earlier, overrides inherited methods (i.e., connect, send, ...), and provides the following services:

– Call **getIncomingCall**(*ID*): provides the service for receiving incoming voice calls.
– Call **setOutgoingCall**(*NUM*): provides the service for setting an outgoing call.

WWAN_GPRS – The GPRS Class does not provide new services but overrides inherited methods (i.e., connect, send, ...) and instantiates all the attributes defined earlier according to its specification.

WWAN_UMTS – The UMTS Class instantiates all the attributes defined earlier, overrides inherited methods (i.e., connect, send, ...), and provides the following services:

- Call **getIncomingCall(*ID*)**: provides the service for receiving incoming voice calls.
- Call **setOutgoingCall(*NUM*)**: provides the service for setting an outgoing voice call.
- void **sendFAX(*MSG*)**: provides the service for sending a Fax.
- MSG **getFAX()**: provides the service for receiving a Fax.

WPAN – WPAN Class identifies a channel implemented by means of a personal area network. It defines some common services and can be further derived into more specific classes:

- [ID] **peerDiscovery()**: provides the service for retrieving the ID of the peers in range. [ID] represents an array containing all the IDs retrieved.
- Call **setVoiceTrasmission(*ID*)**: provides the service for managing audio/voice transmission to the device identified by ID.

3.3   Early Example

In this section, We present a simple example which aims to summarize the characteristics introduced above. Figure 4 shows an SA composed of a number of components: an Application is connected through a generic network to the Web Server that, by using a XParlay connector, is able to interact to different mobile clients (namely GSM Phone, Laptop and UMTS PDA) through WAN networks. Moreover, while the GPRS Mobile Termination (GPRS MT) acts as network access point for the Laptop, the UMTS PDA is directly connected to Application by means of a PAN channel and to Web Server trough the UMTS network. Note that, while Web Server accesses the XParlay connector services by using a CN_Wired channel, the wireless clients are linked to it by using different CNW_WWAN channels. Here, the role of the XParlay connector is to make the set of services implemented within WAN networks (i.e., messaging, presence, localization, phone calls) available to the web server [21].

In this setting, let the UMTS PDA holder want to send an SMS to both the GSM Phone and the Laptop clients. She can choose if sending the SMS by using the WWAN facilities (then paying the cost of two SMS) or using her web account that allows her to send free SMS. In the latter case, she has a further choice: she can browse the web site by using either the UMTS data transfer service (then paying the service cost) or a PAN network in order to use the Application component as router to access Internet and interact to Web Server for free.

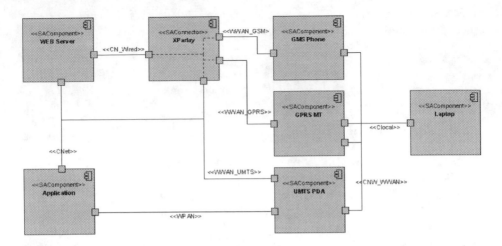

Fig. 4. B3G early example

Even though this example is really simple and the SA is composed of few components, it shows the overall complexity inherent to B3G scenarios. Modeling the same SA by using either ADLs or SA-oriented UML profiles would hide the main characteristics of this type of networks (i.e., QoS properties) and the services they provide (e.g, SMS service).

4   B3G Software Architecture Analysis

As remarked in previous section, SA descriptions allow for analysis and validation of architectural choices obtaining better software quality and shorter time-to-market development [6].

Since SA represents the first, in the development life-cycle, complete description of the system under development, carrying on accurate analysis at this stage would speedup and improve the next life-cycle phases. This is even more important while developing B3G Applications. In fact, since the complexity of these systems comes from both the application itself and the underlay networks, having qualitative and quantitative analysis results allows software engineers to understand in advance the behavior/misbehavior of the system.

To this extent, the B3G UML profile presented in previous section provides the ability to perform the following analysis by using UML-based automated tools: (*i*) *SA Model Checking* which allows for checking architectural model consistency, (*ii*) *Performance Analysis of SA* which allows for making quantitative analysis on SAs, and (*iii*) *SA-driven Testing* which allows for checking whether the implementation under test fulfills the architectural specification, and (*iv*) *Runtime SA-based System Reconfiguration* which allows for monitoring and reconfiguring the system at runtime.

Model Checking Software Architectures – Model-checking is a well known verification technique which aims to validate system specifications against functional properties of interest expressed by means of formal languages [11]. The use of such a technique at the architectural level allows architects to design correct SAs (i.e., system specifications) that satisfy the functional requirements (i.e., properties of interests).

The B3G profile presented in Section 3 exploits the functionalities provided by DUALLY which in turn is fully integrated into the CHARMY tool [10], a framework for specifying and model-checking SAs. This allows us to model-check B3G applications by taking into account the networks low-layer properties usually abstracted by ADLs.

Performance Analysis of SA – *Software performance* is the process of *predicting* and *evaluating* whether a system meet the user performance requirements [4]. Performing such an analysis requires to use modeling languages specifically designed for this purpose - e.g., Queuing Network (QN), Petri Nets (PN), etc.

However, given a UML-based SA specification, it is possible to automatically generate the relative QN model and carry on the analysis [12]. This, allows us to automatically transform B3G-oriented SAs into QNs and then carry on a performance analysis that takes into account also the network QoS properties discussed in Section 2.

SA-based Testing – While SA model-checking allows for an exhaustive and automatic analysis of the system model, SA-based testing aims to validate the implementation conformance to the SA model [7]. In UML-based SA specification, SA-based testing uses UML notations such as *State Diagrams* and *Sequence Diagrams* for describing component/connector behavior and test cases respectively [12].

Hence, casting this to the B3G-oriented SA presented above, allows us to automatically generate test cases that consider also the characteristics of the involved networks.

Runtime SA-based System Reconfiguration – In deploying complex distributed software systems, runtime QoS management is an important issue to address. Self-adaptation, based on on-line monitoring and dynamic reconfiguration, is considered a useful technique to solve it. To this extent, the use of SA performance analysis, for evaluating the actual system status and choosing the next system configuration, achieves fine tuned reconfiguration process that overcomes the observed QoS problems [9].

Thus, using the B3G-oriented UML profile for specifying the SA allows for evaluating the actual performance and for reconfiguring the system also with respect to the QoS properties of the underlay networks. Moreover, this also allows for designing applications able to dynamically negotiate Service Level Agreements (SLA) according to the connectivity and QoS they perceive, as long as properties match the requirements.

5 Conclusions and Future Work

B3G technology conceives the convergence of telecommunication networks with IP based networks for providing enhanced services. This new class of services exploits the ability to transfer both voice data and non-voice data through different kinds of networks, either wired or wireless. This define a new application domain where applications can not only interact with each other, but they can also interact with non-software entities (i.e., humans). This new application domain requires for an adaptation/revision of the software life-cycle and the related tools.

To this extent, we presented our ongoing work on investigating how to address the designing and developing of B3G-oriented applications. In particular, we first described the different network involved in B3G scenarios and their main characteristics. Then, we proposed an extended UML Profile which allows for defining B3G-oriented SA and for performing different kind of analysis which aim to validate B3G-oriented applications with respect to both qualitative and quantitative requirements.

The work discussed herein represents the first step of a long term research. In fact, we plan to use the proposed B3G-oriented UML profile for designing and evaluating the PLASTIC middleware. PLASTIC is a IST Project [26], we are involved in, which aims to construct a platform for delivering software services deployed over B3G networks. Main characteristics of the PLASTIC Services is that they will be adaptive to the environment with respect to resource availability and delivered Quality of Service (QoS), via a development paradigm based on Service Level Agreements (SLAs) and resource-aware programming.

References

1. 3rd Generation Partnership Project Technical Specification Group. Digital Cellular Telecommunications System (Phase 2+) - General Packet Radio Service (GPRS) Service Description - Services and System Aspects - Stage 2, Jan. 2002.
2. 3rd Generation Partnership Project Technical Specification Group. Universal Mobile Telecommunications System (UMTS) - Services and service capabilities, Sept. 2005.
3. 3rd Generation Partnership Project Technical Specification Group. Universal Mobile Telecommunications System (UMTS) - Universal Mobile Telecommunications System (UMTS) - Quality of Service (QoS) concept and architecture, June 2005.
4. S. Balsamo, A. Di Marco, P. Inverardi, and M. Simeoni. Model-based performance prediction in software development: a survey. *IEEE Transactions on Software Engineering*, 30(5):295–310, May 2004.
5. L. Bass, P. Clements, and R. Kazman. *Software Architecture in Practice*. Addison-Wesley, Massachusetts, 1998.
6. M. Bernardo and P. Inverardi. *Formal Methods for Software Architectures, Tutorial book on Software Architectures and Formal Methods*. SFM-03:SA Lectures, LNCS 2804, 2003.

7. A. Bertolino and P. Inverardi. Architecture-based software testing. In *Joint proceedings of the second international software architecture workshop (ISAW-2) and international workshop on multiple perspectives in software development (Viewpoints '96) on SIGSOFT '96 workshops*, pages 62–64, New York, NY, USA, 1996. ACM Press.
8. Bluetooth. Bluetooth core specification v2.0. http://www.bluetooth.com.
9. M. Caporuscio, A. Di Marco, and P. Inverardi. Model-based system reconfiguration for dynamic performance management. *Journal of Systems and Software*, 2006. To appear.
10. Charmy Project. Charmy web site. http://www.di.univaq.it/charmy, February 2004.
11. E. M. Clarke, O. Grumberg, and D. A. Peled. *Model Checking*. The MIT Press, 2001.
12. V. Cortellessa, A. D. Marco, P. Inverardi, H. Muccini, and P. Pelliccione. Using uml for sa-based modeling and analysis. In *Proceedings of Int. Workshop on Software Architecture Description & UML*, Lisbon, Portugal, Oct 2004.
13. D. Di Ruscio, H. Muccini, P. Pelliccione, and A. Pierantonio. Towards weaving software architecture models. In *Proocedings of the MBD-MOMPES 2006 Workshop*, Potsdam, Germany, March 2006.
14. D. Garlan and M. Shaw. An introduction to software architecture. In V. Ambriola and G. Tortora, editors, *Advances in Software Engineering and Knowledge Engineering*, pages 1–39, Singapore, 1993. World Scientific Publishing Company.
15. IEEE 802.11 Working Group. IEEE 802.11 Wireless Local Area Networks (WiFi). http://grouper.ieee.org/groups/802/11/.
16. IEEE 802.3 Working Group. IEEE 802.3 CSMA/CD (ETHERNET) based Local Area Networks. http://grouper.ieee.org/groups/802/3/.
17. P. Inverardi, H. Muccini, and P. Pelliccione. DUALLY: Putting in synergy UML 2.0 and ADLs. In *Proocedings of Int. 5th Working IEEE/IFIP Conference on Software Architecture (WICSA)*, Pittsburgh, November 2005.
18. J. Ivers, P. Clements, D. Garlan, R. N. B. Schmerl, and J. R. O. Silva. Documenting component and connector views with uml 2.0. Technical report, Carnegie Mellon, Software Engineering Institute, Pittsburgh, USA, April 2004.
19. N. Medvidovic, D. S. Rosenblum, D. F. Redmiles, and J. E. Robbins. Modeling software architectures in the unified modeling language. *ACM Trans. Softw. Eng. Methodol.*, 11(1):2–57, 2002.
20. N. Medvidovic and R. N. Taylor. A classification and comparison framework for software architecture description languages. *IEEE Transaction on Software Engineering*, 26(1):70–93, 2000.
21. A.-J. Moerdijk and L. Klosterman. Opening the Networks with Parlay/OSA: Standards and Aspects Behind the APIs. *IEEE Network*, 17(3):58–64, May-Jun 2003.
22. M. Mouly and M. Pautet. Current evolution of the GSM systems. Technical report, IEEE Pers. Commun., 1995.
23. Network Working Group. The Point-to-Point Protocol (PPP). RFC 1661, July 1994.
24. Object Management Group OMG. Unified Modeling Lanauge Specification - UML 2.0 Superstructure Specification. OMG Document: formal/05-07-04, Aug 2005.
25. D. E. Perry and A. L. Wolf. Foundations for the study of software architecture. *SIGSOFT Software Engineering Notes*, 17(4):40–52, Oct 1992.
26. Plastic Consortium. Providing Lightweight and Adaptable Service Technology for pervasive Information and Communication. http://www.ist-plastic.org/. IST STREP Project.

27. S. Roh, K. Kim, and T. Jeon. Architecture modeling language based on uml2.0. In *Proocedings of 11th Asia-Pacific Software Engineering Conference (APSEC'04)*, pages 663–669.
28. M. Vieira and D. Richardson. Analyzing dependencies in large component-based systems. In *Proceedings of the 17th IEEE International Conference on Automated Software Engineering*, pages 241–244, Edinburgh, UK, September 2002.
29. M. Vieira and D. Richardson. The role of dependencies in component-based systems evolution. In *IWPSE '02: Proceedings of the International Workshop on Principles of Software Evolution*, pages 62–65. ACM Press, 2002.
30. T. Zahariadis and B. Doshi. Applications and services for the B3G/4G era. *Wireless Communications, IEEE*, 11(5), Oct 2004.

RTDWD: Real-Time Distributed Wideband-Delphi for User Stories Estimation

Giovanni Aiello[1], Marco Alessi[1,2], Massimo Cossentino[3], Alfonso Urso[3], and Giuseppe Vella[2]

[1] Engisud S.p.A. - Research and Development Lab. - Palermo, Italy
[2] Engineering Ingegneria Informatica S.p.A. - Research and Development Lab. - Palermo, Italy
[3] ICAR-CNR Istituto di Calcolo e Reti ad Alte Prestazioni Consiglio Nazionale delle Ricerche, Palermo, Italy
{giovanni.aiello, marco.alessi, giuseppe.vella}@eng.it
{cossentino, urso}@pa.icar.cnr.it

Abstract. This paper proposes RTDWD (Real-time Distributed Wideband-Delphi), a real-time collaborative web application for user stories estimation through the Wideband-Delphi method. RTDWD realizes, in a lightweight way, virtual meetings for a critical phase of the requirements management in distributed Agile development processes, such as Distributed eXtreme Programming. The web 2.0-based nature of RTDWD adds new communication modes to a distributed Agile development process, where a close real-time collaboration is needed but difficult to realize due to the geographic dislocation of team members. Features of RTDWD allow to take into consideration several scenarios where mobile devices (i.e. Pocket PCs and Smartphones) well substitute desktop and laptop computers. We present our experience in order to point out to the researcher community the usefulness of RTDWD and, generally, of the lightweight real-time collaboration underlining the need to introduce new technologies on practices of distributed Agile processes.

1   Introduction

In the last years, the research area on software engineering aimed at Agile development processes causing great interest both of academic and industrial companies. Moreover, recently, also the embedded software market seems to be interested in Agile methodologies, because they propose lightweight development processes aiming to carry out a logarithmic trend of the requirements change cost according to the project duration [1].

The evaluation both in academic and industrial areas of Agile methodologies has shown very good results if applied to small/medium co-localized working groups. Moreover a common principle of every agile framework is the continuous collaboration and communication among team members and the customer, preferring face-to-face conversations[1]. These considerations help to underline

---

[1] Manifesto for Agile Software Development, http://agilemanifesto.org/

N. Guelfi and D. Buchs (Eds.): RISE 2006, LNCS 4401, pp. 35–50, 2007.

the difficulties to apply agile methodologies in contexts where team members are geographically distributed, and to highlight the need to create tools able to support agile processes even in distributed contexts. In [2] authors propose practices and values of DXP, a distributed version of eXtreme Programming (XP). DXP examines XP practices involved when team members of a software project are geographically distributed, giving importance to the communication. DXP assumes as available certain important conditions enabling a reliable communication among distributed team members; for instance the *application sharing* imposes synchronous communication among team members. In fact, in [3] the synchronous communication is considered as a way to improve the work process of distributed teams. DXP also proposes some challenges related to the communication, highlighting benefits of web technologies in terms of low costs and close involvement of team members. In [4] the importance of having a close communication within the team and tools supporting specific Agile practices is highlighted. Agile methodologies emphasize the direct communication between customers and developers, so that the percentage of information loss, due to the lack of long communication chains within the team, is minimal. Consequently distributed Agile processes emphasize the importance of close communication and collaboration *realizing lightweight techniques for a reliable communication and distributed collaboration.*

Literature presents several works dealing with distributed versions of Agile development processes (i.e. eXtreme Programming [1]). In [6] several patterns supporting the distributed eXtreme Programming are proposed. Two of these patterns (*virtual shared location* and *multiple communication modes*) are particularly important for the communication issue. The *virtual shared location* pattern deals with the need to use collaboration software in order to asynchronously post persistent information and ideas shared among distributed team members. Nevertheless, the virtual shared location pattern does not deal with the real-time communication, on the contrary with our experience where a real-time collaboration was necessary in order to realize reliable synchronous communications between team members and customers for user stories estimation. The multiple communication modes pattern suggests making available as many communication channels as possible, in order to replace, in the best way possible, the face-to-face communication and to maintain tacit knowledge, trust and shared understanding among remote team members.

In this paper we propose RTDWD (Real-time Distributed Wideband-Delphi), a fully web based tool to effectively perform Wideband-Delphi virtual meetings between team members and the customer, also using mobile devices. As both customers and developers can participate to an estimation virtual meeting, their direct interaction minimizes the usual information loss in plan-based development processes, in fact they collaborate in real-time in a work context (a synchronous virtual shared location related to the user stories estimation practice is identified and common useful information is shared by each user) avoiding general misunderstanding. RTDWD realizes also asynchronous collaborations because the results of each virtual meeting are stored in a database. The deployment environment of RTDWD is CONDIVISA, an architecture providing knowledge sharing among nodes forming a network.

The remaining part of the paper is structured as follows: section 2 presents related works in this area, section 3 describes the context of the user stories estimation practice in Agile requirements management, section 4 introduces the deployment environment of RTDWD, section 5 describes RTDWD and its usefulness to perform real-time collaborations for the user stories estimation, section 6 presents the validation of RTDWD within Engisud and a comparison with other tools, finally section 7 traces some conclusions and future works.

2   Related Works

The literature in software engineering presents various works concerning the distributed collaboration. CAISE [5] is a valid architecture for the rapid development of CSE (Real-time Collaborative Software Engineering) tools but it does not support web based collaborative systems.

Existing web based tools supporting distributed Agile processes include XPlanner [7], VersionOne [8], MILOS [3] and MASE [4]. XPlanner is a project planning and tracking tool for eXtreme Programming (XP) teams which provides asynchronous communications among team members. It is a good management tool but it does not deal with the real-time collaboration among distributed team members and provides off-line documentation to the customer. VersionOne is an Agile software management tool supporting multiple Agile processes. MILOS and MASE are collaboration and knowledge sharing tools for Agile teams supporting both asynchronous and synchronous (real-time) collaborations. Precisely, MILOS and MASE realize the real-time collaboration through their integration with Microsoft NetMeeting. Although the usefulness of Microsoft NetMeeting for synchronous collaboration, it has been a heavy-solution for us, due to the necessity of installing stand-alone applications, its operative system dependence, and its lack of supporting specific Agile practices. Since we have used user stories for the requirements elicitation phase, we needed a lightweight way to perform Wideband-Delphi virtual meetings for their estimation.

3   The Estimation Phase in Agile Software Development

Agile methodologies, because of their emphasis on customer satisfaction through continuous delivery of valuable software, suggest to adopt the user story practice in order to gather functional requirements from the customer's point of view [1]. Moreover, Agile methodologies assume that the requirement elicitation and analysis do not take a single time window on the whole development process, but their iterative nature requires periodic meetings with the customer in order to perform an incremental gathering of functional requirements and to always be ready for software requirement changes. This point is of great interest for IT companies because it minimizes several misunderstandings caused by inconstant communications. From this point of view, we share our experience with authors of [9].

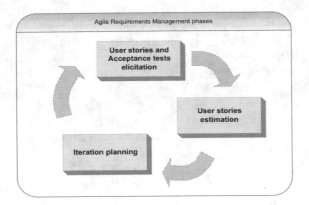

Fig. 1. Agile requirements management phases

When user stories and acceptance tests are gathered, the former have to be estimated from developers through meetings of user stories estimation. Estimates of user stories are necessary in order to perform reliable iteration plannings. The process is shown in figure 1. User stories estimation meetings are easily performable when involved team members (i.e. developers and project managers) and customers are co-localized. The co-localization is very important for these meetings because a continuous interaction related to technical and management issues have to be tackled. Nevertheless, when the team members are geographically distributed, problems concerning the lack of direct and synchronous communication precludes plans, several Agile principles (i.e. Customer On-Site) and values (i.e. Communication).

We use the Wideband-Delphi method to estimate a set of customer user stories. This method, as described in [10], is widely used because it represents a good chance for a close exchange of ideas between developers and the customer.

Agile methodologies, for user stories estimation, use the *ideal time* concept referring to a full devotion of a programmer to the code development during working hours. The unit of effort is the *story point*. The development team and project managers have to agree on the story point meaning taking into consideration a common unit of measure. For instance, an *ideal day* for an archetypal senior programmer defined specifically for the project, or an *ideal week* can represent a single story point. We preferred the former because a senior programmer has a large experience, she/he can debate the estimates with an high level of sureness and, therefore, she/he avoids problems to add calendar days from two or more developers with different levels of proficiency. In our case, the senior programmer is a project manager.

It is a good practice to provide ranges of estimation through two estimates covering different levels of proficiency for each user story. We consider 50% and 90% levels of confidence in respect to the total confidence estimate.

3.1   The Wideband-Delphi Method for User Stories Estimation

The Wideband-Delphi method, as described in [10], is an iterative and collaborative process that a team uses to estimate the effort that will be spent to realize a set of customer user stories. Generally, actors involved in a Wideband-Delphi meeting are developers, project managers and customers. Few days before the beginning of the meeting, project managers provide, to involved developers, user stories which will be estimated so that they can think about them. Therefore, estimators can be both developers and project managers. The participation of the customer is very useful because she/he can directly interact with developers and share opinions concerning user stories. In a Wideband-Delphi meeting a moderator (generally a project manager) manages the order of user stories to be estimated based on their coherence. When the meeting starts, each estimator reads the user story and, in private, provides her/his 50% and 90% levels of confidence estimates in story points (iteration 1). When all estimators are ready, they publish their estimates. Initially, the estimates will be divergent, therefore the estimators will debate on the reasons of their estimates. It represents a good chance for knowledge sharing among several team members and to clear up misunderstandings, involving also the customer. After the group has discussed the story the moderator asks everyone to estimate it again, keeping into consideration old estimates (iteration 2). The estimators erase their old estimates and write new ones on their cards. When all estimators are ready, the estimates are published again. In many cases the estimates will already converge by the second round, otherwise high and low estimators will explain the thinking behind their estimates. Iterations go on until estimate will converge, obtaining the final 50% and 90% levels of confidence estimates. The process is repeated for the following user story until all user stories for the iteration are estimated.

Therefore, the Wideband-Delphi method requires the close communication among all involved actors, making it very difficult when the development team is geographically distributed. For this reason, a specific tool to perform synchronous communications in a *real-time virtual shared location* for user stories estimation is needed. Tools cited in section 1 do not realize this specific virtual shared location. These reasons have provided us with motivations to create RTDWD.

4   CONDIVISA: The Deployment Environment of RTDWD

In this section we show CONDIVISA, a deployment environment of real-time collaborative web applications (i.e. RTDWD). CONDIVISA (Collaborative Object shariNg on Distributed enVIronments based on SOAP and Ajax) is an architecture enabling the sharing of information, represented by XML documents, among several agents. In the CONDIVISA architecture two main agents are identified:

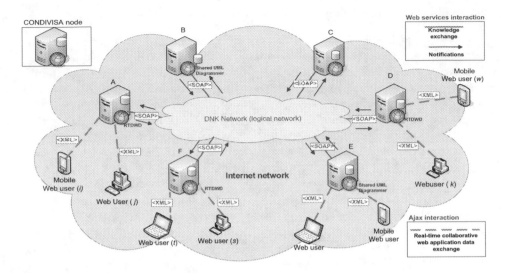

Fig. 2. CONDIVISA architecture according to SOA and Ajax interactions

1. *CONDIVISA node*: it publishes *services* represented by real-time collaborative web applications (i.e. RTDWD) and plays the role of *servent* with other CONDIVISA nodes. For this reason, a CONDIVISA node is both a web server for any web user participating to a virtual meeting and a component of a peer-to-peer network, called CONDIVISA network.
2. *Web user*: It is represented by a desktop/laptop computer or mobile device running a web browser (i.e. Microsoft Internet Explorer and Mozilla Firefox). It communicates with a CONDIVISA node deploying the real-time collaborative web application (i.e. RTDWD) which represents a shared repository for any web user connected.

CONDIVISA nodes exchange SOAP messages with attachments[2] containing XML documents related to the current state of a virtual meeting and several data of common interest for CONDIVISA nodes. For this reason, the communication among CONDIVISA nodes is performed by web services interactions. Precisely, the notification pattern[3] is used so that an information update in a CONDIVISA node is immediately notified and shared with the remaining nodes without a specific request from closest nodes, minimizing the network traffic (the network traffic is generated when updates have to be sent and shared among CONDIVISA nodes).

The interaction between a web user and a CONDIVISA node is performed using the Ajax web technology[4], so that rich client applications are available to

---

[2] W3C SOAP protocol specification, http://www.w3.org/TR/soap/
[3] Technical works about Web Services Notification (WSN) have been provided by the OASIS technical committee, http://www.oasis-open.org/committees/wsn/
[4] W3C XMLHttpRequest object specification, http://www.w3.org/TR/XMLHttp Request

each web user, providing very similar functional features to stand-alone applications, but using http as application protocol and a simple web browser.

The CONDIVISA architecture, shown in figure 2, is a Service Oriented Architecture [12]. In a CONDIVISA network, the *interest* level of a node related to information available on the network identifies two data types:

- *Common interest data*: information shared by all CONDIVISA nodes.
- *Partial interest data*: information shared by a subset of all CONDIVISA nodes.

The CONDIVISA network topology is performed using the Distributed Network Knowledge (DNK) Heuristic [13]. DNK is a lightweight (low computational cost) Heuristic for a simple and robust knowledge distribution among several computers. At this level, the knowledge represents both information concerning a piece of network topology and information made available from each node. All information related to the network topology is represented by all *knowledge spikes* in the network. Each CONDIVISA node holds several knowledge spikes representing its closest nodes. An effective distribution of knowledge spikes among CONDIVISA nodes, performed by the DNK Heuristic, assures the connection of the network graph and an implicit full knowledge to each CONDIVISA node. Therefore, a CONDIVISA node directly communicates with its knowledge spikes through notifications of XML documents concerning both common interest data and partial interest data.

In figure 2 a scenario where nodes A-D-F and B-E have common interests respectively related to two real-time collaborative web applications (RTDWD and Shared UML Diagrammer). If the web user j performs an interaction with the shared Wideband-Delphi environment, several XML documents are notified from the CONDIVISA node A to D and F through the DNK network. Note that the mobile web user i will receive XML documents from the same CONDIVISA node, through Ajax interactions. The notification to nodes D and F involves the synchronization of the environment state visible to web users k, s ,t and mobile web user w. Communication types both among CONDIVISA nodes and web user-CONDIVISA node are based on XML document exchange using http, and two levels of knowledge sharing are identified: intra-CONDIVISA node and inter-CONDIVISA node sharing levels. The former deals with the sharing of XML documents related to deployed real-time collaborative web applications, the latter deals with the sharing of common interest data and partial interest data. An example of common interest data is the list of real-time collaborative web applications available in the CONDIVISA network. The list contains all knowledge fragment of CONDIVISA nodes but it is shared by all. Consequently, a web user communicating with a CONDIVISA node may have access to all public information.

Each real-time collaborative web application realizes a virtual shared location for all participant to a virtual meeting through the sharing of XML documents that contain information related to the current environment state (e.g. the shared web page) and objects within the environment (e.g. user stories).

5 RTDWD: A Tool for Distributed Wideband-Delphi Virtual Meetings

As described in section 3, the user stories estimation phase is performed for each iteration because it provides estimates to be considered during iteration and release plannings. Nevertheless, Agile methodologies assume as normal requirements changes, also related to user stories of the current iteration, involving the need to perform multiple Wideband-Delphi meetings to estimate user stories. Therefore, requirements changes make unpredictable the number of estimation phases within a single iteration. When Agile team members are geographically distributed, the need to perform unpredictable lightweight virtual meetings for user stories estimation become a critical issue. The lightness of virtual meetings is very important because the fully web based solution allows each web user to always be ready to participate to the virtual meeting.

Real-time Distributed Wideband-Delphi (RTDWD) has been integrated with our Agile project management tool, called *eXtreme Project Manager* [11], which supports the Agile development process shown in section 6. RTDWD is a real-time collaborative web application realizing distributed Wideband-Delphi virtual meetings for user stories estimation, realizing a Real-time virtual shared location, and satisfying requirements related to the distributed communication [2]. Although RTDWD was tested for our Agile development process, it can easily be used in any distributed Agile development process, such as in [9], using the user stories estimation practice. RTDWD is not bound to the CONDIVISA architecture because it is an independent real-time collaborative web application performing XML documents sharing among several web users. XML documents describe the current state of the shared Wideband-Delphi virtual location so that the sharing, through Ajax interactions, assures a continuous synchronization of the environment state. Ajax refers to a set of techniques which rely on a layer added between browser and server. Instead of submitting a full page of data to the server, receiving a full page back, an application which uses Ajax techniques can send an individual field value and receive information to update only a single portion of the page. Ajax engine relies its power on JavaScript and CSS, but mainly on *Document Object Model (DOM)* and *XMLHttpRequest* object. DOM enables to modify the user interface on the fly, effectively redrawing parts of the page, while XMLHttpRequest object allows to perform asynchronous requests to the server and manipulate responses as a background activity.

RTDWD, due to its web based features, can be used from mobile devices (i.e. Pocket PCs and Smartphones) running a web browser. This feature is very useful when some potential participant to the virtual meeting, such as the customer, cannot use a desktop or laptop computer. RTDWD realizes a virtual close communication between geographically distributed team members (i.e. developers and project managers) and the customer, in order to provide reliable estimates to customer user stories to be developed in the current iteration.

In order to perform Distributed Wideband-Delphi virtual meetings, RTDWD recognizes the following user types:

- *Moderator*: The moderator holds full ownership to move user stories within the environment, to confirm final estimates and initialize the estimation phase of a customer user story. These features represent the *external state* of user stories. The initialization of the estimation phase of a customer user story will create a shared dynamic table where estimators and generic users can interact in real time. Generally, the moderator does not estimate customer user stories, because she/he is represented by a project manager.
- *Estimator*: The estimator takes part to the iterative estimation phase of a user story in order to perform a real planning for the implementation of the selected customer user story. The estimator can see, in real time, the user story movement within the environment performed by a moderator and she/he can interact both with user stories and a dynamic table where she/he can insert her/his own min and max estimates (in story points) for the current iteration. Moreover, she/he can see estimates published by other estimators in real time. The estimators are, generally, the developers that will have the responsibility to realize customer user stories.
- *Generic user*: A generic user is, for instance, a customer. Customers can easily take part in the Wideband-Delphi session from any geographic location, in a non-invasive way. This user type cannot move on the shared user stories within the environment for order reasons. On the contrary she/he will see actions performed by other user types within the environment at real-time. If a participant associated with this user type wants to communicate with other participants, a chat room with all connected users is available.

RTDWD service is linked to a database containing all defined accounts for each Agile project in progress. As above mentioned, according to a specific account entered during the login phase, RTDWD recognizes the user type and projects where she/he works. Of course, any account can be assigned to multiple projects. The user type establishes the interaction policy that a single participant has on shared objects (e.g. user stories). The logged user can choose the room related to the project in which a Wideband-Delphi session is needed, as shown in figure 3. Figure 3 shows both the desktop/laptop computer and mobile device versions. Figure 4(a) and figure 4(b) show a shared Wideband-Delphi-session web page with customer user stories to be estimated, respectively for desktop/laptop computer and mobile device. Ajax capabilities allow to manage, on the client side, shared XML documents in order to update, "on the fly", the local shared web page. According to the user type, it is possible to change or not the external state of the single user story. If the user type is *moderator* she/he can drag and drop a user story wherever she/he wants within the environment, causing the real-time information propagation, through the notification of XML documents, to others participants which can instantaneously see the state change. Of course, multiple moderators can join a single Real-time Wideband-Delphi session, so they will have full ownership of external user stories states. All user types hold the *internal state* of user stories, so that each participant is owner of her/his local objects, and therefore can explode or collapse internal information sections such as user story description area, tasks area, estimates area (see figure 4(a)). Furthermore,

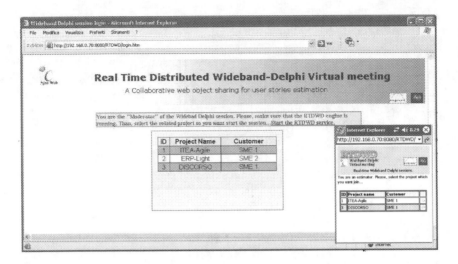

Fig. 3. The logged user can choose the room related to an assigned project

each participant can export messages exchanged in XML format which can be used as documentation support, according to the Agile methodologies principles. RTDWD has been developed considering the situation in which Real-time Wideband-Delphi sessions related to different Agile projects run simultaneously. Each RTDWD node implements all software packages shown in figure 5. The *Security manager* package manages the user login phase through filtering and dispatching of ajax requests to session manager, communication manager and sharing manager packages. The *Session manager* realizes the multi-session capability allowing to simultaneously execute multiple wideband-delphi virtual meetings related to different Agile projects. The *Communication manager* package implements the data access policy based on the user type and communicates with the *Sharing manager* package that manages XML documents related to the shared wideband-delphi environment. The *Wideband-Delphi manager* is the core package of RTDWD because it implements the business logic needed for the user stories estimation phase and provides XML documents shared by web users. The data storage and interactions with the database is accomplished by the *Data persistence manager* package performing the persistence of user stories estimates .

RTDWD can be distributed on multiple CONDIVISA nodes, related to projects of each company branch. Moreover, a single web user can join multiple Real-time Wideband-Delphi virtual meetings published on different CONDIVISA nodes. Figure 5 shows that exchanged documents are XML based and the direction is full duplex for moderator and estimator and half-duplex (from server to client) for generic users. Server side packages are J2EE based and provide, for each session, the storing and the management of the XML documents exchange.

As described in section 3.1, when a moderator begins an estimation phase of a user story, the wideband delphi process starts. For each iteration each

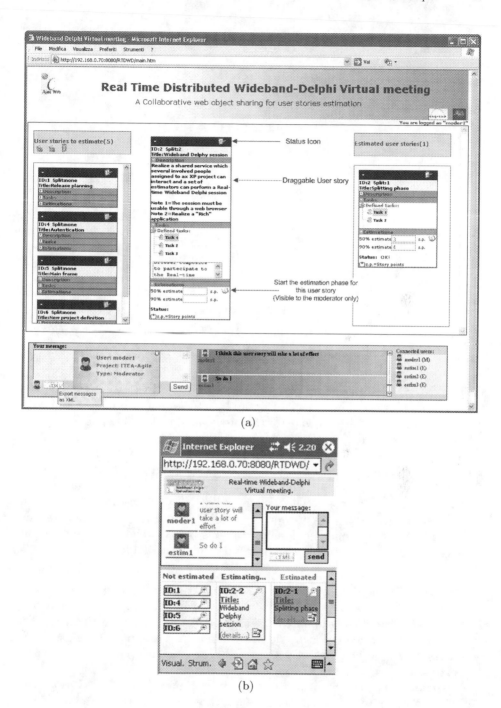

(a)

(b)

Fig. 4. A Real-time Wideband-Delphi virtual meeting for a) a moderator and b) a mobile estimator

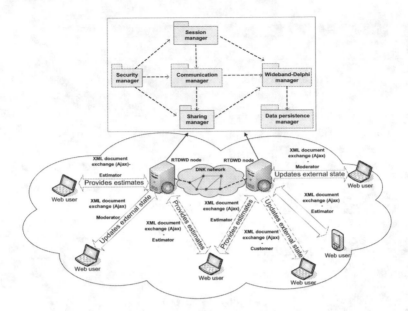

Fig. 5. RTDWD architecture, communication model and server side software packages

estimator provides her/his estimates (50% and 90% levels of confidence estimates) debating her/his reasons with other estimators. If estimates conflict, the moderator will start the next iteration and each estimator provides estimates again, keeping in mind the debate of the previous iteration. The moderator coordinates the several iterations and confirms final estimates when estimators ideas converge. When a moderator starts the estimation phase of a user story using RTDWD, all participants will see a red title background of the user story. RTDWD supports iterative estimation phases putting a shared dynamic table at the participants' disposal. The dynamic table shows all estimation status of user stories and all estimates provided by estimators during the whole real-time Wideband-Delphi session. The dynamic table is built by the Wideband-Delphi Manager software package. For each user type an interaction level with the table exists:

- *Moderator*: The moderator sees the dynamic table containing all estimates submitted by estimators in previous and current iterations. The dynamic table is automatically updated when an estimator submits estimates. This feature is provided through Ajax interactions. The dynamic table is non-invasive within the page because any user can drag, drop and close it whenever she/he wants.
- *Estimator*: The estimator provides her/his estimates for each iteration. She/he can interact with the dynamic table and insert her/his estimate only in the row related to her/him. The Wideband-Delphi manager package, shown in figure 5, recognizes connected users (interacting with the session manager) package, and builds the dynamic table.

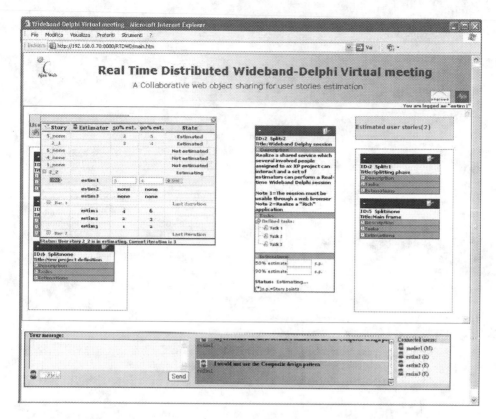

Fig. 6. Iterative estimation phase of a customer user story

- *Generic user*: The generic user (e.g. a customer) can see all submitted estimates by estimators. She/he cannot insert estimates in the table because she/he is not an estimator. The generic user can interact with estimators in order to participate to the estimation phase and debate the estimates.

Figure 6 shows the dynamic table of *estim1* estimator using a desktop/laptop computer; she/he can a)insert her/his own estimates, b)see others estimates of both current and previous iterations and c)know the status of estimation of user stories. In the same way, figure 7 refers to the participation of *estim3* estimator using her/his mobile device. During the virtual Wideband-Delphi all participants share various XML documents containing information related to the current state of both the virtual shared location and the Wideband Delphi session. Figure 8 shows a fragment of the shared XML document containing current estimates related to the figure 6. When estimates for a single user story converge, the moderator will close the estimation phase of the selected user story and the dynamic table will be automatically updated with final estimates. This process goes on until all customer user stories of the iteration have been estimated. The logout of the moderator will cause the storing of all estimates in the database of the CONDIVISA node. Furthermore, RTDWD provides documentation through

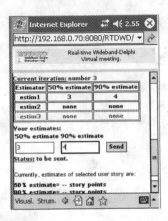

Fig. 7. Iterative estimation phase of a customer user story using a mobile device

Fig. 8. Shared XML document containing current estimates

asynchronous storing, in XML format, of messages exchanged during the virtual meeting. This way, RTDWD also tracks reasons related to user stories estimates.

6 Tool Validation

We have validated the RTDWD tool on the ITEA-AGILE project [14], during the Agile assessment within Engisud that usually outsources its projects to three geographically distributed development laboratories. The assessment has carried out an Agile development process, shown in figure 9. The comparison of RTDWD with tools described in section 2 is shown in table 1. XPlanner is full web based but it does not support the synchronous communication. CAISE tools support both synchronous and asynchronous communications but they are not web based. MILOS and MASE, although support the synchronous communication, depend on a stand-alone application that makes them platform dependent and not full web based. RTDWD is full web based, realizing both synchronous and asynchronous communications. For this reason, RTDWD have provided reliable user stories estimations because team members and the customer have synchronously communicated also when they were geographically dislocated. During our trials RTDWD has shown to be a concrete approach for distributed Agile development processes considerably reducing travel costs and times needed to reach a collective sharing of ideas among several team members and customers. Finally, RTDWD has provided a support to a critical phase of the Agile requirements management keeping simple for the customer to actively take part in the real-time Wideband-Delphi virtual location, using any web enabled device.

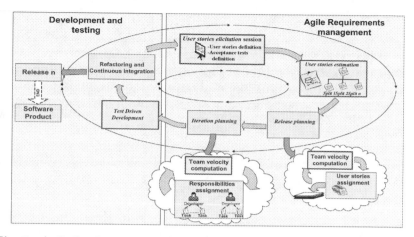

Fig. 9. Agile development process related to the Agile assessment in Engisud

Table 1. Comparison of RTDWD with other collaborative tools

Tool	Communication type	Users interaction	Deployment	Supported practices	Synchronization support
CAISE tools	synch./asynch.	text/voice	stand-alone	generic	-
XPlanner	asynchronous	text	web-based	XP phases	-
VersionOne	asynchronous	text	web-based	several Agile methods	-
MILOS	synch./asynch.	text/voice	web-based	several Agile methods	stand-alone (MS NetMeeting)
MASE	synch./asynch.	text/voice	web-based	several Agile methods	stand-alone (MS NetMeeting)
RTDWD	synch./asynch.	text	web-based	user stories estimation	web-based (Ajax technology)

RTDWD can be adopted independently of its deployment environment due to its versatility, therefore it can support any tool for distributed Agile project management adding a reliable synchronous communication way for a specific Agile practice. RTDWD well meets the DXP assumptions related to the distributed communication, the importance of the reliable distributed collaboration and the availability of tools supporting specific Agile practices.

7   Conclusions and Future Work

In this paper we have proposed RTDWD, a real-time collaborative web application realizing Wideband-Delphi virtual meetings for the Agile requirements management in a distributed environment. We have used RTDWD in our Agile development process providing a suitable communication mode among geographically distributed team members and customers for user stories estimation. Results of

RTDWD motivates us to continue our research in real time collaborative environments for distributed Agile development processes. RTDWD will be extended to the face-to-face communication improving human interaction through vocal and visual supports. RTDWD is part of a real-time collaborative tool suite which aims to effectively support all critical phases of a distributed Agile development process related to synchronous and asynchronous communications. All results will enhance the CONDIVISA architecture in order to take advantage from lightweight real-time collaborative supports.

References

1. Kent Beck: Extreme programming explained. Addison-Wesley (2000).
2. Michael Kicher, Prashant Jain, Angelo Corsaro, David Levine: Distributed eXtreme Programming. XP International Conference (2001).
3. Frank Maurer: Supporting Distributed Extreme Programming. Proceedings of XP/Agile Universe Lecture Notes in Computer Science **2418** (2002).
4. Thomas Chau, Frank Maurer: Knowledge Sharing in Agile Software Teams. Logic versus Approximation (2004) 173–183.
5. Carl Cook, Neville Churcher: Constructing Real-Time Collaborative Software Engineering Tools Using CAISE, an Architecture for Supporting Tool Development. Twenty-Ninth Australasian Computer Science Conference **48** (2006) 267–276.
6. Keith Braithwaite, Tim Joyce: XP Expanded: Extreme Programming and Agile Procesees in Software Engineering. XP International Conference (2005).
7. XPlanner software, http://www.extremeplanner.org
8. VersionOne software, http://www.versionone.net/
9. Paul Prior, Frank Keenan: Requirements Management in a Distributed Agile Environment. Transaction on engineering, computing and technology **4**, (2005).
10. Mike Cohn: User Stories Applied - For Agile Software Development. Addison Wesley (2004).
11. Engisud: eXtreme Project Manager: a tool for Agile project management. Internal document for the ITEA-Agile project (2006).
12. Randall Perrey, Mark Lycett: Service-Oriented Architecture. Proceedings of the Symposium on Applications and the Internet Workshops (SAINT'03) (2003).
13. Engisud: DNK Heuristic for a lightweight knowledge distribution on P2P computer networks. Internal document for the ITEA-Agile project (2006).
14. ITEA-AGILE project web site. http://agile-itea.org
15. Engisud: An Agile development process for Engisud. Internal document for the ITEA-Agile project (2006).

Trust Strategies and Policies in Complex Socio-technical Safety-Critical Domains: An Analysis of the Air Traffic Management Domain

Massimo Felici

School of Informatics, The University of Edinburgh
Edinburgh EH9 3JZ, UK
mfelici@inf.ed.ac.uk
http://homepages.inf.ed.ac.uk/mfelici/

Abstract. The future development of Air Traffic Management (ATM), set by the ATM 2000+ Strategy, involves a structural revision of ATM processes, a new ATM concept and a system approach for the ATM network. This requires ATM services to go through significant structural, operational and cultural changes that will contribute towards the ATM 2000+ Strategy. Moreover, from a technology viewpoint, future ATM services will employ new systems forming the emergent ATM architecture underlying and supporting the European Commission's Single European Sky Initiative. Introducing safety relevant systems in ATM contexts requires us to understand the risk involved in order to mitigate the impact of possible failures. This paper is concerned with trust in technology. Technology innovation supports further (e.g., safety or performance) improvements, although there is often a lack of trust in changes. This paper argues that organizations need to identify trust strategies and policies supporting the delivery of technology innovation. Moreover, the identification of trust strategies and policies supports the understanding of subtle interactions between diverse, often competing, system objectives.

1 Introduction

Computer systems support diverse human activities (e.g., monitoring, decision making, etc.). The introduction of new computer systems, or the upgrade of existing ones, in any environment often modifies work practice. For instance, system operators often need to adjust their procedures around new systems. Moreover, systems may act as a means of communication/mediation between human beings. Complex interactions [17] emerge as results of changes (e.g., environmental changes, new computer systems, adjusted work practices, etc.). The introduction of new technology often requires the re-negotiation of social organizations (e.g., responsibility and accountability) as well as overall system features (e.g., safety). Change gives rise to uncertainties with respect to computer systems. For instance, in the Air Traffic Management (ATM) domain, air traffic controllers often react to system changes or failures by managing less traffic in their air spaces. Uncertainties require of us an extent of *trust* (e.g., with respect

N. Guelfi and D. Buchs (Eds.): RISE 2006, LNCS 4401, pp. 51–65, 2007.

to computer systems). Unfortunately, changes often trigger mistrust. Norman, for instance, reports how the introduction of questioning between pilots in work practice, initially, triggered a lack of trust in the commercial aviation community [46]. However, the new practice, eventually, produced increased safety[1]. Similarly, empirical studies point out the relationship between trust in automation and effectiveness of human intervention in continuous process control [43]. Human Reliability Analysis (HRA) highlights how the *"human component"* affects the overall performance and reliability of heterogeneous systems [29].

Technology involves an extent of *risk* [50], regardless our knowledge or trust in it. Any time we use or rely on technologies we take risks. Understanding trust is very important in presence of uncertainties with respect to computer systems and, generally speaking, socio-technical systems. On the one hand technology supports human activities. On the other hand it is a source of harm. Engineering safety-critical systems involves risk analysis [34,55] as part of safety analysis in order to identify safety requirements, although assessing the benefits of technology exposes the limits of pure technical arguments [25]. Whatever is the risk associated with technology, social aspects constrain risk perception - *"Acceptable risk is a matter of judgement"* [10]. However, social and cultural aspects affect judgement [10]. For instance, MacKenzie analyzes how social connectivities affect global financial markets [37]. In particular, the study highlights how, even, electronic mediated trading relies on trust between traders communicating by computers [37]. This further points out contingencies between cooperation (competition) [44] and emergent trust (mistrust).

This paper analyzes trust in the context of Air Traffic Management (ATM). The future development of ATM, set by the ATM 2000+ Strategy [13], involves a structural revision of ATM processes, a new ATM concept and a systems approach for the ATM network. Despite the overall objectives [13], emerging lack of trust may undermine any improvement in the aviation domain (e.g., increased safety and performance). Ongoing research (see, Section 2) is debating and addressing the notion of trust: *What is trust? How to model trust?* Section 2 acknowledges that it is important to understand trust. But, it argues, too, that it is important to investigate trust dynamics. *Trust strategies* and *policies* should capture how socially constructed risk and knowledge (e.g., system reliability) interact each other. This paper stresses trust strategies (in terms of game theory) and trust policies for the investigation of interaction between *trust, risk* and *knowledge*. This paper is structured as follows. Section 2 reviews models of trust. Section 3 highlights the current developments in ATM. Section 4 introduces trust games and elaborates the motivations for trust strategies and policies in ATM.

---

[1] "Obviously, getting this process in place was difficult, for it involved major changes in the culture, especially when one pilot was junior. After all, when one person questions another's behavior, it implies a lack of trust; and when two people are supposed to work together, especially when one is superior to the other, trust is essential. It took a while before the aviation community learned to take the questioning as a mark of respect, rather than a lack of trust, and for senior pilots to insist that junior ones question all of their actions. The result has been increased safety", p. 145, [46].

Trust games capture processes of negotiating, may be competing, over different objectives (e.g., increased safety or performance) limiting phenomena of *risk homeostasis* (e.g., increased system reliability or safety may imply a decreased risk perception favoring risk-taking strategies or behaviors) [29,30] - *Is trust in technology appropriate to the risk?* Section 5, finally, draws some conclusions.

2   On Trust

Modelling has steadily acquired an important role in presence of uncertainty of software-intensive systems [35]. On the one hand, modelling addresses uncertainty of software-intensive systems. On the other hand, it is necessary to contextualize the trust in modelling, that is, acquire trust in models in context. This section reviews diverse models of trust. The diverse models highlight an ongoing debate on the nature of trust. This points out the complexity of trust. Although it is unfeasible, and may be unnecessary, to take a definitive model of trust, models further support the understanding of underlying mechanisms of trust. McKnight and Cherwany propose a *typology of trust* [39]. The typology consists of six trust constructs: *Situational Decision to Trust, Dispositional Trust, System Trust, Trusting Beliefs, Trusting Intention* and *Trusting Behavior*. Later, McKnight and Cherbany [41] extend the typology of trust to the notion of *distrust*, as opposed to trust. Although the typology addresses the lack of an unified trust definition, it provides limited support to understand the dynamics of trust formation [42].

The shortcomings of security mechanisms [2] have motivated the increasing interest for the formalization of trust in global computing scenarios [6]. Recent research [6,45] proposes formal models that capture to some extent the typology of trust [39]. Trust constructs, therefore, allow believes to emerge [39]. Other formal models [1,59] exploit the trust constructs and the belief formation processes in order to stress trust into design [46]. Furthermore, formal representations investigate the dynamics of trust [16]. In particular, formal models capture how social connectivities [37] influence the formation of trust in situated relationships (or interactions) between peers [16]. Recent research has exploited similar trust models in order to investigate trust in e-commerce [22,24,40] or other domains involving human-machine interactions [8]. Other research has, instead, investigated quantitative aspects of trust [22,24,56]. However, experimental results expose the limits of extending quantitative approaches to human behaviors [48].

Another aspect of trust is related to its role at the organizational level [23,32,36,49]. It is evident how the formation and perception of trust within, and between, organizations follow mechanisms grounded in the social and cultural nature of trust and risk perception [10,54]. Douglas and Wildavsky elaborate risk perception from a social viewpoint [10]. They analyze how social organizations perceive risk differently [10]. They initially take into account four problems of risk [10]. The four problems consider risk as a joint product of *knowledge* about the future and *consent* about the most desired prospects. It is possible to identify the best solution when knowledge is certain and consent complete. The problem, in this case, is technical and the solution is one of calculation. By contrast, if consent is contested, the problem is one of disagreement about how to assess consequences. In this case the solution requires further coercion or discussion. In the case in which the consent is complete and the knowledge is uncertain, the risk is related to insufficient information. Therefore, the solution involves research. The last case (i.e., knowledge is uncertain and consent is contested) is how any informed person would characterize risk assessment. In safety-critical systems [34,55], for instance, safety analysis relies on assessment methodology (e.g., FMEA, HAZOP, FTA, etc.) in order to solve the problem of knowledge and consent. Safety assessment gathers evidence in order to acquire consent and confidence over safety arguments and past experiences. Note that diverse arguments may affect each other (e.g., a negated reliability argument of fault free may invalidate a formal argument of correctness) [4,5].

Trust in technology is therefore an emergent judgement depending of knowledge becoming available eventually. Trust in technology mediates different perspectives (e.g., engineering knowledge or safety arguments) and stakeholders (often interacting by technological artifacts). Trust in technology as emergent socially influenced judgement relates (whether directly or not) knowledge and assessed risk influencing its perception. On the other hand, trust in technology is the result of *complex interactions* [50] shaping (e.g., negotiating) knowledge. This paper pinpoints basic mechanisms capturing emergent trust (strategies and policies) relating technological knowledge and risk.

3   Safety, Risk and Trust in ATM

The ATM 2000+ Strategy [13] involves a structural revision of ATM processes, a new ATM concept and a system approach for the ATM network. The overall objective [13] is, *for all phases of flight, to enable the safe, economic, expeditious and orderly flow of traffic through the provision of ATM services, which are adaptable and scalable to the requirements of all users and areas of European airspace.* This requires ATM services to go through significant structural, operational and cultural changes that will contribute towards the ATM 2000+ Strategy. Moreover, from a technology viewpoint, future ATM services will employ new systems forming the emergent ATM architecture underlying and supporting the European Commission's Single European Sky Initiative.

ATM services, it is foreseen, will need to accommodate an increasing traffic, as many as twice number of flights, by 2020. This challenging target will require the cost-effectively gaining of extra capacity together with the increase of safety levels [38,47]. Enhancing safety levels affects the ability to accommodate increased traffic demand as well as the operational efficiency of ensuring safe separation between aircrafts [50]. Unfortunately, even maintaining the same safety levels across the European airspace would be insufficient to accommodate an increasing traffic without affecting the overall safety of the ATM system [11]. Suitable safe conditions (e.g., increased safety levels) shall precede the achievement of increased capacity (in terms of accommodated flights).

The introduction of new safety relevant systems in ATM contexts requires us to understand involved hazards in order to assess the risk and mitigate the impact of possible failures. Diverse domains (e.g., nuclear, chemical or transportation) adopt safety analysis that originates from a general approach [34,55]. The unproblematic application of conventional safety analysis is feasible in some safety-critical domains (e.g., nuclear and chemical plants). In such domains, physical design structures constrain system's interactions and stress the separation of safety related components from other system parts. This ensures to some extent the independence of failures. Unfortunately, ATM systems and procedures have distinct characteristics (e.g., openness, volatility, etc.) that expose limitations of the approach [17,18,20,19]. ATM systems operate in open and dynamic environments where it is difficult completely to identify system interactions (e.g., between aircraft systems and ATM safety relevant systems) [17,18,20,19]. Unfortunately, these complex interactions may give rise to catastrophic failures. Hence, safety analysis has to take into account these complex interaction mechanisms (e.g., failure dependence, reliance in ATM, etc.) in order to guarantee and, possibly, increase the overall ATM safety as envisaged by the ATM 2000+ Strategy [17,18,20,19].

Trust is steadily acquiring an important role in the design of socio-technical systems [46]. This is also driving recent research in ATM [14]. The interaction of trust with system features (e.g., system reliability) highlights contingencies in understanding the role of trust with respect to system dependability and risk perception. The contextualization of trust in ATM [14] identifies four main relevant aspects: *Automation, Understanding Trust, Trust and Human-Machine Systems* and *Measuring Trust*. The level of automation takes into account to which extent human and machine cooperate in performing an activity. Automation is, defined as [14], *a device or system that accomplishes (partially or fully) a function that was previously carried out (partially or fully) by a human operator.* The notion of automation influences the understanding of trust in the ATM context. Trust is, defined as [14], *the extent to which a user is willing to act on the basis of, the recommendations, actions, and decisions of a computer-based 'tool' or decision aid.* This definition of trust originates from general models of trust. *Complacency*, may be, distinguishes the ATM domain from others. Complacency is a kind of automation misuse, which takes into account those situations characterized by an operator's over-reliance on automation resulting in the failure to detect system faults or errors [14]. Although trust and reliability have an important role in ATM[2], air traffic controllers accept (unreliable) tools as far as they understand the failure modes [14]. Note that the *competence of tool* contributes to the overall trust according to a simple model identified in [14]. Similarly to other domains, ATM is seeking to understand the conceptualization, as well as the quantification, of trust.

---

[2] "Trust is an intrinsic part of air traffic control. Controllers must trust their equipment and trust pilots to implement the instructions they are given. The reliability of new systems is a key determinant of controller trust", [14].

4   Trust Strategies and Policies

The ATM context provides many examples in which trust and risk may exhibit competing behaviors. For instance, the introduction of new ATM tools aims to support air traffic controllers as well as to increase system performance. However, regardless the (safety) assurance given to the controllers, they often exhibit an initial lack of trust[3] (in system evolution) by managing less traffic than planed. This results in economic pressures on the ATM system and customer dissatisfaction. The Short-Term Conflict Detection (STCD) system provides an instance of accepted technology innovation that may result in mistrust or, worst, unsafe behaviors[4]. Figure 1 shows a *Value Net* [44] for the ATM domain.

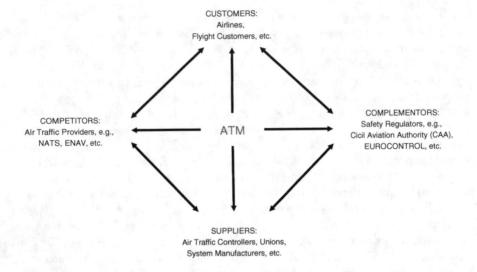

Fig. 1. The value net for ATM

The value net represents all the players and the interdependencies among them. Along the vertical dimension of the value net are *customers* and *suppliers* [44]. Along the horizontal dimension are *competitors* and *complementors* [44]. This section articulates the motivations for trust strategies and policies.

---

[3] "A well-known problem connected with the introduction of a new system (or even changes to an existing system) is that people in the workplace may feel threatened, alienated or otherwise uncomfortable with the change", p. 19, [12].

[4] "Mistrust in automation may develop from annoyance about false alarms, for example. While system tools as Short-Term Conflict Detection (STCD) have generally received widespread acceptance among operators, it is crucial for the operator to develop trust in the system. High trust (overtrust or complacency) in automation may on the other hand lead operators to abandon vigilant monitoring of their displays and instruments.", p. 37, [12].

4.1   Trust, Risk and Knowledge: A Game

Various models capture to some extent the notion of trust, although there has been little attention in the investigation of the dynamics of trust. Social aspects of trust and risk perception [10] stress the interaction between trust, risk and knowledge [23]. Therefore, a social viewpoint provides a convenient intersection between risk, trust and technology. The different relationships (e.g., independence, mediation and moderation) between trust and risk affect emergent behaviors [23]. These relationships between risk and trust highlight different behaviors. The interaction between trust and risk perception founds grounds in the social aspects of technology [10]. The characterization of trust and risk [23] suggests that the underlying constructs interact in the formation of trust and the perception of risk. This interaction origins from the social aspects of trust and risk [10]. Many models address the understanding of trust and risk, although they often treat these aspects in isolation. Whereas, social aspects stress their interdependency. This section presents the interaction between risk, trust and knowledge as a game (in terms of game theory). The underlying idea is to contextualize (i.e., put the risk and trust interdependency into perspective) the conceptualization of risk, with respect to knowledge and consent, in the case of trust in ATM, with respect to system reliability. It is possible to capture the interactions between trust and risk as trust games extending the *Prisoners' Dilemma*.

The Prisoners' Dilemma is a (decision support) game that captures those situations in which there might be competing or cooperative stakeholders having different viewpoints. The prisoners' dilemma has been extensively investigated and used in social, economic, and political contexts [3,9,33,44]. In the Prisoners' Dilemma, two prisoners are placed in separate cells. Both prisoners care much more about their personal freedom than about the welfare of their accomplice. They may choose to confess or remain silent. If they both confess, they will receive reduced convictions (i.e., reward for mutual cooperation). If they both remain silent, they will receive minimal convictions (i.e., punishment for mutual defection). However, if they disagree (i.e., a prisoner confesses and the other remains silent, and vice versa), the silent one will receive the full conviction. Whereas, the one who confessed will be freed. The dilemma here is that, whatever the other does, each is better off confessing than remaining silent. But the outcome obtained when both confess is worse for each than the outcome they would have obtained had both remained silent. Note that different matrices and different rules identify different characterizations (e.g., symmetric, asymmetric, iterative, etc.) of the prisoners' dilemma [33]. The prisoners' dilemma captures those situation in which two players have conflicting interests. Although the two players have their own interests in winning the game, the better strategy corresponds to cooperation [3]. It is possible to identify different heuristics depending on whether or not *dominant strategies* exist [9]. Therefore, the prisoners' dilemma captures those situations that may result in cooperation or competition (i.e., *co-opetition* [44]). The prisoners' dilemma captures trust between individuals (or groups of individuals). People have to collaborate in order to improve their situations. If they trust each other, they have a cooperative strategy.

Trust games as extensions of the Prisoners Dilemma enable the modeling of realistic scenarios [52]. Several studies use the prisoners' dilemma in order to characterize trust, e.g., in computer-mediated communications [52]. Unfortunately, social connectivity [37] exposes the limitations of interpreting the rate of cooperation (measured in terms of collective pay-off) as the level of trust in computer-mediated communications [52]. Characterizations of trust based on the basic prisoners' dilemma partially capture trust complexity. Trust games extend the prisoners' dilemma in order to overcome some of its practical limitations [52]. Trust games capture real scenarios that exhibit asynchronous and asymmetric properties, which expose the limitations of the prisoners' dilemma [52]. In particular, asymmetric games capture differences of risk perceptions among individuals, actors or agents (e.g., systems, business competitors, users, etc.). Risk perception affects interactions. Figure 2 shows a representation of a trust game.

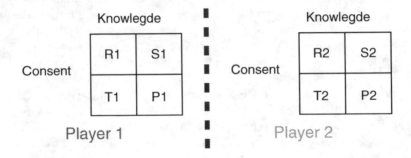

Fig. 2. A Trust Game

The game involves two players: Player 1 and Player 2. The two players have some *common knowledge* [51] about the system (e.g., system reliability). The two players have different strategies according to their expected pay-offs (or convictions). For instance, Player 1 (i.e., *complete-certain*) can have complete consent and being certain of the system reliability. That is, Player 1 trusts the common knowledge and expect a similar behavior from Player 2. This corresponds to $R1$ in the pay-offs matrix (see, Figure 2). The other pay-offs, i.e., $T1$, $S1$ and $P1$, correspond to the different combinations of consent and certainty about knowledge, i.e., *contested-certain*, *complete-uncertain* and *contested-uncertain*, respectively.

Although the two players partially have some common knowledge about the system, the two players will normally choose their dominant choice (i.e., defection: $P1$ and $P2$). Thus, each will get less than they both could have gotten if they had cooperated (i.e., cooperation: $R1$ and $R2$) [3]. If they play a known finite number of times, the players would have none incentive to cooperate. By contrast, if the players will interact an indefinite number of times, cooperation can emerge [3]. Each player chooses the preferred strategy independently (that is, without knowing each other strategy). Player 1 would like to have a dominant strategy such to have correct trust in technology. However, `Player 2` would prefer to have a dominant strategy such to have complete consent in the risk associated with technology. Once the two players have decided their strategies, `Player 1` exhibits the chosen trust in technology and exhibits relevant evidence (e.g., high reliability or low reliability). `Player 2`, then, according to the chosen strategy (i.e., certain or uncertain knowledge), can have a contested or complete consent of the knowledge exhibited (e.g., high or low reliability). The unfolding of the game identifies different strategies (e.g., trust as well as risk taking). The two players may have different overall objectives or cooperate towards common objectives. The next section shows how the game allows the understanding and the characterization of the relationship between trust, risk and knowledge. Moreover, playing the game identifies trust strategies.

4.2 Trust Strategies

This section highlights that trust games allow the characterization of trust in situated (risk) contexts. Trust games take into account that risk perception and trust may behave as opponent (or competing) forces, regardless the (system) knowledge (e.g., system reliability). Playing trust games shows whether the two players exhibit cooperative or competing strategies [44]. Once the players have chosen their strategies (i.e., trust or mistrust, and certain or uncertain), they both have limited choices for the next move. For instance, if `Player 1` has trust in technology, whatever the knowledge about it. `Player 1` can only exhibit partial knowledge about the system (e.g., high reliability or low reliability). Although, it seems a contradiction there are cases in which people have trust in technology, despite low reliability, because they understand it. Similarly, `Player 2` may have a contested or complete consent over the knowledge in alternative strategies of certain or uncertain knowledge.

Figure 3 shows an example of possible choices (in terms of decision tree) when both players have trust in knowledge about the system. The decision tree shows the different combinations and identifies the different outcomes. In this case, full cooperation between the ATM service provider and Air Traffic Controllers is a possible outcome. Let us assume that both players `Player 1` and `Player 2` (e.g., ATM provider and Air Traffic Controllers) have certain knowledge of system reliability. `Player 1`, therefore, can be in two situations: $R1$ or $T1$. Similarly, `Player 2` can choose $R2$ or $T2$. Figure 3 shows the different cases. For instance, the combination $T1$ and $R2$ may result in a risk taking strategy, because there is a complete consent on over-trusting the system according to certain knowledge. This could be the case, when unreliable technology is still adopted, because the air traffic controllers understand the failure modes. Therefore, they systematically work-around faulty conditions. Another example is the situations in which there is a complete consent in technology trust according to certain available knowledge (i.e., $R1$ and $R2$). This would be the optimal case in practice for trust strategies - people have trust in reliable technology.

The combination of the different conditions allows the identification of potential strategies. However, any strategy may require further commitments in terms

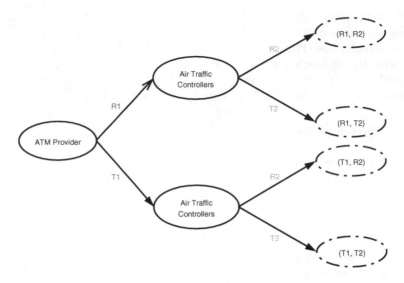

Fig. 3. A decision tree

of resources (e.g., financial investment) and activities (e.g., gathering further evidence). Similarly, it is possible to explain and analyze the other conditions and the cases of mistrust in technology. Note that the players may engage two different types of games: a cooperative game or a competitive game. The cooperative game corresponds to situations in which both players have common objectives, despite that they might have different understanding how to achieve them. The competitive game corresponds to those situations in which both players have different objectives (e.g., customer vs. supplier, regulator vs. service provider, etc.).

4.3   Trust Policies

Cooperation or competition among ATM actors stress the characterization of trust strategies in terms of (multi-agent) trust games. Policy-based frameworks (e.g., KAoS [57,58]) differently support the building on trust (strategies) within organizations. For instance, KAoS policy supports the specification, analysis, disclosure and enforcement for semantic web services [57,58]. KAoS provides a framework in which agents will discover, communicate and cooperate with other agents and services. Therefore, KAoS enables the specification of trust policy-based management systems. Hence, trust policy-based management systems extend trust management systems [31,53]. However, trust policies, in this way, represent and extend security mechanisms within specific virtual organizations. Trust policies would enhance to a certain extent trust, although they provide limited support for organizational trust.

Policies in safety-critical domains, for instance, are differently decomposed in order to constrain the behavior of a System of Systems (SoS) [27]. A goal-based approach is used to decompose safety policies, which represent a means for achieving safety. Although structured notations support the decomposition process, they face evolution [20]. However, It is possible to captures emergent complex interactions [17]. Modeling enables the characterization of evolutionary structures [21], although it is still required the identification of change strategies. This stresses the interactions between trust strategies and (structured) trust policies.

4.4   A Matter of Knowledge

This section points out a characterization of trust games in a logical framework for reasoning about knowledge and uncertainty [15,28] . The logical framework allows the characterization of knowledge (uncertainty) in multi-agents systems [15]. Therefore, the framework easily captures trust games. The basics consist of well-established results in modal logic [7,15]. Although the theoretical results in modal logic extend over several levels of expressiveness (e.g., intuitionistic, propositional, first-order, etc.), this section refers to a simple propositional modal logic. Modal logic allows the formalization of the intuitions about necessity and possibility. There exist many different representations that describe modal logic. Most of them are equivalent from a theoretical viewpoint. A semantics for propositional modal logic relies on the *possible worlds* framework, *Kripke structures* or *Kripke frames*. This allows us to define a notion of validity for modal logic, hence *Kripke models*. Intuitively, the Kripke semantics interprets modal formulas like worlds that are related each other by an accessibility relationship.

The basic framework of modal logic allows the modeling of multi-agents systems [15]. For instance, in a group of agents (or players) G, given current information, an agent may not be able to tell which of a number of possible worlds describes the actual state of affairs. An agent is then said to know a fact, if the fact is true at all the possible worlds (according to given knowledge). It is possible to extend the modal logical framework in order to express the notions of *common knowledge* and *distributed knowledge* [15]. To express these notions, the language is extended with the modal operators *"everyone in the group G knows"*, *"it is common knowledge among the agents in G"* and *"it is distributed knowledge among the agents in G"* [15]. This allows the modeling of multi-agents systems or trust games.

5   Conclusions

The social aspects of trust and risk perception highlight the interactions between trust, risk and knowledge. These interactions exhibit different behaviors situated in contexts. The analysis of trust with respect to risk perception and knowledge allows the characterization of practical situations in which trust, or mistrust, emerges. This paper presents a trust game that captures the interdependency between trust and risk perception. The trust game is an extension of the prisoners' dilemma. Unfolding the game corresponds to different trust strategies. Moreover, the game captures the interdependency between trust and risk perception into contextualized (system) knowledge. Trust games capture the interactions between risk, trust and knowledge that emerge in practice. Organizational (e.g., social and cultural) aspects constrain the game, that is, the movements available to each player. Trust policies may capture these organizational constraints. Therefore, it could be the case that some practical situations lack any achievable solution, that is, none of the player has a dominant strategy. It is possible to formalize the game in a logical framework for reasoning about knowledge (and uncertainty) [15,28].

In conclusions, this paper analyzes the interaction of trust, risk and knowledge in the context of Air Traffic Management (ATM). It is possible to characterize the emergence of trust strategies and policies. Trust games highlight that trust plays a crucial role with respect to risk and knowledge in order to achieve overall objectives [13] in the ATM domain. Although trust games capture the interaction between trust, risk and knowledge, in practice, it is still challenging the instantiation and construction of trust games (e.g., identification of the decision matrix, rules, etc.). However, the paper stresses and justifies future investigations of trust strategies and policies. Moreover, it provides a game-oriented characterization for the analysis of trust strategies and policies. Future formalization of the game in theoretical terms would allow the identification of game conditions. Future work aims to formalize the rules underlying trust games. Moreover, the instantiation of trust games in situated context would allow the identification of heuristics [26]. Future work intends to use trust games in order to investigate relationships between different strategies (e.g., adoption of technology innovation, system testing and validation, etc.) and policies. This would further support the understanding and generalization of the notion of trust. However, organizations may, already, use and instantiate trust games in order to understand and investigate how trust, risk and knowledge interact within their contexts.

Acknowledgements

This work has been supported by the UK EPSRC Interdisciplinary Research Collaboration in Dependability, DIRC - http://www.dirc.org.uk - grant GR/N13999.

References

1. Alfarez Abdul-Rahman and Stephen Halles. A distributed model of trust. In *Proceedings of the New Security Paradigms Workshop*, pages 48–60. ACM, 1997.
2. Ross Anderson. *Security Engineering: A Guide to Build Dependable Distribute Systems*. Wiley Computer Publishing, 2001.
3. Robert Axelrod. *The Evolution of Co-operation*. Penguin Books, 1990.
4. Robin Bloomfield and Bev Littlewood. Multi-legged arguments: the impact of diversity upon confidence in dependability arguments. In *Proceedings of the 2003 International Conference on Dependable Systems and Networks, DSN'03*, pages 25–34. IEEE Computer Society, 2003.

5. Robin Bloomfield and Bev Littlewood. On the use of diverse arguments to increase confidence in dependability claims. In Denis Besnard, Cristina Gacek, and Cliff B. Jones, editors, *Structure for Dependability: Computer-Based Systems from an Interdisciplinary Perspective*, chapter 13, pages 254–268. Springer-Verlag, 2006.
6. Marco Carbone, Mogens Nielsen, and Vladimiro Sassone. A formal model of trust in dynamic netwotks. In *Proceedings of the First International Conference on Software Engineering and Formal methods (SEFM'03)*. IEEE Computer Society, 2003.
7. Alexander Chagrov and Michael Zakharyaschev. *Modal Logic*. Number 35 in Oxford Logic Guides. Oxford University Press, 1997.
8. I. Dassonville, D. Jolly, and A. M. Desodt. Trust between man and machine in a teleoperation system. *Reliability Engineering & System Safety*, 53:319–325, 1996.
9. Avinash K. Dixit and Barry J. Nalebuff. *Thinking Strategically: The Competitive Edge in Business, Politics, and Everyday Life*. W. W. Norton & Company, 1991.
10. Mary Douglas and Aaron Wildavsky. *Risk and Culture: An Essay on the Selection of Technological and Environmental Dangers*. University of California Press, 1982.
11. John H. Enders, Robert S. Dodd, and Frank Fickeisen. Continuing airworthiness risk evaluation (CARE): An exploratory study. *Flight Safety Digest*, 18(9-10):1–51, September-October 1999.
12. EUROCONTROL. *Human Factor Module - Human Factors in the Development of Air Traffic Management Systems*, 1.0 edition, 1998.
13. EUROCONTROL. *EUROCONTROL Air Traffic Management Strategy for the years 2000+*, 2003.
14. EUROCONTROL. *Guidelines for Trust in Future ATM Systems: A Literature Review*, 1.0 edition, 2003.
15. Ronald Fagin, Joseph Y. Halpern, Yoram Moses, and Moshe Y. Vardi. *Reasoning about Knowledge*. The MIT Press, 2003.
16. Rino Falcone and Cristiano Castelfranchi. The socio-cognitive dynamics of trust: Does trust create trust? In R. Falcone, M. Singh, and Y.-H. Tan, editors, *Trust in Cyber-societies*, number 2246 in LNAI, pages 55–72. Springer-Verlag, 2001.
17. Massimo Felici. Capturing emerging complex interactions - safety analysis in atm. In Chris Johnson, editor, *Proceedings of the 2nd Workshop on Complexity in Design and Engineering, GIST Technical Report G2005-1*, pages 120–129, 2005.
18. Massimo Felici. Evolutionary safety analysis: Motivations from the air traffic management domain. In R. Winther, B.A. Gran, and G. Dahll, editors, *Proceedings of the 24th International Conference on Computer Safety, Reliability and Security, SAFECOMP 2005*, number 3688 in LNCS, pages 208–221. Springer-Verlag, 2005.
19. Massimo Felici. Capturing emerging complex interactions: Safety analysis in air traffic management. *Reliability Engineering & System Safety*, 91(12):1482–1493, 2006.
20. Massimo Felici. Modeling safety case evolution - examples from the air traffic management domain. In Nicolas Guelfi and Anthony Savidis, editors, *Proceedings of the Second International Workshop on Rapid Integration of Software Engineering Techniques, RISE 2005*, number 3943 in LNCS, pages 81–96. Springer-Verlag, 2006.
21. Massimo Felici. Structuring evolution: on the evolution of socio-technical systems. In Denis Besnard, Cristina Gacek, and Cliff B. Jones, editors, *Structure for Dependability: Computer-based Systems from an Interdisciplinary perspective*, chapter 3, pages 49–73. Springer, 2006.
22. David Gefen, Elena Karahanna, and Detmar W. Straub. Inexperience and experience with online stores: The importance of tam and trust. *IEEE Transactions on Engineering Management*, 50(3):307–321, August 2003.

23. David Gefen, V. Srinivasan Rao, and Noam Tractinsky. The conceptualization of trust, risk and their relationship in electronic commerce: The need for clarifications. In *Proceedings of the 36th Hawaii International Conference on Systems Sciences (HICSS'03)*. IEEE, 2003.
24. David Gefen and Detmar W. Straub. Consumer trust in b2c e-commerce and the importance of social presence: experiments in e-products and e-services. *Omega: The International Journal of Management Science*, 32:407–424, 2004.
25. Gerd Gigerenzer. *Reckoning with Risk: Learning to Live with Uncertainty.* Penguin Books, 2002.
26. Gerd Gigerenzer, Peter M. Todd, and The ABC Research Group, editors. *Simple Heuristics That Make Us Smart.* Oxford University Press, 1999.
27. Martin Hall-May and Tim Kelly. Defining and decomposing safety policy for systems of systems. In R. Winther, B.A. Gran, and G. Dahll, editors, *Proceedings of SAFECOMP 2005*, number 3688 in LNCS, pages 37–51. Springer-Verlag, 2005.
28. Joseph Y. Halpern. *Reasoning about Uncertainty.* The MIT Press, 2003.
29. Erik Hollnagel. *Human Reliability Analysis: Context and Control.* Academic Press, 1993.
30. Chris W. Johnson. *Failure in Safety-Critical Systems: A Handbook of Accident and Incident Reporting.* University of Glasgow Press, Glasgow, Scotland, October 2003.
31. Audun Josang, Claudia Keser, and Theo Dimitrakos. Can we manage trust? In P. Herrmann et al., editors, *Proccedings of iTrust 2005*, number 3477 in LNCS, pages 93–107. Springer-Verlag, 2005.
32. Eva C. Kasper-Fuehrer and Neal M. Ashkanasy. Building trus in cross-cultural collaborations: Toward a contingency perspective. *Journal of Management*, 27:235–254, 2001.
33. Steven Kuhn. Prisoner's dilemma. In Edward N. Zalta, editor, *The Stanford Encyclopedia of Philosophy*, http://plato.stanford.edu/archives/fall2003/entries/prisoner-dilemma/, 2003.
34. Nancy G. Leveson. *SAFEWARE: System Safety and Computers.* Addison-Wesley, 1995.
35. Bev Littlewood, Martin Neil, and Gary Ostrolenk. The role of models in managing the uncertainty of software-intensive systems. *Reliability Engineering & System Safety*, 46:97–95, 1995.
36. Yadong Luo. Building trust in cross-cultural collaborations: Toward a contingency perspective. *Journal of Management*, 28(5):669–694, 2002.
37. Donald MacKenzie. Social connectivities in global finalcial markets. *Environment and Planning D: Society and Space*, 22:83–101, 2004.
38. Stuart Matthews. Future developments and challenges in aviation safety. *Flight Safety Digest*, 21(11):1–12, November 2002.
39. D. Harrison McKnight and Norman L. Chervany. The meanings of trust. Technical Report 96-04, University of Minnesota, 1996.
40. D. Harrison McKnight and Norman L. Chervany. Conceptualizing trust: A typology and e-commerce customer relationships model. In *Proceedings of the 34th Hawaii International Conference on System Sciences*, pages 1–9. IEEE, 2001.
41. D. Harrison McKnight and Norman L. Chervany. Trust and distrust definitions: One bite at a time. In R. Falcone, M. Singh, and Y.-H. Tan, editors, *Trust in Cyber-societies*, number 2246 in LNAI, pages 27–54. Springer-Verlag, 2001.
42. D. Harrison McKnight, Larry L. Cummings, and Norman L. Chervany. Trust formation in new organizational relationships. Technical Report 96-01, University of Minnesota, 1996.

43. Neville Moray, Douglas Hiskes, John Lee, and Bonnie M. Muir. Trust and human intervention in automated systems. In Jean-Michel Hoc, Pietro C. Cacciabue, and Erik Hollnagel, editors, *Expertise and Technology: Cognition & Human-Computer Cooperation*, chapter 11, pages 183–194. Lawrence Erlbaum Associates, 1995.
44. Barry J. Nalebuff and Adam M. Brandenburger. *Co-opetition*. HarperCollinsBusiness, 1996.
45. Mogens Nielsen and Karl Krukow. Towards a formal notion of trust. In *Proceedings of PPDP'03*. ACM, 2003.
46. Donald A. Norman. *Emotional Design: Why We Love (or Hate) Everyday Things*. Basic Books, 2004.
47. Michael Overall. New pressures on aviation safety challenge safety management systems. *Flight Safety Digest*, 14(3):1–6, March 1995.
48. Alberto Pasquini, Giuliano Pistolesi, and Antonio Rizzo. Reliability analysis of systems based on software and human resources. *IEEE Transactions on Reliability*, 50(4):337–345, 2001.
49. Paul A. Pavlou, Yao-Hua Tan, and David Gefen. The transitional role of institutial trust in online interorganizational relationships. In *Proceedings of the 36th Hawaii International Conference on Systems Sciences (HICSS'03)*. IEEE, 2003.
50. Charles Perrow. *Normal Accidents: Living with High-Risk Technologies*. Princeton University Press, 1999.
51. Eric Rasmusen. *Games and Information: An Introduction to Game Theory*. Blackwell, second edition, 1989.
52. Jens Riegelsberger, M. Angela Sasse, and John D. McCarthy. The researcher's dilemma: evaluating trust in computer-mediated communication. *International Journal of Human-Computer Studies*, 58:759–781, 2003.
53. Sini Ruohomaa and Lea Kutvonen. Trust management survey. In P. Herrmann et al., editors, *Proccedings of iTrust 2005*, number 3477 in LNCS, pages 77–92. Springer-Verlag, 2005.
54. J.N. Sorensen. Safety culture: a survey of the state-of-the-art. *Reliability Engineering & System Safety*, 76:189–204, 2002.
55. Neil Storey. *Safety-Critical Computer Systems*. Addison-Wesley, 1996.
56. Ananth Uggirala, Anand K. Gramopadhye, Nrain J. Melloy, and Joe E. Toler. Measurement of trust in complex and dynamic systems using a quantitative approach. *International Journal of Industrial Ergonomics*, 34(3):175–186, 2004.
57. Andrzej Uszok et al. Applying KAOS services to ensure policy compliance for semantic web services workflow composition and enactment. In S.A. McIlraith, editor, *Proceedings of ISWC 2004*, number 3298 in LNCS, pages 425–440. Springer-Verlag, 2004.
58. Andrzej Uszok et al. KAOS policy management for semantic web services. *IEEE Intelligent Systems*, pages 32–41, July/August 2004.
59. Eric Yu and Lin Liu. Modelling trust for system design using the i^* strategic actors framework. In R. Falcone, M. Singh, and Y.-H. Tan, editors, *Trust in Cyber-societies*, number 2246 in LNAI, pages 175–194. Springer-Verlag, 2001.

Development of Extensible and Flexible Collaborative Applications Using a Web Service-Based Architecture[*]

Mario Anzures-García[1], Miguel J. Hornos[2], and Patricia Paderewski-Rodríguez[2]

[1] Facultad de Ciencias de la Computación, Benemérita Universidad Autónoma de Puebla,
14 sur y avenida San Claudio. Ciudad Universitaria, San Manuel,
72570 Puebla, Mexico
anzures@correo.ugr.es
[2] Dept. de Lenguajes y Sistemas Informáticos, E.T.S. de Ingenierías Informática y de
Telecomunicación, Universidad de Granada, C/ Periodista Saucedo Aranda, s/n,
18071 Granada, Spain
{mhornos,patricia}@ugr.es

Abstract. This paper presents a study of the main current collaborative applications and shows how their architectural models focus on the interactive aspects of the systems for very specific applications. It also analyses state-of-the-art web service-based collaborative applications and shows how they only solve specific problems and do not provide an extensible and flexible architecture. From this study, we conclude that there is currently no standard architecture (and even less a web service-based one) which can be taken as a model for collaborative application development. We therefore propose a web service-based architectural model for the development of this type of application. This model provides flexible collaborative sessions in order to facilitate collaborative work in a consistent way and with group awareness mechanisms. The proposed architecture enables applications, components or tools to be added and can be extended with new web services when required without the need to modify existing services. The resulting collaborative applications are therefore flexible and extensible.

1 Introduction

As a result of technological progress (especially in telecommunications) and also the development of new software technologies and globalization, there has been a strong trend towards distributed groupwork, crossing (for example) geographical, organizational and cultural boundaries. For this, software systems are needed that support, contribute and strengthen groupwork, and such systems must be supported by models, methodologies, architectures, and platforms that allow CSCW (Computer Supported Cooperative Work) applications to be developed with respect to current needs.

Development of groupware applications is based on different approaches including object-oriented, component-oriented, aspect-oriented, and agent-oriented ones. Each groupware system has been designed to support a particular form of cooperative work or a specific range of cooperative work forms. In recent years, the use of SOA

---

[*] This work is financed by the Spanish project CICYT (TIN2004-08000-C03-02).

N. Guelfi and D. Buchs (Eds.): RISE 2006, LNCS 4401, pp. 66–80, 2007.
© Springer-Verlag Berlin Heidelberg 2007

(Service-Oriented Architecture) for the development of distributed collaborative applications has increased since it provides an abstract interface that supplies a set of loosely coupled, asynchronous, document-based services. This makes the resulting applications reusable, efficient and adaptable [10]. The most common way to implement SOA is with web services and since they have been developed under a series of standard protocols and open technologies, the resulting applications are interoperable, portable, and easy to integrate [9]. For this reason, the computer industry has increasingly focused on web services as an alternative for the construction of open distributed Internet systems since any web-accessible program can be wrapped as a web service, and the system components can therefore be implemented as services. Web service technology is ideal for implementing collaborative work because it is based on the notion of building new applications by combining network-available services.

An architectural model is necessary, however, for the development of flexible and extensible collaborative applications and which supports the three key characteristics of CSCW systems: communication, coordination, and collaboration [8]. For this purpose, we present a web service-based architecture which enables flexible (i.e. able to support different ways of organizing the groupwork) and extensible (i.e. able to increase the functionality of the application according to new requirements) collaborative systems to be developed.

In Section 2 of this paper, we present the conclusions of the analysis carried out on the main architectural models and environments for the development of collaborative applications, in addition to a study on a series of web service-based collaborative applications. Section 3 shows our architecture and describes its main elements. Section 4 briefly explains the use of our architecture for developing collaborative applications. The final section presents our conclusions and future lines of research.

2 Related Work

A wide range of applications, prototypes, and products have been developed to support groupwork. Each groupware system has been designed to support a particular form of cooperative work or a specific range of cooperative work forms. There are also a wide variety of architectural models and environments which help us develop collaborative applications, such as the ones analysed in Section 2.1. In recent years, web services have been the technological basis for the development of CSCW applications. The study carried out on nine of the most representative web service-based applications of this type is presented in Section 2.2.

2.1 Models and Environments for Developing Collaborative Applications

Architectural models attempt to model the system as a group of components and the relationships between them, e.g. Interactor Models [18], PAC [6], and MVC (Model-View-Controller) [16]. Extensions have also been proposed for CSCW systems, e.g. PAC* [4] and Dewan's generic architecture [7], and new models such as Patterson's taxonomy [23], COCA (Collaborative Objects Coordination Architecture) [20], Clock [14] and Clover [19]. One disadvantage of these models is that they focus on the interactive aspects of the system (with the exception of COCA, although this is mainly directed towards designing independent coordination policies in a declarative language). None of these architectures provide a consistent model which allows third-party components to be added.

Although a number of environments have been developed to simplify the inherent complexity of developing groupware applications, these do not provide all the aspects required to develop flexible and extensible collaborative applications. We will now indicate the main disadvantages of the analyzed development environments. While Groupkit [24] provides a library of components for the construction of multi-user interfaces, these are not easy to customize and cannot interoperate with each other. Habanero [5] enables their single-user applications to be converted into collaborative applications and collaborative applications to be developed with group awareness mechanisms, but extra effort is needed to implement different group awareness mechanisms and it is not platform independent. JSDT (Java Shared Data Toolkit) [3] provides a set of APIs to construct collaborative applications with group awareness mechanisms, but these applications are tightly coupled with the environment and are dependent on it. COAST (Cooperative Application Systems Technology) [27] allows document-based synchronous collaborative applications to be developed by means of a general architecture and the corresponding classes; however, it does not provide any consistency mechanisms, and this can result in conflicts and loss of work. TOP (Ten Objects Platform) [17] enables the development of collaborative applications using the definition of ten objects, but it does not establish mechanisms for integrating other applications. ANTS [13] facilitates the development of CSCW systems by providing monitoring and group awareness services and a three-layer architectural model; its main disadvantage is that it does not allow third party components to be added. CoopTEL [12] defines collaborative applications based on a model of components and aspects; however, it does not allow other applications to be integrated.

2.2 Web Service-Based Collaborative Applications

In terms of the use of web services for the development of collaborative applications, nine applications have been analyzed, including three from the CAROUSEL group (CollAboration fRamewOrk for UniverSal accEssibiLity): the universal accessibility infrastructure in collaboration services [26], the framework for collaboration and audio/videoconferencing [11], and collaborative web services and the W3C Document Object Model [25]. The remaining six applications are: dynamic service cooperation [28], processes of virtual plant production [29], distributed collaborative CAD systems based on web services [21], using web services implementing collaborative design for CAD systems [22], handling of exceptions [15], and providing context information to CSCW applications [2]. Analysis was carried out according to the three main characteristics of CSCW systems and to the implementation, architecture, and technologies used for the web services. In accordance with all three key characteristics of CSCW systems, we observed the following:

- **Communication:** In general, this is implemented using HTTP, XML and SOAP messages. The CAROUSEL group has developed certain subsystems to solve specific problems, e.g. they implemented an adapter with a definite protocol to support communication between applications and mobile devices.

- **Collaboration:** Seven out of the nine applications implement asynchronous and synchronous collaboration. The application for handling exceptions has two cooperation models: simple (whereby a partner controls the cooperative process) and cooperative (integrating locally available web services or those provided by external partners). In the dynamic service cooperation application, collaboration is carried out in the cooperative process and this consists of activities and transitions and is used to orchestrate the execution of a specific aspect of cooperation.
- **Coordination:** Four out of the nine applications define a session explicitly. The three CAROUSEL group applications define the XGSP (XML-based General Session Protocol) [11] which provides a general session layer, enabling different users of the same application to interact with each other and the incorporation of different collaboration applications in the system; this protocol also defines various floor control policies. The fourth application which establishes a session is the collaborative CAD system. This is based on web services and defines a session manager which is responsible for coordinate the designer's participation. Applications for providing context information to CSCW use a repository to store, recover, and exchange context information, thereby supplying group awareness.

In terms of web service use, we should mention:

- **Web service implementation:** A web service is built for each component, service, characteristic, or collaborative application. Each application differs in the way it is implemented as a web service.
- **Collaborative architecture:** This is implemented by each application according to the needs and application domain, and therefore results in different architectures.
- **Technologies and standards:** The applications generally use web service technology and standards: XML, SOAP, WSDL, and HTTP.

In conclusion to the study and analysis of the collaborative applications based on web services, we have observed that there is currently no architecture for developing extensible and flexible CSCW systems based on this type of service. The use of web services generally offers the possibility of establishing asynchronous and synchronous communication; however, it would be advisable to use standard web services technologies to enable shared access control, notification and group awareness mechanisms to be established. For coordination purposes, it would be advisable to develop a session manager that allows a session to be created, joined, or left in real time, and to provide a repository that serves as the basis for group awareness and notification mechanisms in order to ensure the consistency of shared information.

3 Architecture

We propose a web service-based architecture for developing collaborative systems, directed towards overcoming the shortcomings of current architectural models. Figure 1 presents the general outline of the architecture proposed, showing its main layers, modules, and services. The design of our proposal allows the collaborative aspects to be separated from the functional components of the application. Consequently, there are two layers: the Group Layer (which contains all the information relating to collaboration aspects and comprises the Session Management and Shared Control Access modules, and the Group Awareness and Registration services) and the Application Layer (which allows components, tools or applications to be integrated in the architecture without the need to modify it. Both layers are independent but are interconnected by the communication mechanisms.

3.1 Group Layer

This is the central layer of the architecture where all the activities relating to groupwork are carried out. Firstly, it is important to provide the user with mechanisms that allow him/her to start groupwork through the Registration service. Secondly, a shared workspace is established through the sessions, which are sufficiently flexible to be adapted to different forms of groupwork organization. Thirdly, a series of policies to facilitate

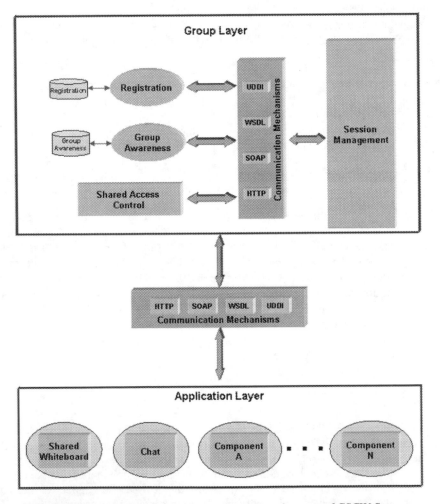

Fig. 1. Web Service-based Architecture for the Development of CSCW Systems

interaction between users and with the shared resources is defined; these policies avoid conflicts leading to information inconsistencies. Fourthly, mechanisms are supplied that give the user information about what the other users are doing and what is happening in the shared space. We will now describe the elements that carry out these tasks.

- **Registration Service:** This service registers a new session and the user who creates it, and the users in a current session. During user registration, an authentication mechanism enables user identification (by entering the login and password) for session participation, but only when necessary and in persistent sessions, i.e. those that keep the session state until the next connection. Users initiate a session by invoking the Registration service, which stores session information (session name, user id, location, etc.) in the repository called Registration. This repository is also used as a local repository (instead of a UDDI repository) when it is necessary to execute constant location requests on the Registration service and to avoid important limitations, especially in the case of synchronous sessions which require an immediate response. The Registration service provides the user with information about how to register a session, currently open sessions, number of users in each one, and detailed information about each user (name, alias, occupation, photograph, etc.). The Registration service notifies the different Group Layer components of any changes (when a new session or a new user is registered) by means of a notification mechanism. This mechanism is based on the interchange of XML documents through messages, providing relations that are loosely coupled between services; since the web service interface adds an abstraction layer to the environment, the connections are flexible and adaptable [1]. For this reason, each component carries out the following tasks in order to adapt to the new groupwork conditions (we consider the two cases mentioned):

1. Registration of a new session and the user who creates it; each component is notified when there is a new session and a participant in it.
2. Registration of a new user in an existing session. The Registration service interacts with the other Group Layer components (see Figure 1) as follows:

    - *Session Management Module:* The Registration service notifies this module of the existence of the new user in order to assign a role to him/her according to the session management policies currently being used. Simultaneously, this module notifies the Registration service when a user leaves the session in order to update the Registration repository and to report this new situation to the Shared Access Control module and to the Group Awareness service.
    - *Shared Access Control Module:* This module is notified when a user registers in a session so that the access control policies may be adapted to the new situation.
    - *Group Awareness Service:* The Registration service supplies it with all the necessary information (user data, name and type of open sessions, etc.) in order to provide a shared workspace context where each user knows which users are in a session, what sessions are currently open, whether a user has entered the session, type of session (asynchronous or synchronous), and whether this is a synchronous persistent session.

■ **Session Management Module:** This module supplies facilities for adapting to the different needs and working styles of the various groups. For this reason, it manages the users (registration and group membership) and orchestrates the session (see Figure 2). The Session Management module provides a user interface (web page) in order to register a new session or a user in an existing session; to enable users to join, leave, invite someone to, and exclude someone from a session; to define the type of session (synchronous or asynchronous), deciding whether the synchronous session is persistent; to establish how the groupwork will be organized by means of the session management policies; to provide information about the session state; to invoke the application to be used (e.g. a shared whiteboard) and/or some tool that is needed; and to facilitate elements that allow the collaborative work to be suspended, resumed and stopped. The first three tasks correspond to the User management module and the remaining tasks correspond to the Session Orchestrating module. The collaborative session can be asynchronous or synchronous. Since the asynchronous sessions are based on SOA, they present a service requester, for example the user who requests the service

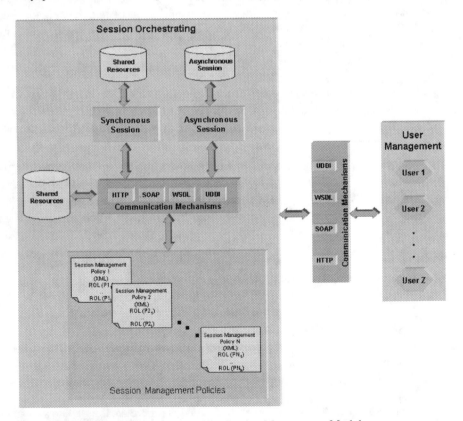

Fig. 2. Components of the Session Management Module

(such as an e-mail). The user invokes the asynchronous application (service provider) through the interface provided by this module. The service description is in a local repository called the Asynchronous Session (for an immediate response in the case of many requests) as well as in a UDDI repository. The local repository also stores user-generated information or information that will be shared and accessed by other participants.

The synchronous session provides a shared space that allows connected users to work together on shared resources to carry out a specific task in a certain time. In order to achieve this:

- It provides a repository of shared resources, where it registers the shared resources, their state (free or busy), the names of the users using them and the roles that these are playing, the information associated with each resource, as well as the waiting list of potential users associated to each one.
- It facilitates session management policies. We currently consider two kinds of policies: the first is a moderate session, where a moderator or president controls and coordinates the session, selects the appropriate tools and establishes turns for user participation; and the second is a brainstorming session which functions in a similar way to instant messaging applications. The group can change the session management policy in run time. Each policy is implemented by an XML file and determines the roles that users can play. Each role represents the set of access rights that users have on shared resources and the actions or tasks that they can perform. The roles are dynamic, since a user can play several roles during a session as long as the new role satisfies the current session management policy.
- It informs the users when a change has occurred (a user joins or leaves a session, a resource is free or busy, any modification of the session state or the information of the shared resource, etc.) through the notification mechanism. In order to do so, it uses the user interface to invoke the Application Layer containing the application, component or tool to be used in the collaborative session.

The Session Management module is the core of the architecture since it interacts with the rest of the Group Layer components (see Figure 1) in the following way:

- *Registration Service:* The Session Management module invokes this service to register a new session or a new user (and also to notify when a user leaves a session and when a session ends) so as to keep the information used by this service up-to-date.
- *Shared Access Control Module:* The Session Management module reports two types of situations to this module: when a user joins a session (so that it can grant the user access rights to the shared resources according to their role and can determine whether these rights allow them to use the shared resource) and when a user leaves the session (so that this module can adapt to the new situation and can therefore liberate the resources used by the user in order to assign them to the following user on the list).
- *Group Awareness Service:* The Session Management module informs this service of all the changes that have occurred, stores them in the Group Awareness repository, and transmits the changes to each user participating in the collaborative session or in the task that is being carried out (only certain group members can be involved in a task).

This module facilitates the development of flexible collaborative applications, i.e. applications that can adapt to different groupwork organizational styles as they allow:

- Synchronous and asynchronous communication;
- Various groupwork practices, by supplying different session management policies that can change in run time;
- Dynamic roles for group members so that users can play various roles during a session;
- Different users in a session as users can join and leave a session during application execution.

■ **Shared Access Control Module:** This module coordinates interaction between users to avoid conflicts in the shared workspace (because of cooperative and competitive activities) by supplying dynamically generated, temporary permissions to collaborating users. In this way, the race conditions are lessened, mutually exclusive resource usage is guaranteed, and safety, timeliness, fairness, adaptability, and stability are provided to session participants. The permissions granted to users depend on their possible roles, and specify which user is allowed to send, receive, or manipulate shared data at a given moment. The default policy is "free for all", where conflicts are resolved by serialization of access requests to shared resource on a first-come-first-served basis. The access request is made to the Shared Resources repository (see Figure 2), which verifies whether:

1. The user has the rights needed to use the resource:
   - If the resource is free, the user is allowed to use the resource in order to carry out the task, reflecting any modification in the interface of the users involved in this task.
   - If the resource is busy, the user requesting the resource is informed and is put on the waiting list. If the users do not want to wait for the resource, they can remove themself from the waiting-list. Once the resource is free (because the user using it has finished their task or left the session), it is assigned to the next user on the list. This process is repeated until either all the users on the waiting list have used the resource or the session ends.

2. The user does not have the rights to use the resource. The permission is therefore refused and the resource is granted to the following user with suitable rights on the waiting list.

This module interacts with the following elements (see Figure 1):

- *Registration Service:* Every time a user registers, this service informs the Shared Access Control module that it can assign the corresponding permissions to the user according to their role so that they can use the shared resources. This service also notifies this module when a user leaves the session so that it can liberate the resource assigned to him/her and assign it to the next user on the waiting list. If the user leaving the session was not assigned a resource, this module adapts to the new situation.
- *Session Management Module:* This notifies the Shared Access Control module of the role played by the user (so that they can be assigned access rights for a certain

shared resource), and also of the current state of the shared resources (so that they could be used by users fulfilling the restrictions imposed by their roles).
- *Group Awareness Service:* This service is notified when a resource is modified or assigned to a new user by means of the Session Management module.

- **Group Awareness Service:** For users to be able to cooperate, they must be aware of the presence of other members in the session and of the actions that each one has carried out and is carrying out. One of the main tasks of any CSCW system is to provide the users with the necessary information to support group awareness, and this helps session participants establish a common context and coordinate activities, thereby avoiding surprises and reducing the probability of conflicts in the group. This service therefore stores each action carried out by the users in the session in the Group Awareness repository; in this way, the other participants are notified by means of the notification mechanism. This service interacts with the other Group layer components (see Figure 1) in the following way:

  - *Registration Service:* It informs the Group Awareness service when someone joins or leaves a session so that other users are aware of which users can carry out the collaborative task. It also provides a list of the users who are participating in a session, the name and type of the open sessions, and personal information for each user (e.g. name, alias, occupation, photograph, etc.).
  - *Session Management Module:* It informs this service of all the changes that occur in each session (when a user joins or leaves a session, whether a resource is free or busy, information about modifications made to the shared resources, when a session is initiated, suspended, resumed, stopped, etc.) using the notification mechanism. In this way, users know the state of the shared resources as well as who is using them, and each user's state is shown with an icon.
  - *Shared Access Control Module:* When a resource is modified or assigned to a new user, these changes must be reflected in each user's interface in order to maintain group awareness.

3.2 Application Layer

This layer contains the specific collaborative applications which users are interested in, i.e. those that they want to use for carrying out groupwork (e.g. a shared whiteboard). Since this has been designed using a service-oriented architectural style, other applications, components or tools that are wrapped as web services may be added to provide the functionalities needed for carrying out the groupwork or corresponding collaborative task. These services must be described and later published in a UDDI repository and also a local repository to avoid any limitation in run time and to give an immediate response to a large number of requests. We must follow two steps to add another application, component or tool.

  1. To invoke the corresponding web service:
      - the required service must be chosen from the list of available services;
      - the invoked service must provide the name of the application and the resources that will be shared so that the new application can add them to the collaborative environment.

2.   Once the web service has been obtained:
  • the shared resources are registered in the Shared Resources repository so
    that they can be used by users with roles with the corresponding
    permissions;
  • the Session Management module informs the Registration service of the
    presence of the new application so that this service can send the list of users
    participating in the session;
  • the Session Management module provides the roles played by each user
    with their respective access rights to the shared resources and notifies the
    Group Awareness service of the existence of the new application;
  • the added application appears in a new window of each user's web page
    with the application name at the top, and with the names of the users and
    shared resources in the main part of the window.

The functionality of the architecture can therefore be extended with new web services
when needed without having to modify existing services. The addition of services is
simple and quick since it is only necessary to invoke the service through an interface and
(if the service contains the necessary information) to display the window with the new
collaborative application. It will not be possible to add a service which does not have the
necessary information (name of the application and resources to be shared).

3.3 Communication Mechanisms

The communication mechanisms (see Figure 3) allow groupwork by enabling
sessions to be implemented in such a way that users can join and leave a session, and
different coordination policies can be established; they also provide group awareness
mechanisms. These mechanisms manage external communication (communication
between layers) and internal communication (communication between modules
and/or services of a layer) by interchanging documents through messages.

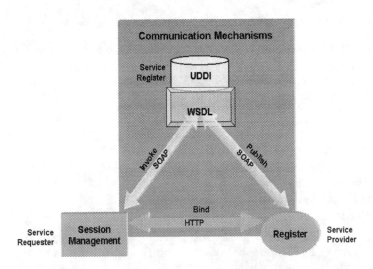

Fig. 3. Communication Mechanism Elements

The use of an XML document-based communication model provides relations which are loosely coupled between services, and this results in flexible and adaptable connections. We use the following standard web services technologies: HTTP, SOAP, WSDL and UDDI.

The HTTP protocol enables the user to access the web page of the architectonical proposal. With this page, users are connected with the Session Management module so that they may either create a new (asynchronous/synchronous) session or join a session in progress. Consequently, this module invokes the Registration service with the SOAP protocol for registering either the new session and the user who creates it or a new user in the session in progress. The Registration service must obviously be described in WSDL in order to specify what this service does, where it is located, and how it is invoked, and it must be published in the UDDI repository.

4 Development of Collaborative Applications

Thanks to the design of the proposed architecture, each new collaborative application may be assembled with reusable parts, e.g. the Registration service, Session Management module, shared access control policies, Group Awareness service and Application Layer. This is achieved as a result of the following features:

- Each element of the architecture is based on SOA and is designed independently (this enables the responsibilities of each to be perfectly separated, thereby facilitating their reuse).
- SOA is implemented with web services which are based on a series of standard protocols and open technologies (the collaborative application can therefore be used on any platform and operative system).
- The architecture can be used to develop any collaborative application by assembling its reusable elements.

Our architecture reduces the time and effort devoted to the development of a collaborative application since it is only necessary to select and/or invoke its elements through the user interface (in this case, a web page). The steps to be followed from the user interface are:

1. To register a new session and the users who will take part in this by means of the Registration service;
2. To choose how the groupwork will be organized, defining the type of session, session management policies, and roles that users can play. This is carried out by the Session Management module.
3. The Shared Access Control module automatically assigns the access rights to the shared resources for each user according to their role.
4. The Group Awareness service provides personal information of each user, the list of users, session type and state, and notifies of every change that occurs (e.g. when a user joins or leaves a session).
5. To invoke the collaborative application that the user wants to work with.
6. Finally, once the application has been obtained, it is possible to carry out the groupwork.

5   Conclusions and Future Work

In this paper, we have presented an architecture that reduces the time and effort necessary for the development of collaborative applications with group awareness mechanisms. This reduction is due to the fact that the application is built by assembling every element of the architecture with a user interface (web page). By means of this interface, a user can register a session and the users who will participate in it, determine the type of session (even to define a synchronous session as persistent), establish how collaborative work will be organized (by means of the session management policies), define access rights to the shared resources according to these policies, and invoke the collaborative application they want to work with. In addition, each user interface (web page) shows the necessary information to provide group awareness so that every user perceives a group context.

Our architecture allows collaborative applications to be developed with the following characteristics:

- **Flexibility:** since the resulting application allows changes to be made to the way in which users organize the groupwork. This is possible because the architecture provides elements to change the group size, session participants, session management policies, roles played by the user and therefore his/her access rights to the shared resources.
- **Extensibility:** since the architecture allows functionalities to be added according to the new requirements of the collaborative work. In order to achieve this, it allows applications, components or tools to be added that are wrapped as web services in the Application Layer. Extending the functionality of the collaborative application is simple as we need only invoke the required functionality from the list of available web services. As soon as the service has been bound, a window is displayed showing the new application and the information needed to carry out the collaborative work (such as the list of users, each user's roles with his/her respective access rights to the shared resources, state of the session, etc.). This window can be closed when the corresponding part of the collaborative work has finished.

We have studied and analyzed the main existing collaborative applications, and we have ascertained that most have been developed for specific applications. This means that in order to create a new application, we must start from scratch, something which entails a great deal of effort for developers. There are other applications that support the development of these applications, but none is perfect, e.g. some require extra effort in order to customize the application, others are not platform independent or do not provide consistency mechanisms. We have also analysed the state-of-the-art web service-based collaborative applications and shown how they only solve specific problems and do not provide an extensible and flexible architecture.

By way of future work, we intend to increase the number of shared access control policies and to design the session management policies by means of models in order to provide more flexible sessions, which are more suitable for the many ways in which groupwork can be organized. We also want to establish notification mechanisms for the exchange of documents by means of messages to reinforce group awareness and to redefine authentication mechanisms using XML standards, such as XML-Encryption [30] or XML-Signature [31].

References

1. Alonso, G., Casati, F., Kuno, H., and Machiraju, V.: Web Services: Concepts, Architectures and Applications. Springer–Verlag, Berlin Heidelberg (2004).
2. Bulcao, R., Jardim, C., Camacho-Guerrero, J., and Pimentel, M.G.: A Web Service Approach for Providing Context Information to CSCW Applications. Proc. of American Web Congress (2004) 46-53.
3. Burridge, R.: Java Shared Data Toolkit User Guide version 2.0. Sun Microsystems, JavaSoft Division (1999).
4. Calvary, G., Coutaz, J., and Nigay, L.: From Single-User Architectural Design to PAC*: A Generic Software Architecture Model for CSCW. Proc. of CHI (1997) 242-249.
5. Chabert, A., Grossman, E., Jackson, L., Pietrowicz, S., and Seguin, C.: Java Object Sharing in Habanero. Communications of the ACM, Vol. 41-6 (1998) 69-76.
6. Coutaz, J.: PAC-ing the Architecture of your User Interface. Proc. of the Fourth Eurographics Workshop on DSVIS. Sringer-Verlag (1997) 15-32.
7. Dewan, P.: Multiuser Architectures. Proc. of the IFIP TC2/WG2.7 Working Conference on Engineering for Human-Computer Interaction (1995) 15-32.
8. Ellis, C.A., Gibas, S.J., and Rein, G.L.: Groupware: Some Issues and Experiences. Communications of the ACM, Vol. 34-1 (1991) 39-58.
9. Erl, T.: Service-Oriented Architecture: A Field Guide to Integrating XML and Web Services. Prentice Hall. (2004).
10. Erl, T.: Service-Oriented Architecture: Concepts, Technology, and Design. Prentice Hall. Crawfordsville Indiana (2005).
11. Fox, G., Wenjun, W., Ahmet, U., and Hasan, B.: A Web Services Framework for Collaboration and Audio/Videoconferencing. Proc. of the International Multiconference in Computer Science and Computer Engineering, Internet Computing (2002).
12. Fuentes, L., Pinto, M., Amor, M., and Jimenez, D.: CoopTEL: A Component-Aspect Middleware Platform. Proc. of ACM/IFIP/USENIX Int. Middleware Conference (2003).
13. García, P., and Gómez, A.: ANTS Framework for Cooperative Work Environments. IEEE Computer Society Press, Vol. 36-3. Los Alamitos CA USA (2003) 56-62.
14. Graham, T.C.N., and Urnes, T.: Integrating Support for Temporal Media in to an Architecture for Graphical User Interfaces. Proc. of the International Conference on Software Engineering (ICSE). ACM Press, Boston USA (1997) 172-182.
15. Greiner, U., and Rahm, E.: Quality-Oriented Handling of Exceptions in Web Service Based Cooperative Enterprise Application Integration. GITO-Verlag (2002) 11-18.
16. Goldberg A.: Smalltalk-80: The Interactive Programming Environment. Addison Wesley, (1984).
17. Guerrero, L.A., and Fuller, D.: CLASS: A Computer Platform for the Development of Education's Collaborative Applications. Proc. of CRIWG (1997) 51-60.
18. Harrison, M., and Thimbleby, H. (eds.): Formal Methods in Human-Computer Interaction, Cambridge University Press (1990).
19. Laurillau, Y., and Nigay, L.: Clover Architecture for Groupware. Proc. of the ACM Conference on CSCW. New Orleans Louisiana USA (2002) 236-245.
20. Li, D., and Muntz, R.: COCA: Collaborative Objects Coordination Architecture. Proc. of CSCW. ACM Press (1998) 179-188.
21. Ouyang, Y., Tang, M., Lin, J., and Dong, J.: Distributed Collaborative CAD System Based on Web Service. Journal Zhejiang University Science, Vol. 5-5. (2004) 579-586.
22. Pan, Y., Duanqing, X., Chun, C., and Ying, Z.: Using Web Services Implementing Collaborative Design for CAD Systems. Proc. of Services Computing (2004) 475-478.

23. Patterson, J.F.: Taxonomy of Architectures for Synchronous Groupware Applications. Proc. of the CSCW'94 Workshop on Software Architectures for Cooperative Systems, Vol. 15-3. ACM SIGOIS, Chapel Hill North Carolina (1994) 27-29.
24. Roseman, M., and Greenberg, S.: Building Realtime Groupware with GroupKit: A Groupware ToolKit. ACM Trans. Computer-Human-Interaction, Vol. 3 (1996) 66-106.
25. Sangmi, L., Geoffrey, F., Sunghoon, K., Minjun, W., and Xiaohong, Q.: Ubiquitous Access for Collaborative Information System Using SVG. SVG Open. Zurich, Switzerland (2002).
26. Sangmi L., Sunghoon K., Geoffrey F., Kangseok K., and Sangyoon, O.: A Web Service Approach to Universal Accessibility in Collaboration Services. Proc. of 1st International Conference on Web Services. Las Vegas (2003).
27. Schuckmann, C., Kirchner, L., Schümmer, J., and Haake, J.M.: Designing Object-Oriented Synchronous Groupware with COAST. Proc. of CSCW (1996) 30-38.
28. Shaohua, L., Jun, W., Yinglong, M., and Yu, L.: Web Service Cooperation Ideology. Proc. of IEEE/WIC/ACM International Conference on WI (2004) 20-24.
29. Woerner, J., and Woern, H.: Distributed and Secure Co-operative Engineering in Virtual Plant Production. Proc. of Advanced Production Management Systems: Collaborative Systems for Production Management (2002) 175-187.
30. XML-Encryption Working Group. World Wide Web Consortium (2001). http://www.w3.org/Encryption/2001/
31. XML-Signature Working Group. Internet Engineering Task Force (IETF) and World Wide Web Consortium (2002). http://www.w3.org/TR/xmldsig-core/

Build, Configuration, Integration and Testing Tools for Large Software Projects: ETICS

Marc-Elian Bégin[2], Guillermo Diez-Andino Sancho[2], Alberto Di Meglio[2], Enrico Ferro[1], Elisabetta Ronchieri[1,*], Matteo Selmi[1], and Marian Żurek[2]

[1] INFN, Italy
[2] CERN, Switzerland
elisabetta.ronchieri@cnaf.infn.it

Abstract. Software development within geographically dispersed and multi-institutional projects faces challenges in the domain of validation and quality assurance of software products. Experience in such projects, especially in the area of Grid computing, has shown that the lack of appropriate tools and procedures may cause high overall development costs and delays in the deployment, development and maintenance of the software. In this paper, we introduce ETICS, an integrated infrastructure for the automated configuration, build and testing of Grid and distributed software. The goal of the infrastructure is to provide a service for software projects by integrating well-established procedures, tools and resources in a coherent framework and adapting them to the special needs of distributed projects. A set of versatile tools and best-practice guidelines for quality assurance implementation are also provided to maximize the project's chances of delivering reliable and interoperable software.

1 Introduction

Several large-scale open-source software projects have to deal with the need to organize complex software life cycle management infrastructures and processes in order to guarantee required levels of quality, interoperability and maintainability. Often these projects have to face resource, skill, time and budget constraints that may lead to the risk of releasing software difficult to deploy, maintain, understand and integrate with other applications. Fixed-term research projects such as DILIGENT [1], [2] and EGEE [3], [4] have to focus on developing software of increasing functionality through their lifetime, but cannot always guarantee that the software will still be accessible, maintainable and documented after the conclusion of their mandate. In such distributed development environments, ensuring that components developed by different developers, in different languages, on different platforms and with non homogeneous tools and processes is often a daunting challenge that may lead to software difficult to manage. Furthermore permanent projects such as QUATTOR [5] suffer from the lack of well-defined build procedures and this makes it difficult for other institutes to

---

* Corresponding author.

N. Guelfi and D. Buchs (Eds.): RISE 2006, LNCS 4401, pp. 81–97, 2007.

adopt them. Under the pressure of short deadlines and large requirement sets, project managers may have to face the decision of cutting testing and quality assurance verifications, which can be a cause of delaying the release or impairing the usability of the software because of the excessive number of undetected problems. Even when functional tests are performed, the nature itself of complex middleware, such as that developed for the computational Grid[1], render costly the provision of adequate hardware and network resources. When middleware and applications are deployed on tests or certification testbeds a lot of time is usually spent trying to make middleware suites and applications to interoperate due to the different configuration assumptions and different versions of common libraries.

In this work, we introduce ETICS, an integrated infrastructure for the automated build, configuration, integration and testing (BCIT) of software [6], specifying its requirements and architecture. ETICS aims to support such research and development initiatives by integrating existing procedures, tools and resources in a coherent infrastructure, additionally providing an intuitive access point through a Web portal and a professionally-managed, multi-platform capability based on Grid technologies [7]. Consequently, developers and software managers will be able to integrate their code, libraries and application, validate the code against standard guidelines, run extensive automated tests and benchmarks, produce reports and improve the overall quality of the software. ETICS goal is not to develop new software but to adapt and integrate already existing capabilities, chiefly open source, providing other research projects with the possibility of focusing their efforts in their specific research field and to avoid wasting time and resources in such required, but expensive, activity. Nevertheless, ETICS also adds any missing features, such as a consistent schema in order to configure, build and test software projects with different characteristics (e.g., platforms, development languages).

This paper is organized as follows. Section 2 describes the requirements of the system, whilst Section 3 documents the related work, explaining what ETICS can add to the state of the art. Section 4 details the certification process. Section 5 describes the architecture. Section 6 presents a rigorous definition of the basic concepts, whilst Section 7 reports useful user's operations supported in the ETICS infrastructure. Few use cases are provided in Section 8. Section 9 reports the conclusion and future activities.

2   Requirements for the Design of the BCIT Framework

In this section, we describe the requirements for the design of the build, configuration, integration and testing framework for distributed software. First of all, it is fundamental to establish an international and well-managed capability for software configuration, integration, testing and benchmarking for the scientific community (for what concerns the software configuration in a complex testbed,

---

[1] Computational Grid provides a set of services that allow a widely distributed collection of resources to be tied together into a computing framework.

it is of major importance to keep the configuration as simple as possible). Secondly, it is also important to deploy, and if necessary to adapt, engineering tools and support infrastructures developed by other projects such as EGEE, NMI [8], LCG [9] and other open-source or industrial entities and organize them into a coherent easy-to-use set of on-line tools. The creation of a repository of libraries is also a requirement in order to allow the ETICS framework to link against and consequently to validate their software in different configuration conditions. A distributed infrastructure of computing and storage resource to support the software in different configuration conditions is a crucial ETICS objective. Collecting, organizing and publishing middleware and application configuration information is another requirement in order to facilitate interoperability analysis at the early stages of development and implementation. The collection from the scientific community of sets of test suites is necessary to help users to validate deployed middleware, applications and their products for specific uses. Another requirement is to increase the awareness of the need for high-quality standards in the production of software and to promote the identification of common quality guidelines and principles and their application to software production in open-source academic and research organization. The international collaboration between research projects and establishment has to be promoted and a virtual community in the field of software engineering has to be established in order to contribute to the development of standards and advancement in the art of quality assurance.

Via the ETICS service, users can explore meaningful metrics pertaining to the quality of their software. Furthermore, the ETICS service also offer a repository of ready-built components, services and plug-ins, with a published-quality level. The quality metrics provided by the ETICS services and available for each package in the repository help guide the user in selecting reliable software dependencies. Finally, the repository also contain pre-built packages for specific hardware platforms and operating systems, which will help the developers to assess the platform independence of their entire service, including each and every dependency the service is relying on.

The task of building Grid applications that run reliably and efficiently on Grid resources remains extremely difficult. In general those applications consist of a heterogeneous collection of sub-applications that are handled together in order to form a large distributed application. From the perspective of Grid application developers, the ETICS service should allow them to automate their build and test procedures, and to verify that all the pieces work together. Developers should not be equipped with a programming framework in order to have details of most Grid services. In addition they should work by using a consistent, non-complex model in which their application could be composed from well tested, reliable sub-units. Most Grid and distributed software projects invest in a build and test system in order to build and test automatically their software and monitor key quality indicators. ETICS takes requirements from many Grid and distributed software projects (e.g., QUATTOR, EGEE, DILIGENT) and offers a generic yet powerful solution for building and testing software. Building software via such a systematic process can provide a rich pool of published quality components, services and plugins, which the next generation of Grid and distributed applications could be based on and composed of.

ETICS aims to establish a distributed and managed infrastructure providing common software engineering tools and processes. Therefore, integrated pools of resources also have to be maintained and managed for running automated builds and test suites. For this reason, a centre of exchange for software configuration information and documentation is required in order to allow projects to best organize their software. In addition, a repository of standard benchmarks and interoperability information that new projects can use to validate their products has to be defined.

To fulfill ETICS requirements, firstly, it is fundamental to identify a number of existing resource pools with adequate network, hardware and software capabilities that can be federated to run builds and test suites. The next step consists of promoting the definition and adoption of common configuration management and quality assurance guidelines to foster software interoperability and reliability. This activity lead to the establishment of the "quality certificate" for the software developed by the research community. Then, it is mandatory to run a professionally managed service in support of software projects and offload them from the need of setting up dedicated infrastructures and help improve the overall quality of the software. Finally, it is required to set up a repository of software configuration information, documentation, benchmarking data and reference test cases that projects can use to validate their products and ultimately produce increasingly better and more efficient software. The ETICS services must be rapidly and efficiently accessible by users from different locations and platforms. A Web-based portal is therefore considered to be the right choice as a means of accessing the services and resources provided by ETICS.

3   Related Work

In the area of software development management, we consider *Gump* and *Maven* [10] sponsored by the Apache software Foundation [11]. Gump is a distributed software build service, whilst Maven is a software build and project management tool. These projects are often referred as "social experiments", since they try to address not only the technical problems but also the issues that arise when software is developed by several communities. Gump supports the build of software for a particular technology (i.e., Java), and does not support testing tools.

Tools that provide customizable portals for software project management are also available such as *Sourceforge* [12], *Savannah* [13] and *GForce* [14]. Sourceforge is provided as a service, whilst Savannah (like GForge) is supplied as a software package that can be installed and customized by users. Moreover, GForge automatically creates a repository and controls access to it depending on the role settings of the project. These projects give a Web-based portal that users can access to register their software, track its evolution and interact with the user community. They do not provide, for example, automated software build and testing.

ETICS, compared with Gump, integrates in a single framework of build, testing and reporting functionality. It also gives the provision of software engineering functionalities such as the software build and testing, compared with Sourceforge, Savannah and GForge. Within EGEE, the *gLite Configuration and Build System* [15], [16] was set up to build automatically the software and support the integration activities. *OMII Europe* [17] (acronym for Open Middleware Infrastructure Institute) identifies, proposes and promotes middleware and applications that want to improve their quality and be part of a coherent development effort at pan-European and international level. ETICS profits from the gLite experience to lay the foundations of a more general configuration, integration and build system to match the needs of distributed software development. OMII and ETICS projects are to complement each other. The latter, in fact, can provide the underlying development process and quality assurance facility.

4   Quality Assurance Certification Process

As with other major issues, the ETICS project must deliver a feasibility study for the implementation of a Quality Assurance (QA) certification process for Grid and distributed software projects which want to adopt a quality label and promote their products. In fact, software products need to be certified in order for them to be accepted by other projects and user communities. In most cases, it is very difficult to assess the quality of software and most standards address the problem by specifying various statistical methods of calculating the defect density of the software or by setting the following equation: `quality of the software` $= quality\ of\ the\ company/institute$. Although such metrics [18] are certainly of great importance in the evaluation of software quality, there are no agreed definitions of such concepts based on usability or suitability principles. Such a task is of great difficulty and the ETICS infrastructure is in a strategic position to participate in and promote discussions on the definition of more qualitative rather than quantitative standards. For example, "is the software good enough for what I need to do?", rather than, "it has passed a set of reference tests?", or "it has less than 0.9 defects per thousands lines of code".

Some useful metrics are: 1. the number of implemented requirements based on the requirements that can be tracked in a project tracker. Since the percentage is relative to the number of requirements in the tracker, which is supposed to increase in time, a small increase in percentage may still imply a large number of implemented requirements. This metric must therefore be accompanied also by the real number of received and implemented requirements; 2. defect and usage correlation: this is a metrics that tries to correlate the usage of a package or a system (e.g., number of users, number of days between updates, number of packages depending or using this package, number of bugs per package, trends) with the number of defects found before releasing; 3. the number of lines, classes, methods counts and stats fragility, complexity, hierarchy size. The idea is to demonstrate in practice that the application of proper software engineering and QA techniques has a measurable impact on the final quality and usability of the software.

The ETICS study is a full assessment of what procedures, tools and rules maximize the project's chances of delivering reliable [19], interoperable software based on the real data collected in two years of activity. ETICS wants to propose the results of this study as the starting point of a coordinated QA Certification activity in the context of a more permanent Grid infrastructure initiative. The investigation is conducted using as benchmarks the software developed by some of the ETICS partners in other projects. Currently, the EGEE-gLite software, the DILIGENT software and the VDT [20] software use the ETICS service. Additional software packages (e.g., QUATTOR) have already been selected in order to start using ETICS services and to be deployed by using ETICS infrastructure. The ETICS system performs both static and dynamic analysis: the former consists of evaluating the adherence to user defined coding conventions and the source code, and making custom analysis (e.g., IPv6 compliance); the latter consists of for example evaluating the code coverage for unit and system tests, compliance tests, stress tests, performance tests.

5   ETICS System Architecture

The ETICS system architecture is based on the requirements described in Section 2. It is split into several entities, as shown on Figure 1: Web Service; Web Application; command line interfaces; data model and storage; job execution engine. The *Data Model and Storage* is designed to organize a software project by using the high-level entities such as the project structure, the build configuration, the security information, the build and job result set. The data model describes explicitly the objects and the relationships between objects. In addition, the model allows representing the results of running a build and test job in a way that can be consumed by the Web Application to generate reports. The

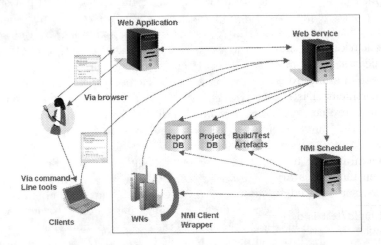

Fig. 1. The ETICS System Architecture

data storage back-end holds the persisted data model and supports different deployment models. For example, as the number of requests increases, with more users using the service, a potential use cases require database to be hosted on different machines via a load balancing algorithm and/or several instances of the Web Service to be deployed in parallel on multiple hosts. The *Web Service* is the entity providing business logic for the entire service, used by both the client and the Web Application. An important goal of the Web Service is to abstract the data storage backend, which holds the persisted version of the ETICS data model. For simplicity and better scalability, the Web Service is stateless. This means that it does not use a stateful Web Service paradigm, such as Web Services Resource Framework (WSRF), which still has to prove itself in high-availability applications. The *Web Application* is responsible for allowing the user to view, monitor, configure and execute automated builds and tests. It is stateful in order to maintain the security credentials and session information, which improves the ergonomics of the interface. The *Command Line Interfaces* provide a similar functionality as the Web Application and makes use of the same Web Service interface for simplicity and symmetry (i.e., they have some tasks in common). The command line interfaces can be used directly by the user on local resources (e.g., a developer machine). Furthermore, the same client is used in an almost identical context by the NMI build and test framework. This similarity is crucial to avoid context switching between local and remote builds/tests[2], which would reduce the usability and reliability of the system. The *Job Execution Engine* allows the ETICS service to offer the user the automation of builds and tests, possibly on a regular schedule, on a large set of different resources and platforms. The engine is provided by the NMI build and test framework, which builds on top of Condor [21], a specialized workload management system for computing intensive jobs.

5.1   Security in ETICS

The underlying security infrastructure is based on digital certificates. Both the Web Application and the client authenticate themselves using standard *x.509* [22] certificates. Users are modeled as fully qualified *x.509* principal names as they appear in standard *x.509*-compliant certificates. The Web Service verifies the user certificate Distinguished Name (DN) in the database of existing users involved in a project, and it allows or denies the operation based on the roles (summarized in Figure 2) assigned to the users. From that point onwards, the Web Service uses a service certificate to interact with other internal services. The access control list on the persisted data will be enforced by the Web Service.

The identified roles are described in the following list: *Administrator* (A) is a super user enabled to perform all the operations allowed in the ETICS

---

[2] A local build/test is performed, for instance, by the developer on his/her personal workstation whenever he/she wants. A remote build/test is submitted, for instance, by the developer on a remote system that will process it when possible (i.e., the developer does not have a total control of the resources that may be used by other users).

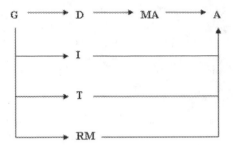

Fig. 2. The Hierarchy of Roles. Figure has to be read from left to right. The role G is the lowest important respect to the role A. The arrow points out that the destination role can perform the same action of the source one.

infrastructure; *Module Administrator* (MA) is responsible for handling the project by using the ETICS services; *Developer* (D) works on the implementation of the software; *Integrator* (I) runs software verifying if it works and register packages; *Tester* (T) submits and stores test; *Release Manager* (RM) is responsible for defining the release candidate of the project, publishing packages, creating release notes and other documentation; *Guest* (G) has only read access.

6   A Rigorous Definition of the Basic Concepts

In this section we introduce in a rigorous way the basic concepts and the definitions of the ETICS data model. The schema has been designed to model a generic software project, its internal structure and its relationships and the operations required to build and test such a project. The model is inspired by the Common Information Model (CIM) Application model [23] and the Object Management Group (OMG)'s Model Driven Architecture [24], but it adds definitions for the operations of software construction (build) and verification (testing) which are missing from the above mentioned models. The ETICS data model is composed by several elements which can be organized in *software structure, build configuration* and *security information*.

6.1   Software Structure Definitions

We provide the software structure definitions, characterized by the concepts of component, subsystem and project. We start by defining the concept of component that is different from the same definition used in the object-oriented programming:

Definition 1. *A component c is defined as a collection of objects providing a well-defined more limited functionality within the system architecture.*

A proper understanding of this definition requires investigation of the concepts of *object* and *functionality*. The former can be at least a source file, or a configuration file or a document, whilst the latter is the sum or any aspect of what a software application can do for a user[1]. The software application can be formalized in the following way:

Definition 2. *A software application SA is a set of non-ordered components SA = $\{c_1, c_2, ..., c_m\}$ with $m \in \mathbb{N}$.*

The set of all subset of SA is called the power set of SA and specified as $\mathcal{P}(SA)$. Taking into consideration the previous two definitions, we introduce the subsystem, a logical portions of the overall architecture in more specific subsets of functionalities, as follows:

Definition 3. *A subsystem SS is a non empty subset of the software application, defined as a set of non-ordered components $SS = \{c_{s1}, c_{s2}, ..., c_{sn}\}$, where c_{si} (si=1, ...,n with $n \in \mathbb{N}$) are components defined in SA.*

Definition 4. *Let SSS be a set of subsystems $SSS = \{ss_1, ss_2, ..., ss_n\}$ where ss_i (i=1, ...,n with $n \in \mathbb{N}$) are subsystems defined in SA, so that $SSS \subseteq \mathcal{P}(SA)$.*

For the sake of simplicity in the definition of subsystem we neglect the fact that it could be composed not only of components but also of other subsystems. Taking into account the component, software application and subsystem definition, we formalize the project, a complete software package providing well-defined high level functionalities according to predefined user requirements, as follows:

Definition 5. *A project P is a non empty subset of subsystems and components of the software application, defined as a set of non-ordered elements $P = \{p : p \in SSS \vee p \in SA\}$.*

Definition 6. *Let PRJ be the set of projects $PRJ = \{prj_1, prj_2, ..., prj_h\}$ where prj_j (j=1, ...,h with $h \in \mathbb{N}$) are projects defined in SA, so that $PRJ \subseteq \mathcal{P}(SA)$.*

For instance, a project can be composed of one or more components, of one or more subsystems, of a combination of components and subsystems.

Definition 7. *A module m is a generic entity, where entity can be a project, a subsystem or a component. Let M e the set of modules $M = \{m_1, m_2, ..., m_n\}$ where m_i (i = 1, ...,n with $n \in \mathbb{N}$) are modules defined in M and $M = \{PRJ \cup SSS \cup SA\}$.*

6.2   Build Configuration Definitions

In this section we provide the build configuration definitions, composed of platform, resource, commands, and configuration concepts. An example of platform is *slc4_x86_64_gcc345* where *slc4* is the operating system, *x86_64* is the machine architecture and *gcc345* is the compiler.

---

[1] Szyperski [25] gives the definition of software component, commonly used in the object-oriented programming.

Definition 8. *Let OS be the set of operating systems. Let CMP the set of compilers. Finally, let MA be the set of machine architectures. PLT = OS × CMP × MA is a set of platforms.*

Definition 9. *Let R be the set of resources $R = \{r_1, r_2, ..., r_b\}$ with $b \in \mathbb{N}$.*

We now define the applications f and g. The former enables to define the concept that it is possible to have several resources with the same platform, and exactly one platform for each resource. The latter enables to define the concept that a project runs on several resources, and a resource can run more than one projects.

Definition 10. *The application $f \colon R \to PLT$ from R to PLT is a correspondence between R and PLT such that for each resource $r \in R$, $\exists$ exactly one platform $plt \in PLT$ such that $f(r) = plt$.*

We observe that given the resources r_j and r_k with $j \neq k$ (i.e., $r_j \neq r_k$) and r_j, $r_k \in R$ and the platform $plt \in PLT$, it could be that $f(r_j) = ptf$ and $f(r_k) = ptf$, so that the application f is not *injective*.

Definition 11. *Consider the application $g : R \times PRJ \to \{0, 1\}$ such that*

$$g(r, prj) = \begin{cases} 1 & \textit{if prj runs on } r, \\ 0 & \textit{otherwise.} \end{cases}$$

We observe that given:

- the resources r_j and r_k with $j \neq k$ (i.e., $r_j \neq r_k$) and r_j, $r_k \in R$ and the project $prj \in PRJ$, it could be that $g(r_j, prj) = 1$ and $g(r_k, prj) = 1$;
- the projects prj_j and prj_k with $j \neq k$ (i.e., $prj_j \neq prj_k$) and prj_j, $prj_k \in PRJ$ and the resource $r \in R$, it could be that $g(r, prj_j) = 1$ and $g(r, prj_k) = 1$.

EV environment variables are a set of dynamic values that can affect the way running processes will behave.

Definition 12. *A configuration conf collects some information needed to download, build and test a subset of software for each supported platform. Let CONF be the set of configurations.*

The *PRP* property is a set of custom attributes that a configuration requires at build-time such as compilation flags.

Definition 13. *Let VCSC be the set of version control system commands. Let BC be the set of build commands. Finally, let TC be the set of test commands. CMN = VCSC × BC × TC is a set of commands.*

Subversion [26] and Control Version System [27] are examples of version control systems. An example of version control system command is *cvs co component*. The build commands are used to configure, build, package, create documentation, remove generated build files (e.g., *make clean, make doc*), whilst the test commands are involved in running, for example, specialized unit test, coverage test, coding conventions test, functional test, stress test and performance test. We introduce the formal definition of relationship between platform and configuration:

Definition 14. *Consider the case* $h : CONF \times PLT \rightarrow CMN \times EV \times PRP$ *such that*

$$
h(conf, plt) = \begin{cases}
(cmn, ev, prp) & \text{if plt is defined for conf,} \\
(cmn_d, ev, prp) & \text{if plt is not defined for conf} \\
& \text{but } plt_d \text{ is associated with conf,} \\
\emptyset & \text{if plt is not defined for conf} \\
& \text{and } plt_d \text{ is not associated with conf,}
\end{cases}
$$

where plt_d *is the default platform, and* cmn_d *is the default command and* $\{CMN \times EV \times PRP\} \bigcup \{\varnothing\}$.

Definition 15. *Consider the case* $k : CONF \times PLT \times M \rightarrow \{0, 1\}$ *such that*

$$
k(conf, plt, m) = \begin{cases}
1 & \text{if m is defined for conf and m,} \\
0 & \text{otherwise}
\end{cases}
$$

where m *represents the dependency by which* $conf$ *depends on.*

We formalize the relationship between modules and configurations as follows:

Definition 16. *The application* $w : CONF \rightarrow M$ *from CONF to M is a correspondence between CONF and M such that for each configuration conf* $\in$ *CONF,* $\exists$ *exactly one module* $m \in M$ *such that* $w(conf) = m$.

We observe that a module can have more than one configuration.

6.3 Security Information Definitions

Finally, we provide definitions for security information. Let U be the set of users. Let RL be the set of roles RL={A, MA, D, I, T, RM, G}. We now define four applications v, z, t, q that enables a user to act on a configuration, project, subsystem, and component respectively with a specific role.

Definition 17. *Consider the case* $v : U \times RL \times CONF \rightarrow \{0, 1\}$ *such that*

$$
v(u, rl, conf) = \begin{cases}
1 & \text{if the user u has the role rl for the configuration conf} \\
0 & \text{otherwise.}
\end{cases}
$$

Definition 18. *Consider the case* $z : U \times RL \times PRJ \rightarrow \{0, 1\}$ *such that*

$$
z(u, rl, prj) = \begin{cases}
1 & \text{if the user u has the role rl for the project prj} \\
0 & \text{otherwise.}
\end{cases}
$$

Definition 19. *Consider the case* $t : U \times RL \times SSS \rightarrow \{0, 1\}$ *such that*

$$
t(u, rl, ss) = \begin{cases}
1 & \text{if the user u has the role rl for the subsystem ss} \\
0 & \text{otherwise.}
\end{cases}
$$

Definition 20. *Consider the case* $q : U \times RL \times SA \to \{0, 1\}$ *such that*

$$q(u, rl, sa) = \begin{cases} 1 & \text{if the user } u \text{ has the role } rl \text{ for the component } sa \\ 0 & \text{otherwise.} \end{cases}$$

7   Supported Operations

The operations supported by the existing ETICS implementation are classified in two main categories: read only and edit. The former one allows users to get information about software, build it and test it, whilst the latter one allows users to interact with ETICS services, such as data storage. In this section we provide more details on the set of the read only and edit categories that are the most meaningful for users, through two list of operations that are respectively able for instance to build software and to support different actions on the ETICS data elements. Table 1 describes the type of the edit operations and their meanings.

Get a Project(prj). *This operation gets information about the project prj.*
   Prereq: The project $prj \in PRJ$.
   Result: prj is returned back to the user.

Checkout a Configuration(conf). *This operation checkouts the configuration conf.*
   Prereq: The operation *Get a Project(prj)* has to be performed with success and the configuration $conf \in CONF$.
   Result: $conf$ with its dependencies and subset of software are returned back to the user.

Build a Configuration(conf). *This operation builds the configuration conf.*
   Prereq: The operation *Checkout a configuration(conf)* has to be performed with success.
   Result: The subset of software associated to that $conf$ is built.

Test a Configuration(conf). *This operation tests the configuration conf.*
   Prereq: The operation *Checkout a configuration(conf)* has to be performed with success.
   Result: The subset of software associated to that $conf$ is tested.

Add a User(a). *This operation adds a new user a.*
   Prereq: The user $u \in U$ who performs this operation has the role $A \in RL$.
   Result: $a \in U$.
Remove a User(a). *This operation remove the user a.*
   Prereq: The user $u \in U$ who performs this operation has the role $A \in RL$, $a \in U$ and the applications $v(a, rl, plt) = z(a, rl, plt) = t(a, rl, plt) = q(a, rl, plt) = 0$, $\forall\ rl \in RL$ and $plt \in PLT$.
   Result: $a \notin U$.

Table 1. Type of edit operations

Operations	Meaning
add	insert new element in the ETICS data model
modify	change some element parameters in the ETICS data model
remove	delete the element in the ETICS data model
clone	copy an element of the ETICS data model
prepare	prepare a template file with element parameters

Add a Platform(plt). *This operation adds a new platform plt.*
Prereq: The user $u \in U$ who performs this operation has the role $A \in RL$.
Result: $plt \in PLT$.

Modify a Platform(plt). *This operation modifies the platform plt.*
Prereq: The user $u \in U$ who performs this operation has the role $A \in RL$, and $plt \in PLT$.
Result: $plt \in PLT$.

Remove a Platform(plt). *This operation removes the platform plt.*
Prereq: The user $u \in U$ who performs this operation has the role $A \in RL$, $plt \in PLT$, and the applications $h(conf, plt) = v(b, rl, plt) = z(b, rl, plt) = t(b, rl, plt) = q(b, rl, plt) = 0, \forall \ conf \in CONF, \ b \in U$ and $rl \in RL$.
Result: $plt \notin PLT$.

Add a Resource(r). *This operation adds a new resource r.*
Prereq: The user $u \in U$ who performs this operation has the role $A \in RL$.
Result: $r \in R$.

Modify a Resource(r). *This operation modifies the resource r.*
Prereq: The user $u \in U$ who performs this operation has the role $A \in RL$, and $r \in R$.
Result: $r \in R$.

Remove a Resource(r). *This operation removes the resource r.*
Prereq: The user $u \in U$ who performs this operation has the role $A \in RL$, $r \in R$ and the application $g(r, plt) = 0, \forall \ plt \in PLT$.
Result: $r \notin R$.

Add a Project(p). *This operation adds a new project p. It also associates to p a configuration conf.*
Prereq: The user $u \in U$ who performs this operation has the role $A \in RL$.
Result: $p \in PRJ$ and $conf \in CONF$.

Modify a Project(p). *This operation modifies the project p.*
Prereq: The user $u \in U$ who performs this operation has the role $A \in RL$, and $p \in PRJ$.
Result: $p \in PRJ$.

Remove a Project(p). *This operation removes the project p. It also removes all its configurations $conf_i$, i=1,...,n, $n \in \mathbb{N}$.*

Prereq: The user $u \in U$ who performs this operation has the role $A \in RL$, and $p \in PRJ$.

Result: $p \notin PRJ$, and $conf_i \notin CONF$, i=1,...,n, $n \in \mathbb{N}$.

Add a Module(m). *This operation adds a new module m. It also associates to m a configuration conf.*

Prereq: The user $u \in U$ who performs this operation has either the role A or the role MA with A, $MA \in RL$.

Result: $m \in \{M \setminus PRJ\}$ and $conf \in CONF$.

Modify a Module(m). *This operation modifies the module m.*

Prereq: The user $u \in U$ who performs this operation has either the role A or the role MA with A, $MA \in RL$.

Result: $m \in \{M \setminus PRJ\}$.

Remove a Module(m). *This operation removes the module m. It also removes all its configurations $conf_i$, i=1,...,n, $n \in \mathbb{N}$.*

Prereq: The user $u \in U$ who performs this operation has either the role A or the role MA with A, $MA \in RL$, and the application $k(conf, plt, m) = 0$, $\forall conf \in CONF$ and $plt \in PLT$.

Result: $m \notin M$, and $conf_i \notin CONF$, i=1,...,n, $n \in \mathbb{N}$.

Add a Configuration(m, conf). *This operation adds a new configuration conf to the module m.*

Prereq: The user $u \in U$ who performs this operation has either the role A or the role MA or the role D with A, MA, $D \in RL$, and $m \in M$.

Result: $conf \in CONF$.

Modify a Configuration(m, conf). *This operation modifies the configuration conf of the module m. It also associates to conf, if there is at least one plt for that conf, environment ev, property prp, command cmn, dependency.*

Prereq: The user $u \in U$ who performs this operation has either the role A or the role MA or the role D with A, MA, $D \in RL$, $m \in M$, and $conf \in CONF$.

Result: $conf \in CONF$, and if $\exists$ at least one plt in PLT for $conf$, $cmn \in CMN$, $en \in EV$ and $prp \in PRP$.

Remove a Configuration(m, conf). *This operation removes the configuration conf of the module m. It also removes all its environments ev_i, properties pr_j, commands cmn_h, i=1,...,n, $n \in \mathbb{N}$, j=1,...,m, $m \in \mathbb{N}$ and h=1,...,c, $c \in \mathbb{N}$.*

Prereq: The user $u \in U$ who performs this operation has either the role A or the role MA or the role D with A, MA, $D \in RL$, and the application $k(conf, plt, m) = 0, \forall m \in M$.

Result: $conf \notin CONF$, and $ev_i \notin EV$, i=1,...,n, $n \in \mathbb{N}$, $prp_j \notin EV$, j=1,...,n, $n \in \mathbb{N}$, and $cmn_h \notin EV$, h=1,...,n, $n \in \mathbb{N}$.

8   Use Cases

A number of use cases have been identified in the framework of the EGEE, DILI-
GENT and VDT projects. The selection of user community applications that are
willing to start using ETICS from the very beginning is an important asset to
ETICS in order to gather feedback on the impact and value of the proposed
service on the entire project lifecycle. Some of the use cases are: building and
testing software locally and remotely by using both the Web Application and the
Command Line Interfaces. In addition to perform the remote building and testing ETICS interacts with NMI framework; register resources as public or private.
This means users can steer their build and test jobs to their private resources, or
add resources in the public pool, in order to share them with other ETICS users;
download the source and build a patched package by using different ways: source
tarballs, source packages and source rpms, checked out source against checked
out binaries: build everything from source; parallel build of software on different
platforms and automatic distribution of the packages in different formats (e.g.,
tarballs, rpms, and debs).

9   Conclusion

In summary, we described how ETICS performs build, configuration, integration
and test for Grid and distributed software projects. Requirements for designing
the service were also described, taking into account the perspective of application
developers and the needs of user communities. We mentioned other systems and
products used for managing software development such as Gump and Maven; we
briefly talked about projects interested in providing customizable portals for software project management such as Sourceforce and Savannah, and also hinted to
other similar initiatives involved in improving the quality of Grid middleware such
as OMII Europe, and configuring and build code such as the EGEE gLite Configuration and Build System. The ETICS architecture was explained, together with
the formalization of the basic concepts of the ETICS data model and of the edit
operations, that belong to the most meaningful category of operations.

Using the valuable feedback from DILIGENT, EGEE, QUATTOR and VDT
we will improve ETICS expanding the number and type of metrics and collected
data. Future work will include investigation of hardware virtualisation. In particular, the possibility of instantiating on-demand virtual machines tailored to
match job requirements is seen as a powerful tool to introduce flexibility and
strict reproducibility in the system. In addition, it may help overcome security
concerns that arise when test jobs require running as root or Administrator on
the target node. An additional area of investigation is the co-scheduling of multiple test jobs onto separate resources. Of particular interest is the case of jobs
with dependencies on the availability of external services. In this case, the system should be able to pause a job, deploy the required services, propagate the
relevant configuration information to the paused job and resume it, cleaning all
resources after the execution of the job. Again the use of virtualisation may help
in this task.

Acknowledgement

We would like to thank colleagues from the ETICS project, Peter Couvares, Paolo Fabriani, Istvan Forgacs, Anatoly Karp, Andrea Manieri, and Cristina Vistoli, who have provided useful suggestions to complete this paper. This work is partially funded by the European Commission under contract number INFSOM-RI-026753.

References

1. Diligent - A Digital Library Infrastracture on Grid ENabled Technology, `http://diligentproject.org/`.
2. D. Castelli and L. Candela and P. Pagano, and M. Simi, DILIGENT: a DL infrastructure for supporting joint research, *In Proceedings of 2nd IEEE-CS International Symposium Global Data Interoperability*, IEEE Computer Society, pages 56-59, 2005.
3. EGEE Middleware Architecture, August, 2004, `https://edms.cern.ch/file/476451/1.0/architecture.pdf`.
4. F. Gagliardi, The EGEE European Grid Infrastructure Project, In *Lecture Notes in Computer Science*, volume 3402, pages 194-203, Jan, 2005.
5. R. A. Garca Leiva, M. Barroso Lopez, G. Cancio Meli, B. Chardi Marco, L. Cons, P. Poznanski, A. Washbrook, E. Ferro and A. Holt, Quattor: Tools and Techniques for the Configuration, Installation and Management of Large-Scale Grid Computing Fabrics, In *Journal of Grid Computing*, Vol 2, N. 4, pages: 313-322, December 2004.
6. M. Fewster, and D. Graham, *Software Test Automation*, Addison-Wesley, 1999.
7. B. Allcock, I. Foster, V. Nefedova, A. Chervenak, E. Deelman, C. Kesselman, J. Lee, A. Sim, A. Shoshani, B. Drach, and D. Williams, High-performance remote access to climate simulation data: A challenge problem for data Grid technologies. *In Proceedings of SC2001 Conference*, Denver, CO, November 2001.
8. NSF Middleware Initiative, `http://www.nsf-middleware.org`.
9. WorldWide LHC Computing Grid - Distributed Production Environment for Physics Data Processing, `http://lcg.web.cern.ch/LCG/`.
10. V. Massol, and T. O'Brien, *Maven: A Developer's Notebook*, O'Reilly Media, Inc., 1 Edition, June 2005.
11. The Apache Software Foundation, `http://www.apache.org/`.
12. The Sourceforge Home, `http://sourceforge.net/`.
13. The Savannah Home, `http://savannah.nongnu.org/`.
14. GForge helps you manage the entire development life cycle, `http://gforge.org/`.
15. A. Di Meglio, Developers' Guide For the gLite EGEE Middleware, `https://edms.cern.ch/file/468700/0.7/`.
16. A. Di Meglio and J. Flammer and R. Harakaly and M. Zurek, and E. Ronchieri, A Pattern-Based Continuous Integration Framework For Distributed EGEE Grid Middleware Are Development, In *Proceedings of Computing in High Energy and Nuclear Physics (CHEP) 2004*, Interlaken, Switzerland, volume 1, pages 579-582, 27 September - 1 October, 2004.
17. OMII-Europe Introduction, `http://www.omii-europe.com/`.
18. S. H. Kan, *Metrics and Models in Software Quality Engineering, II Edition*, Addison-Wesley Professional, 2002.

19. QSM (Model Explanation & Behaviors), `http://www.qsm.com/reliability.pdf`.
20. The Virtual Data Toolkits, `http://vdt.cs.wisc.edu/`.
21. D. Thain, T. Tannenbaum, and M. Livny, Distributed Computing in Practice: The Condor Experience, *Concurrency and Computation: Practice and Experience*, volume 17, No. 2-4, pages 323-356, February-April, 2005.
22. R. Housley, W. Ford, W. Polk, and D. Solo, *Internet X.509 Public Key Infrastructure - Certificate and CRL Profile*, January 1999, `http://www.ietf.org/rfc/rfc2459.txt`.
23. Common Information Model (CIM) Standards, `http://www.dmtf.org/standsrds/cim/`.
24. The Architecture of Choice for a Changing World, `http://www.omg.org/mda/`.
25. C. Szyperski, *Component Software: Beyond Object-Oriented Programming*. 2nd ed. Addison-Wesley Professional, Boston 2002.
26. B. Collins-Sussman, B. W. Fitzpatrick, and C. Michael Pilato, *Version Control with Subversion*, `http://svnbook.red-bean.com/en/1.1/index.html`.
27. J. Vesperman, *Essential CVS (Paperback)*, O'Reilly Media, Inc., 1 Edition, June 2003.

Architectural Verification of Black-Box Component-Based Systems

Antonia Bertolino[1], Henry Muccini[2], and Andrea Polini[1]

[1] Istituto di Scienza e Tecnologie della Informazione "Alessandro Faedo"
Consiglio Nazionale delle Ricerche
via Moruzzi, 1 – 56124 Pisa, Italy
{antonia.bertolino, andrea.polini}@isti.cnr.it
[2] Dipartimento di Informatica,
University of L'Aquila
Via Vetoio, 1 - L'Aquila, Italy
muccini@di.univaq.it

Abstract. We introduce an original approach, which combines monitoring and model checking techniques into a comprehensive methodology for the architectural verification of Component-based systems. The approach works by first capturing the traces of execution via the instrumented middleware; then, the observed traces are reverse engineered into Message Sequence Charts, which are then checked for compliance to the Component-based Software Architecture, using a model checker. The methodology has been conceived for being applied indifferently for validating the system in house before deployment and for continuous validation in the field following evolution. A case study for the first case is here illustrated.

1 Introduction

Two antithetical approaches which emerge today for the verification of large complex distributed systems are *model-based* and *monitoring*. These two approaches are generally used in different stages of the software life cycle, and serve different purposes. The former enforces the rigorous derivation of a set of test cases from the system model, and aims at validating before deployment that the implemented system behaviour actually conforms to the modeled one. The latter collects and analysis runtime data during system execution to identify failures and to evaluate critical quality and performance attributes in the field.

In this paper we describe an original approach we are working on, which draws from both model-based verification and monitoring concepts, and combines their respective strengths into a comprehensive methodology for verification in a continuum between in-house and in the field. In particular we describe here how the behaviour of a component assembly is validated against the corresponding Software Architecture.

A Software Architecture (SA) provides high-level abstractions for representing the structure, behavior, and key properties of complex software systems [12]. SA-driven development assigns to the SA specification a central role in the software

N. Guelfi and D. Buchs (Eds.): RISE 2006, LNCS 4401, pp. 98–113, 2007.

life cycle, both to the phase of design and integration, and to analysis and testing activities. Most methodologies for SA-based analysis and testing generally assume a model-driven approach, in which the SA specification constitutes the reference model and the system is subject to a thorough and accurate validation of the required architectural properties before being deployed.

Advances in SA have greatly contributed to the advent of the *Component-Based paradigm* of development. In fact, the SA specification provides the blueprint for developing systems by properly composing "pieces" of software against it. A Component-Based Software System (CBS) can be roughly considered as an assembly of reusable components, designed to meet the quality attributes identified during the architecting phase [9]. A component can be defined [20] as a unit of composition, with contractually specified interfaces. In a CB approach, a big challenge is posed by the scarce information that is generally available about the components. Various approaches for testing CBSs have been recently proposed spanning over a varying spectrum of assumptions made on the metadata accompanying the component, which can be merely in form of pre- and post-conditions, or even as detailed as state machines. However, such a paradigm needs also to assume there is a time for validation before deployment; with the fast and ceaseless increase of systems complexity and pervasiveness, and the consequent emergence of dynamic global SAs, such a model need to be revised.

In antithesis to a proactive approach to testing such as model driven, several proposal for monitoring, or passive testing, are today spreading. Referred to with differing terminology, such as "monitoring", "tracing", and similar, what this approach to verification foresees is to observe the system during execution and to profile the obtained traces with different purposes. Hence, while in model-based testing the system must be stimulated so to reproduce some predefined behaviour, in monitoring the actual behaviour is observed and a posteriori analysed to see whether this conforms to desired properties. This prevents the burden of reproducing preselected test sequences as in model driven testing; we adopt the model-based approach in that we derive some architectural properties from the specification that we want to verify, and we verify the collected traces against these properties. In particular, for the latter purpose, we apply model-checking techniques, by which we check that the CBS derived traces conforms with the expected event sequences in the CBSA model.

The goal of such an approach is to ensure that the "core" of the implemented system fulfills the SA expectations, as figuratively illustrated in Figure 1; so, for instance, the approach can help to verify that by adding a new plugin component to a given CBS, its overall behaviour does not deteriorate. In light of the evolutionary properties of modern CBS, the same approach is meant to be used both at development stage, and after deployment.

In the next two sections we provide an overview of the proposed approach, and of related work. Then, in Sections 4 and 5 we describe the monitoring and model-checking steps, and in Section 6 we discuss the application of the approach to a case study. Finally some conclusions of results reached so far are drawn in Section 7.

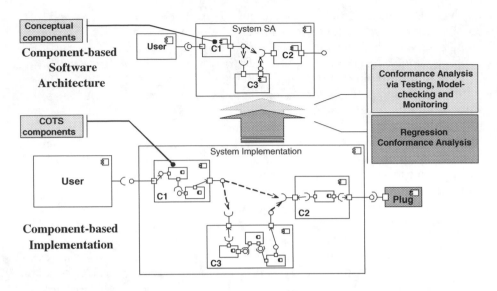

Fig. 1. Architectural Verification of Component-based Systems

2   Related Work

As discussed in the introduction of this paper, our approach wants to integrate, in a novel approach, (model-based) verification applied at the architecture level, monitoring applied during system execution and model-checking techniques covering implementation and software architectures. Much research has been conducted in these areas, and main results are briefly surveyed in this section.

Monitoring and Black-Box Monitoring: Due to the complexity of understanding and configuring modern complex systems, several different approaches to monitor their functioning on-line have been recently proposed. For a recent comprehensive assessment of strategies and testing opportunities for profiling deployed software we refer to [10], while for a quite interesting approach that shares many of the problems and goals with our approach we mention [1]. In the latter, the authors however adopt a different solution, since they instrument the architectural description, and not the middleware. Moreover, they require the developers to define a set of rules used to analyse the traces. Another interesting approach to derive execution traces using Aspect-Oriented Programming is presented in [15]. However even in this case no analysis technique is proposed.

SA-based Model-Checking: Software Model-Checking [8] analyzes concurrent systems behavior with respect to selected properties by specifying the system through abstract modeling languages. Model-checking algorithms offer an *exhaustive* and *automatic* approach to *completely* analyze the system. When errors are found, counterexamples are provided. Initial approaches for model-checking at the architecture level have been provided by the Wright architectural language [5] and the Tracta approach [16]. More recently, Fujaba [3], Æmilia [6], and CHARMY [19] have been proposed. Fujaba is an approach tool supported for real-time model-checking of component-based systems: the system structure is modeled through UML component diagrams, the real-time behavior is modeled by means of real-time statecharts (an extension to UML state diagrams), properties are specified in TCTL and the UPPAAL model-checker is used as the real-time model checker engine. Æmilia is an architectural description language based on the stochastic process algebra EMPAgr: initially introduced for performance analysis, it permits to apply symbolic model-checking. TwoTowers 5.1 is a software tool for the verification of Æmilia specifications. CHARMY [19] is our proposal to model-check software architecture compliance to certain functional temporal properties. The software architecture is specified according to the CHARMY UML-based specification of software architecture. More details will be provided in Section 5.

Integration of analysis techniques: Integration of analysis techniques is a topic which is recently receiving some attention in the software engineering community (e.g., [4]). In [17] the authors integrate testing and monitoring activities, both applied over component-based systems. While testing is used to collect information on components interaction, monitoring is successively employed to identify anomalous interactions when components are added or modified in the original system. More related to some of the authors experience [7], we recently integrated model-checking and testing activities during the life-cycle, where model-checking techniques have been used to validate the SA model conformance with respect to selected properties, while testing techniques have been utilized to validate the implementation conformance to the SA model.

3   Approach Overview

A big synergy relates CB development and SA (the latter being the model that should lead the assembly of a set of components to form the required system): when developing components, our focus is on identifying reusable entities, with well defined interfaces and proved quality. When building component-based systems (CBS), we move our focus to assemble the components so to build a high-quality system. When modeling the software architecture of a component-based system (CBSA), our goal is to provide a high-level blueprint on how real components are supposed to be assembled (according to styles and patterns, constraints, and rules).

Therefore a CBSA specification plays a major role in validating the quality of the assembly (even before the CBS components are developed or bought). The main objective of the approach we propose is to verify the coordination properties of components which are part of a CBS, against the specified CBSA. The verification process we propose is composed by different steps, where:

CBSA Specification for Analysis: The CBSA of the system under analysis is specified in terms of a structural model (which describes components, connectors, interfaces, and ports) and a behavioral model (which specifies the internal expected behavior and coordination of the CBS components).

Operational testing: How do we select the test cases to be executed? As the basis assumption of this approach is that a detailed component model is not available (assuming the component is off the shelf), we use the only information that is anyhow available (it may be in various forms): the expected Input/Output functions of the components. This information has to be available in some form, otherwise we could not even use the components.

Monitoring Black-box Component-Based Systems: We execute the implementation on the selected test cases, by observing the traces of execution via monitoring techniques. Traditionally, monitoring techniques are realized by instrumenting the component code in order to capture desired information from execution. However, since components can be black box with no available code, we cannot instrument the component in traditional ways. For this purposes, we adopted a middleware instrumentation.

Model-Checking CBS conformance to CBSA: The execution traces are used to check the CBS conformance to the CBSA specification. We remind here that while the CBSA specification described the intended/expected system usages, the CBS execution traces (obtained via monitoring) represents how the implemented CBS works. Model-checking techniques are then utilized to compare expected and real behavior.

In this paper we will focus our attention on the Monitoring and Model-Checking activities, while future work will investigate how such technologies can be used for verifying dynamically evolving CBSs. For this purpose, we will distinguish, as showed in Figure 1, among *architectural components* (the abstract ideal components of the SA, specified by their interfaces and their expected model of interactions), *concrete components* (the components of the implemented CBS, obtained by refining SA components or by adapting existing components), and *real components* (the building blocks of the concrete components, and can be, for instance, Commercial-off the Shelf – COTS – components). Concrete and real components may coincide, or a concrete component could be obtained by the assembly or wrapping of real components.

4   Monitoring Black-Box CB Systems

Monitoring is the activity intended to collect and check information about specific properties and behavior of a system during its real execution. Different elements and issues can be recognised in a monitoring setting:

1. the **monitored system** is the software whose behaviour and properties are of interest. The functionalities provided by such system are those that are in general relevant for an external user.
2. the **monitoring system** is the software that collects specific information on the monitored system. In general the monitoring system accepts as input

the information to be observed and collected, and the constraints on the behaviour/properties of the system that must be respected.

3. If a violation is detected, the monitoring system communicates the anomaly to a **controlling component**. The latter, that in some cases can also be a human agent, should put in place a set of actions to manage the anomalous condition and restore the system to a correct state (note this step is out of the scope for the proposed approach).

Observability of the monitored system is certainly the basic element constraining what can be monitored: it refers to what an external observer can notice about the system/component behaviour and properties evolution. In the fortunate case that the system has been developed having already in mind what is necessary to check, the set of information that can be observed generally encloses the set of what is necessary to monitor. Unfortunately this is not the general case.

Monitoring becomes particularly tough when the source code of a software component cannot be directly accessed and modified, as it is the rule when black-box reuse of software components externally acquired is considered. In such a situation the only information that can be accessed by an external agent are those expressly made available by the component developer. In CB programming this will generally only include the information passed trough the public interface.

Our approach requires to collect specific information for checking that the interactions among the concrete components are actually allowed by the architectural description. Two basic elements are needed to put in place this kind of verification activity:

1. a technique for representing the concrete interactions in a way that will be suitable for the architectural checking step
2. a mechanism for observing component interactions as they happen at runtime

In our approach the execution traces are abstracted to Message Sequence Charts (MSCs) reporting the whole signature for each invoked method. It is worth noting that these diagrams will not report any internal interactions within a *concrete component* implementation, given that its implementation is transparent to the system integrator.

The most obvious mechanism to observe component interactions might seem wrapping each concrete component with code that in some way records all the incoming and outgoing invocations. However, a concurrent behaviour of the wrapped component (e.g., the simultaneous invocation of different methods exposed by the component by at least two different threads of execution, or the internal activation, within the invoked component, of another thread) hinders the identification of the correct relations among incoming and outgoing call to and from the component. An example can aid to understand the problem. In Figure 2 component B invokes (b) component C while this component is already processing an invocation (a) from component A. In this situation a standard Wrapper of the C component could not recognize the thread that gave rise to the invocation "c" towards component D. So when situations such as that represented in the figure happen, it becomes impossible, using only a "wrapping" approach, to correctly associate outgoing invocations with the corresponding incoming ones.

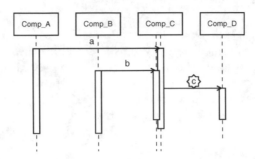

Fig. 2. Wrapping cannot easily manage concurrent invocations

An alternative way to monitoring, the one we chose, is to base such activity on the run-time environment of the application under verification, finding suitable mechanisms to observe the inteactions among the components "following" threads of executions. In a local approach based on Java, for instance, this would mean that we have to base the monitoring on direct interactions with the Java Virtual Machine (JVM) or we have to define an appropriate version of the JVM directly inserting monitoring features on it. In a distributed setting, instead, this would mean to insert the monitoring activity as part of the middleware level and not at the application level as in the case of the wrapping approach. At this point the problem to solve is how it is possible to retrieve the needed information to derive meaningful execution traces. As stated before we can assume the knowledge only of the interfaces to be implemented by the concrete component. However inserting monitoring mechanisms within the application run-time support (JVM for the java application) will permit to increase the observability of the executed application to all the invocations that the components composing the application exchange among them. At this point the idea is that the only additional information we need is to observe all the actions and interactions on and among the processes (thread of execution) activated by the execution of the application. So starting with the "main" thread of the application we should observe, behaving as a sort of debugger, when new processes are activated, when they interact or when they stop. At the same time we should be able to record when a process during its execution "hits" one of the methods of the interface implemented by one concrete component. For each process the invocation sequence are stored in different files successively used to recreate the traces that have been actually executed. Considering the scenario in Figure 2, the result of the monitoring will be two different files, the first reporting the sequence of invocations "C.a", "D.c" and the second the sequence "C.b", providing the precise information on the call sequences.

The above approach is implemented into a proof-of-concept monitoring tool called Theseus, from the mythological character that used a thread to trace the path to the way out from the minotaur's maze. In the current version Theseus can only monitor the execution of non distributed CBS (implemented using the Java language); we are currently working to add support also for Java Remote Method Invocations.

Theseus implementation is based on the Java Platform Debugger Architecture (JPDA) API (Application Programming Interface). The tool takes as input the .class files containing the interfaces defined for the concrete components, then using the API defined in the JDA, it asks to the JVM to notify when methods on this interfaces are invoked. When this happens the JVM is stopped and all the information concerning the invocation are retrievied and stored in the corresponding file; then the machine can then be restarted. The JVM bloking behaviour is consequence of the fact that the API and the JVM have not been explicitly developed for monitoring purpose, and a non stopping behaviour will raise the risk of loosing relevant information given the occurence of successive method calls.

The tool Theseus also records all the invocations made on objects of the java.lang.Thread class, that in Java are the abstraction of processes. In such manner the tool can recognize when a Thread interacts with another via a notify, or also when it activates another thread creating and starting it, permitting to manage the issues raised by the presence of concurrency. In Figure 3 the main window of Theseus is shown.

5   Model-Checking CBS Conformance to CBSA

As soon as execution traces have been collected after monitoring the component-based system implementation, they have to be checked for consistency to expected architectural behaviors. This validation phase has to identify if and how much the (behavior of) realized system complies to what has been previously specified at the architecture level. In fact, while execution traces denote the real system behavior when submitted to certain inputs, architecture-level behavioral models identifies the expected behavior.

The architectural model-checking approach we take in place here is CHARMY, a model-based approach for architectural checking.

CHARMY[2] enables the **specification** of a software architecture through diagrammatic (UML-based) notations, and the *verification* of the architectural specification conformance with respect to certain temporal properties, representing how architectural elements are supposed to be coordinated. By focussing on CHARMY main features, we have that:

Specification: CHARMY allows the specification of a software architecture by means of both a topological (static) description and a behavioral (dynamic) one [11]. The specification of the SA topology is realized in terms of stereotyped UML 2.0 component diagrams, where components represent abstract computational subsystems and connectors formalize the interactions among components.

Fig. 3. Theseus start interface

The internal behavior of each component and the coordination of the interacting components is specified in terms of stereotyped UML 2.0 state machines.

Verification: once the SA specification is available, a translation engine automatically derives from the model-based SA specification, a formal executable prototype in Promela (the specification language of SPIN) [13]. On the generated Promela code, we can use the SPIN standard features to find, for example, deadlocks or parts of states machines that are unreachable.

Figure 4 graphically summarizes how the tool supporting the CHARMY approach works: the CHARMY tool editor allows the graphical specification of the SA topology and behavior and the properties in terms of UML diagrams. In step 1, component state machines are automatically translated into a Promela formal prototype. Once the Promela model is produced SPIN standard checks may be performed. In Step 2, scenario specifications (in the form of extended Sequence Diagrams) are automatically translated into Büchi automata (the automata representation for LTL formulae). Such automata describe properties to be verified. Finally, in Step 3 SPIN evaluates the properties validity with respect to the Promela code. If unwanted behaviors are identified, an error is reported.

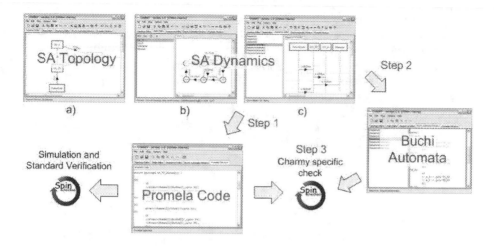

Fig. 4. Tool Support for CHARMY Main Features

6   Applying the Approach to the CHARMY Plugin System

As a case study to experiment the approach we have taken the CHARMY plugin system. We provide an outline of the CHARMY software architecture and its specification (Section 6.1). Then, we identify some monitored traces and show how CHARMY can check some properties over its architectural model (Section 6.2). We conclude this section with some considerations and evaluation of results (Section 6.3).

6.1   The CHARMY Plugin Architecture and Its Specification

The CHARMY architecture is composed by two main parts: the CHARMY `Core` and the `Plugin Package`.

The CHARMY `Core` macro-component is composed of the `Data Structure` component, the `Plugin Manager` and `File Manager` which allows the handling of plugins of type editor and file, respectively, the `GUI` which receives stimuli from the system users, and the `Event Handler` which handles all those events generated by plugins. The CHARMY `core` handles the plugin management by specifying: *i*) how a new plug should be implemented, *ii*) how the core system has to recognize the plug and use it, and *iii*) how the core and plug components should interact. Figure 5 graphically summarizes the interfaces to be implemented in order to plug a new component in the system. Details on how to implement and recognize a new plug, and plugs interaction are provided in [14].

The `Plugin Package` contains a set of plugins to specify and analyze software architectures. The *Topology, State*, and *Sequence* editors permit to edit the software architecture topology, the architectural state machines and the scenarios, respectively. The *PSC2BA* and *Promela Translation* plugins allow an automatic translation from sequence diagrams to Büchi automata and from state machines to Promela code. Such translations permit the application of model-checking techniques at the software architecture level. The *TesTor* component allows the generation of architectural test specifications. The *Composit* component allows for compositional analysis of middleware-based SA. For more details, please refer to [19].

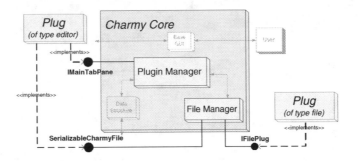

Fig. 5. Plug and Core

By means of the Promela Translation plugin, the CHARMY architectural specification has been automatically translated into a formal executable prototype in Promela, and checked through SPIN standard checks (step 1 in Figure 4). After few modeling and checking iterations, we produced a stable correct (with respect to SPIN checks) architectural specification.

6.2   Validating the CHARMY Implementation with Respect to Its Architectural Specification

The CHARMY core and plugs implementation has been realized in the last three years at the Computer Science Department, University of L'Aquila. When moving from version 0 to version 1, the tool implementation has been re-structured to make it plugin-based. More recently, when moving from version 1 to the current version 2.0 beta, some minor modifications have been made, while re-thinking some interfaces and adding some utilities. Many plugins have been created and unit tested. Since many of them have been realized thanks to students support, our confidence on the plugin-core integration correctness has been mainly based on beta testing.

We then decided to use the approach as a means to validate the plugin-core integration (i.e., to check if the integration of a new plug in CHARMY may violate the CHARMY core standard behavior). We submitted the CHARMY system implementation (together with its plugins) to three different analysis: *i*) we plugged the Topology Editor component to monitor and check its correct integration into the CHARMY system, *ii*) we monitored an initially faulty version of the ExplodePlugin component, in order to obtain an error trail enabling the localization of the fault, and *iii*) we injected a fault on the Topology Editor final version, in order to evaluate the approach ability to precisely localize an expected fault.

Analysis of type i): When running CHARMY with the Topology Editor plugged into the system, we can observe via Theseus only a subset of the entire flows of events (since Theseus in its current version can monitor only interfaces). In particular, it can collect information on how the CHARMY Core loads the plugin, how the copy/cut/undo operations are performed, how the resulting topology diagram is stored and closed.

Figure 6 shows one of the typical traces produced when monitoring the Topology Editor/Core integration. As we can see from the figure, the scenario is quite complex, since it records a quite long list of events. In any case, all the internal (to the plug) operations are not observed, since they are implemented without any specific interface.

Indeed, analyzing the scenario by hand, will be extremely expensive. Instead, the scenario has been drawn into CHARMY, automatically translated into a Büchi automaton representation, and the SPIN verification has been run. No errors have been detected.

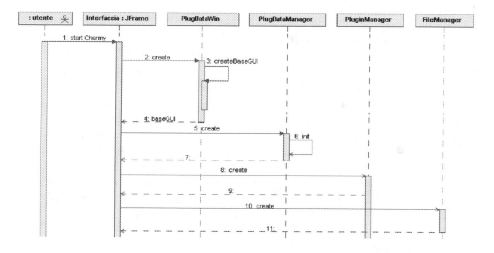

Fig. 6. Monitoring the Topology Editor interaction with the CHARMY Core

Analysis of type ii): In this second scenario, we selected the ExplodePlugin plugin we knew had a bug. This plugin has been realized for testing purposes. It creates incrementally a multitude of plugins to be loaded in CHARMY. Our goal was to evaluate how much CHARMY scales and performs when a multitude of plugins are plugged into the CHARMY Core. We knew in advance the plugin was buggy, but we did not know where the fault was localized.

When running the Theseus monitoring activity, many scenarios have been recorded. For sake of space, we do not report them here. When applying the CHARMY model-checking approach to this scenario, the expected error trail has been detected, highlighting the location of the first undesired (with respect to the architectural model) interaction.

Analysis of type iii): Ultimately, we tested the monitoring + model-checking ability to precisely localize faults. While analysis *ii)* permits to localize the fault, analysis *iii)* allows approach users to check how much the localized fault corresponds to the expected (injected) one. Then, this activity represents a validation of the approach precision in localizing faults.

A fault has been injected in the Topology Editor component. When loading this faulty version into CHARMY, and after Theseus monitoring, many traces have been collected (not reported for space limits). When running the SPIN verification feature, an error trail has been raised, indicating the unwanted behavior.

Indeed, we cannot expect the approach to identify all possible injected faults. Only architectural coordination faults can be detected. Moreover, the fault localization ability of the approach strongly depends on the Theseus ability to monitor events. Since in its current version Theseus monitors only such services implemented via interfaces, the approach localizes the first architectural interaction affected by the injected fault.

An interesting discover we made thanks to the application of the approach has been that the students introduced many architectural mismatches using direct reference to classes instead of using the defined interfaces. By executing the CHARMY tool in a monitored environment we did not notice any strange behaviour; but subsequently the traces collected by Theseus did not expose all the interactions we expected. Indeed we could see all the initial invocations made by the core components to correctly initialise all the installed plug-ins, but after these invocations we could observe less invocations with respect to the expected ones. Initially we thought there was an error in the Theseus implementation previously tested only on small case studies. After having analysed the code of Theseus without finding a solution to the problem we tried to investigate whithin the CHARMY code. During this investigation we discovered that often students preferred to use direct casting on objects or however direct reference to external classes. So we were faced with an implementation containing many architectural mismatches affecting the possibility of substituting components with new versions implemented by different classes. Clearly this architectural mismatches strongly affected our capability of analysis since Theseus is only able to trace invocations occurring through interfaces. Indeed this kind of mismatches could be discovered through static analysis, assuming any tool is available for code-level checking of architectural properties.

6.3   Considerations and Evaluation of Results

With the use of teh approach, we can test the system coordination, by integrating monitoring and model-checking techniques. If the system implementation behaves accordingly to the system specification, an ok message is raised. Otherwise, an error trace identifies where the execution trace differs from the expected one.

When an anomalous behavior is known, the approach allows the detection and localization of known but unwanted faults. It acts as a sort of debugger, identifying which components are behaving incorrectly when integrated.

In both cases, the ability of the approach to detect and precisely localize a fault can be evaluated via fault injection.

Moreover, with respect to traditional specification-based testing techniques, the approach permits to analyze the implementation conformance to external input/output (as in traditional IOLTS-based testing) and also the implementation conformance to the entire architectural trace (by model-checking the execution scenarios compliance to the architectural model).

According to the experiment conducted over the CHARMY system, we here propose some initial considerations and evaluation of results (being conscious more deeper investigation is required to provide more informative insights):

Automation: So far, a quite relevant part of the approach is supported by tools. The architectural specification is made through the CHARMY editors. Test cases generation can be realized according to [18]. The monitoring activity has been supported by the Theseus tool. The model-checking activity is realized through the integration of CHARMY features and the model-checking engine SPIN;

Costs: Monitoring black box components is generally an invasive and expensive activity. Since Theseus requires to stop the JVM at each time an information needs to be collected, the monitoring activity for a complex execution may required up to ten minutes. However, we are working on modifying the JVM in order to reduce the monitoring time. Regarding the model-checking activity, time effort is quite limited, since properties of interest "p" are submitted to an existential check (i.e., check if "p" exists in the system model "m").

Scalability: Even if more experimental results are needed for a finer evaluation, the approach seems to be able to scale to larger systems (assuming an improvement on the monitoring activity performance).

7   Conclusions and Future Work

We have presented a novel approach to the SA-driven verification of CBSs, in that it combines the strengths of either approaches, trying to overcome the inherent difficulty of reproducing a predefined sequence of events of model-based testing, but enriching the power of monitoring with a rigorous model-check stage of the obtained traces. The goal of the approach is to verify that some important SA properties are indeed satisfied by the implemented CBS, and continue to be so even after evolution. The approach is in fact conceived as a comprehensive methodology to be used without interruption both for in-house validation (off-line testing), and for continuous verification in use (on-line testing). The goal we pursue is quite ambitious, and of course we are not yet done, but several pieces of the approach are already implemented. In this paper we have already presented some promising results by applying the approach for off-line testing of the CHARMY architecture. Even though the approach proposed can show appealing opportunity, its usage should be carefully evaluated, particularly for the case of on-line testing. Monitoring being executed concurrently with the application strongly affects performance. The monitoring technique we propose seems to be particularly powerfull but if not supported by adequate tools particularly expensive. In the current implementation performance can be reduced up to ten times when many threads are started. We are currently investigating some tool improvements in order to make it applicable for the run-time monitoring of multi-threades applications.

Acknowledgements

The authors wish to thank Alessia Bardi and Ezio Di Nisio for their important contribution to the implementation of part of TANDEM tools.

This work is partially supported by the PLASTIC Project (EU FP6 STREP n.26955): Providing Lightweight and Adaptable Service Technology for pervasive Information and Communication. http://www.ist-plastic.org.

References

1. An Approach for Tracing and Understanding Asynchronous Systems. ISR Tech. Report UCI-ISR-02-7, 2002.
2. CHARMY Project. Charmy Web Site. http://www.di.univaq.it/charmy, 2004.
3. Fujaba Project. http://wwwcs.uni-paderborn.de/cs/fujaba/publications/index.html, 2005. U.Paderborn, Sw Eng. Group.
4. *Rapid System Development via Product Line Architecture Implementation*, Heraklion Crete, GREECE, September 2005. LNCS.
5. R. Allen and D. Garlan. A Formal Basis for Architectural Connection. *ACM Trans. on Software Engineering and Methodology*, 6(3):213–249, July 1997.
6. M. Bernardo, L. Donatiello, and P. Ciancarini. *Performance Evaluation of Complex Systems: Techniques and Tools*, chapter Stochastic Process Algebra: From an Algebraic Formalism to an Architectural Description Language. LNCS, 2459:236-260, September 2002.
7. A. Bucchiarone, H. Muccini, P. Pelliccione, and P. Pierini. Model-Checking plus Testing: from Software Architecture Analysis to Code Testing. In *Proc. International Testing Methodology workshop*, LNCS, vol. 3236, pp. 351 - 365 (2004), October 2004.
8. E. M. Clarke, O. Grumberg, and D. A. Peled. *Model Checking*. The *MIT Press*, Cambridge, second edition, 2000.
9. I. Crnkovic and M. Larsson, editors. *Building Reliable Component-based Software Systems*. Artech House, July 2002.
10. S. Elbaum and M. Diep. Profiling Deployed Software: Assessing Strategies and Testing Opportunities. *IEEE Trans. on Software Engineering*, 31(8):1–16, August 2005.

11. D. Garlan. Software Architecture: a Roadmap. In *ACM ICSE 2000, The Future of Software Engineering*, pages 91–101. A. Finkelstein, 2000.
12. D. Garlan. Formal Modeling and Analysis of Software Architecture: Components, Connectors, and Events. In *Formal Methods for Software Architectures*, pages 1–24. LNCS, 2804, 2003.
13. G. J. Holzmann. *The SPIN Model Checker: Primer and Reference Manual.* Addison-Wesley, September 2003.
14. P. Inverardi, H. Muccini, and P. Pelliccione. CHARMY: An Extensible Tool for Architectural Analysis. In *ACM Proc. European Software Engineering Conference/the Foundations of Software Engineering (ESEC/FSE)*, September 2005.
15. Kimmo Kiviluoma, Johannes Koskinen, and Tommi Mikkonen. Run-time monitoring of architecturally significant behaviors using behavioral profiles and aspects. In *Proceedings of the International Symposium on Software Testing and Analysis (ISSTA '06)*, pages 181–190, July 17-20 2006. Portland, Maine, USA.
16. J. Magee, J. Kramer, and D. Giannakopoulou. Behaviour Analysis of Software Architectures. In *I Working IFIP Conf. Sw Architecture, WICSA1*, 1999.
17. Leonardo Mariani and Mauro Pezze'. Behavior Capture and Test: Automated Analysis of Component Integration. In IEEE Computer Society, editor, *In 10th IEEE International Conference on Engineering of Complex Computer Systems*, Shangai (China), 16-20 June 2005.
18. H. Muccini, A. Bertolino, and P. Inverardi. Using Software Architecture for Code Testing. *IEEE Trans. on Software Engineering*, 30(3):160–171, March 2003.
19. P. Pelliccione. *CHARMY: A framework for Software Architecture Specification and Analysis*. PhD thesis, Computer Science Dept., U. L'Aquila, May 2005.
20. C. Szyperski. *Component Software. Beyond Object Oriented Programming*. Addison Wesley, 1998.

Systematic Generation of XML Instances to Test Complex Software Applications*

Antonia Bertolino, Jinghua Gao, Eda Marchetti, and Andrea Polini

Istituto di Scienza e Tecnologie della Informazione "Alessandro Faedo"
Consiglio Nazionale delle Ricerche
Via Moruzzi, 1 – 56124 Pisa, Italy
{antonia.bertolino, jinghua.gao, eda.marchetti,
andrea.polini}@isti.cnr.it

Abstract. We introduce the XPT approach for the automated systematic generation of XML instances which conform to a given XML Schema, and its implementation into the proof-of-concept tool TAXI. XPT can be used to automatize the black-box testing of any general application that expects in input the XML instances. We generate a comprehensive set of instances by sampling all the possible combinations of elements within the schema, applying and adapting the well known Category-Partition strategy for functional testing. Originally, XPT has been conceived for application to the e-Learning domain, within which we briefly discuss some examples.

1   Introduction

Increasingly today complex software systems are developed according to a modular architecture, within which precise features can be identified and separately implemented. Main objective of this "componentization" trend is to permit the development of the different features of a complex composite application by diverse stakeholders while maintaining the possibility of integrating the subsystems into a unique working system. Nevertheless the integration clearly presupposes the definition of a rigorous and checkable format of the data exchanged between the components.

One of the most important innovations that strongly contributes to solve this issue has been the introduction of the eXtensible Markup Language (XML) [1]. In few years this language has established itself as the *de facto* standard format for specifying and exchanging data and documents between almost any software application. Immediately following, the XML Schema [2] has then spread up as the notation for formally describing what constitutes an agreed valid XML document within an application domain. Thus, XML Schemas are used for expressing the basic structure of data and parameters that remote components exchange with each other, and restrictions over them, while XML instances, formatted

---

* This work has been supported by the European Project TELCERT (FP6 STREP 507128).

N. Guelfi and D. Buchs (Eds.): RISE 2006, LNCS 4401, pp. 114–129, 2007.
© Springer-Verlag Berlin Heidelberg 2007

according to the rules of the referred XML Schema, represent the allowed naming and structure of data for components interaction and for service requests.

The introduction of XML for specifying standard format of exchanged data is certainly fundamental and strongly increases the possibility of correct interactions, nevertheless XML related technologies do not solve the interoperability problem per se. No information concerning the interpretation of data can be associated to an XML description, leaving the room for different interpretations by the various developers. Trying to make a further step toward guaranteeing interoperability, our proposal here is to combine the great potential of XML Schema in describing input data in open and standard form, with testing activity to assess the common understanding of interacting e-Learning systems. In doing this, our intention is to take advantage of the special characteristic of the data representation suitable for automated processing, which is clearly a big advantage for testing.

We find that the adoption of the XML Schema leads quite naturally to the application of *partition testing*, a widely studied subject within the testing community, since it provides an accurate representation of the input domain into a format suitable for automated processing. The subdivision of the input domain into subdomains, according to the basic principle of partition testing, can be done automatically by analyzing the XML Schema elements: from the diverse subdomains identified, the application of partition testing amounts to the *systematic derivation* of a set of XML instances. Systematic generation of XML instances, differently from a random based approach, clearly has important consequences on the effectiveness of the generated test suite permitting to derive meaningful statistics on the kind of instances generated, and then on the covered features.

This paper introduces our proposed XML-based Partition Testing (XPT) approach for the systematic generation of XML instances. Also a short overview on a proof-of-concept tool, called TAXI (Testing by Automatically generated XML Instances), is provided. Such tool inputs an XML Schema and automatically generates a set of XML instances for the black box testing of a component, whose expected input conforms to the taken schema. At the same time the paper reports a preliminary qualitative evaluation of the approach to the generation of instances for the IMS Learning Information Package specification.

In the remainder of this paper we discuss some related work in Section 2, and summarise the well known Category Partition method in Section 3; then we provide a description of the proposed strategy in Section 4 and of the tool implementing it in Section 5. Section 6 finally reports some preliminary considerations on application of the methodology; in particular in 6.1 we provide quantitative motivations to the application of a systematic approach, then in 6.2 a simple qualitative comparison of TAXI with another existing tool (XMLSpy) is presented. Some conclusions are finally drawn in Section 7.

2   Related Work

Our research is aimed at automatically generating a comprehensive suite of XML instances from a given XML Schema. The generated XML instances can then be used for the black-box testing of applications that expect such XML instances as input.

Notwithstanding the intense production of XML-based methods and tools in the latest years, to the best of our knowledge there do not exist other XML-based test approaches comparable to ours. Indeed, the existing "test tools" based on XML can be roughly classified under three headlines:

- testing the XML instances themselves;
- testing the XML Schemas themselves;
- testing the XML instances against the XML Schema.

Regarding the first group, a basic test on an XML file instance is *well-formedness*, which aims at verifying that the XML file structure and its elements possess specified characteristics, without which the tested file cannot be even classified as an XML file. Diverse sets of test suites (for instance [3], [4]) and various tools aiming at validating the adequacy of a document instance to a set of established rules, such as [5], have been implemented.

With regard to the testing of XML Schemas themselves (second group), several validators exist for checking the syntax and the structure of the W3C XML Schema document (for instance, [6], [7], [8] [9], and [10]).

The third group encloses tools for automatic instance generation based on XML schema, which is what we also do. Relevant tools of this group are [11], [12] and [13]. However for all of them the XML instances generation only implements random or ad hoc generation; the instances are not conceived so to cover interesting combinations of the schema. Indeed this characteristic is where our approach tries to provide a comprehensive solution. Adopting a systematic criterion in generating instances will have a double positive side effect: the generation of more accurate and mindful XML instances and the automatization of black box test suite specification.

So far no proposal has really succeeded in pushing the widespread adoption of automated black box testing as it would deserve. The well known Category Partition method [14] provides a procedural approach to analyse the input domain and to systematically derive a comprehensive test suite (see a brief description in the next section). It has been previously applied by many authors to requirements specifications expressed in various notations (for instance also by authors of this paper to UML specifications [15]). We propose here to apply it to XML schema. We think in fact that the widespread acceptance of XML, and its pragmatic flavor, associated to the Category Partition methodology could finally be the winning instrument to achieve fully automated black-box testing.

3   Category Partition

Introduced in the late 80's and today widely known and used, the Category Partition (CP) [14] provides a systematic and semi-automated method for test data derivation, starting from analysis of specifications until production of the test scripts, through the following series of steps:

1. Analyze the specifications and identify the *functional units* (for instance, according to design decomposition).
2. For each unit identify the *categories*: these are the environment conditions and the parameters that are relevant for testing purposes.
3. Partition the categories into *choices*:[1] these represent significant values for each category from the tester's viewpoint.
4. Determine *constraints* among choices (either properties or special conditions), to prevent the construction of redundant, not meaningful or even contradictory combinations of choices.
5. Derive the *test specification*: this contains all the necessary information for instantiating the test cases by unfolding the constraints.
6. Derive and evaluate the *test frames* by taking every allowable combination of categories, choices and constraints.
7. Generate the test scripts, i.e. the sequences of executable test cases.

The XML Schema provides an accurate representation of the input domain which leads quite naturally to the application of the Category Partition. In particular the subdivision of the input domain into functional units and the identification of categories can be done by exploiting the formalized representation of the XML Schema.

4 Automatic Instances Generation

In this section we briefly describe our original XML instances generation approach, which is called XML-based Partition Testing (XPT) [16]. A proof-of-concept tool called TAXI (Testing by Automatically generated XML Instances) implementing the proposed methodology is also described.

The XPT methodology is composed by two components: XML Schema Analysis (XSA), and Test Strategy Selection (TSS). The former, detailed in Section 4.1, implements a methodology for analyzing the constructs of the XML Schema and automatically generating the instances. The latter, described in Section 4.2, implements diverse test strategies useful both for selecting those parts of the XML Schema to be tested and for opportunely distributing the instances with respect to the Schema elements. These two phases work in agreement, as shown in Figure 1, to realize the application of the Category Partition method.

4.1 XML Schema Analyzer

In this section we introduce the functions realized by the XSA Component as schematized in Figure 1. Specifically XSA takes as an input the weighted version of the original XML Schema that is provided at the end of the first activity (details in Section 4.2) and foresees a *Preprocessor* activity in which the XML Schema constructs, like `all`, `simpleType`, `complexType` and so on, and the

---

[1] Note the usage of the same term "choice" both in XML schema syntax (written as <choice>) and in the CP method (written as *choice*), which is purely accidental.

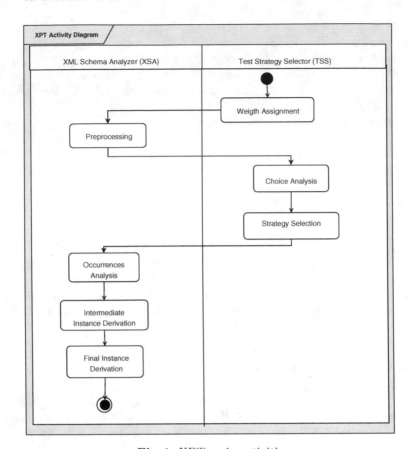

Fig. 1. XPT main activities

shared elements, like `group`, `attributeGroup`, `ref`, and `type`, are analyzed and manipulated. The `choice` elements are excluded from the Preprocessor activity because they will be analyzed by the TSS component.

Considering, for instance, the `all` elements, one of the possible sequences of their children elements is randomly chosen [2] and used for generating instances; for each `group` element, instead, its body is copied wherever it is referenced. These preprocessing operations of course do not contribute to the definition of the test instances, but simplify their successive automatic derivation.

As detailed in Section 4.2 the next two activities by the TSS component have the purpose of: extracting the Functional Units (i.e. a list of subschemas) from the original XML Schema, by means of the analysis of `choice` elements, and selecting the test strategy that must be implemented (i.e. either covering a certain percentage of subschema functionalities or distributing a fixed number of instances among all the extracted subschemas, or a combination).

---

[2] A random selection algorithm which provides the elements ordering has been implemented for this purpose.

The implementation of the Category Partition methodology proceeds with the *Occurrences Analysis* activity, which analyzes the occurrences declared for each element in the subschema and, applying a boundary conditions strategy, derives the border values (*minOccurrences* and *maxOccurrences*) to be considered for the final instances generation.

The results of this activity are combined together during the last steps of the XPT methodology by deriving a set of intermediate instances structures. Values are given to the elements listed into each intermediate instance structure. For this purpose in the current version of TAXI a set of specific algorithms have been implemented to provide the required number of random values for each specific element type. In the current implementation, predefined values available in the Schema and various constraints (for instance `facets`), have been considered. Finally, according to the selected test strategy, the *Final instance derivation* activity produces the final set of instances, which corresponds to the test suite.

4.2   Test Strategy Selection

Testing is an essential, but expensive part of development. Hence test cases need to be prioritized, although generally it is not easy to decide on which parts of the application the testing effort should be concentrated and the amount of test cases to dedicate to each of them. The XML Schema representation of the input domain can help in this regard, by making it possible to implement a practical and automatic strategy for planning a suitable set of test instances.

The component of the XPT methodology which is in charge of this task is the Test Strategy Selection. It completes the implementation of the Category Partition by allowing for the selection of three specific test strategies. Referring to Figure 1 these include: *Weights Assignments*, which assigns weights to the children of the `choice` elements; *Choice Analysis*, which derives a set of subschemas the original XML Schema by means the analysis of the `choice` elements and first level elements; and *Strategy Selection*, which selects the test strategy to be implemented. We describe them in detail in the following.

Weights Assignments. The idea underneath the *Weights Assignments* activity is that the first level element or the children of the same `choice` may have not the same importance for instances derivation. There could be options rarely used or others having critical impact into the final instance derivation. Specifically considering with `choice` elements, according to their definition, only one child per time can appear into the set of final instances, hence from the user point of view the possibility of selecting those more important could be very attractive. He/she can pilot the automatic instance derivation forcing it to derive more instances including the most critical `choice` options.

The XML Schema does not provide the possibility of explicitly declaring the criticality of the diverse options, but often this information is implicitly left to the judgement and expertise of the human agent. The basic idea is that the XML Schema users are asked to make explicit this knowledge. In particular XPT explicitly requires to annotate each child of a `choice` element with a value, belonging to the [0,1] interval, representing its relative "importance" with respect to the other children of the same `choice`. This value, called the weight, must be assigned in such a manner that the sum of the weights associated to all the children of the same `choice` element is equal to 1. A node more critical has greater weight. Several criteria for assigning the importance factors could be adopted. Obviously this aspect in the proposed approach remains highly subjective, but here we are not going to provide a quick recipe on how numbers should be assigned. We only suggest expressing in quantitative terms the intuitions and information about the peculiarity and importance of the different options, considering that such weights will correspondingly affect the testing stage.

Once the weights have been assigned, XPT uses them to derive, for each option in the diverse `choice` elements, the relative importance factor, called the final weight, in terms of how risky is that child and how much effort should be put into the derivation of instances containing it. In a simplified version the final weight of every child is then computed as the product of the weights of all nodes on the complete path from the root to this node. Note that the sum of the final weights of the leaves is still equal to one.

Choice Analysis. As shown in Figure 1, after the *Preprocessor* activity the XPT methodology foresees the analysis of `choice` elements for deriving a set of subschema. These allow only one of the elements contained in their declaration to be present within a conforming instance. This means that for any alternative within a `choice` construct, a separate sub-XML Schema containing it can be derived. Stretching somehow the original meaning of a functional unit, each possible sub-schema is put in correspondence with the notion of a Category Partition functional unit. In other terms, in XPT functional units are meant as "domain units" and are thus assimilated to subsets of XML Schema elements that can originate correct testing instances by managing separate set of data inputs.

Obviously now the problem is the possible occurrence of several `choice`s within one schema, which gives rise to several possible combinations. In this case during the *Choice Analysis* activity as many subschemas as the number of the possible combinations of the children of the `choice` nodes are produced. In Figure 2 we report an example (for simplicity we omit from thew figure the assigned weights). In this case element a is a choice element, which includes a simple element b and another choice element c which has two children: x and y. In particular a transform to three sequence elements, one from element b, and two from the children element of c. In this way the original schema is divided into three subschemas.

During this operation the final weights previously derived are not modified: they will be used once derived the set of possible substructures. Using the final weights of the leaves in each substructure, it is possible to derive a unique value, called the *subtree weight*, useful for test strategy selection, as described in the next subsection. Specifically considering each substructure, starting from its root, the set of the partial subtree weights is normalized so that the sum of the subtree weights over the entire set of substructure is equal to 1.

Original XML Schema	1ˢᵗ Transformation	2ⁿᵈ Transformation	3ʳᵈ Transformation

`<element name="a">`
`<complexType>`
`<choice>`
`<element`
`   name="b".../>`
`<element`
`   name="c"...>`
`<complexType>`
`<choice>`
`<element`
`   name="x".../>`
`<element`
`   name="y".../>`
`</choice>`
`</complexType>`
`</element>`
`</choice>`
`</complexType>`
`</element>`
	`<element name="a">`
	`<complexType>`
	`<sequence>`
	`<element`
	`   name="b".../>`
	`</sequence>`
	`</complexType>`
	`</element>`
		`<element name="a">`
		`<complexType>`
		`<sequence>`
		`<element`
		`   name="c"...>`
		`<complexType>`
		`<sequence>`
		`<element`
		`   name="x".../>`
		`</sequence>`
		`</complexType>`
		`</element>`
		`</sequence>`
		`</complexType>`
		`</element>`
			`<element name="a">`
			`<complexType>`
			`<sequence>`
			`<element`
			`   name="c"...>`
			`<complexType>`
			`<sequence>`
			`<element`
			`   name="y".../>`
			`</sequence>`
			`</complexType>`
			`</element>`
			`</sequence>`
			`</complexType>`
			`</element>`

Fig. 2. Diverse subschema derived by the tag `<choice>`

Strategy Selection. Following the steps described so far each set of substructures has been defined, and a specific subtree weight has been assigned to each of them [3]. Now it is necessary to determine the test strategy to be adopted for test cases derivation. For this we consider three different situations: either a certain number of instances to be derived is fixed, or the percentage of functional coverage is chosen, or both are selected as a stopping rule. The first is the case in which a fixed number of instances must be derived from a specific XML Schema. In this case XPT derives the most suitable distribution of the derivable final instances among the subschemas previously defined. The second situation considers the occurrences with a certain percentage of subschemas, in other words the functionalities must covers a certain percentage of testing purposes. In this case XPT selects those subschemas that will be more suitable for testing purposes. Finally the last case is a mixed test strategy: it proposes a certain number of instances over a fixed percentage of functional coverage.

From a practical point of view, let us discuss the implications of each strategy:

– **Applying XPT with a fixed number of instances:** XPT strategy can be used to develop a fixed number NI of final instances out of the many that could be conceived starting from the original XML Schema. This could be in practice the case in which a finite set of test cases must be developed. Using the subtree weights associated to each substructure, the number of instances that will be automatically derived for each of them is calculated as NI times the subtree weight.
– **Applying XPT with a fixed functional coverage:** this corresponds to the case that a certain percentage of functional test coverage (e.g. 80%) is established as an exit criterion for testing. In this case considering the fixed coverage C, the selection of the substructures to be used can be derived by

---

[3] Of course if the original XML Schema did not include any `choice` element, at this point only one structure is available having *1* as subtree weights.

ordering in a decreasing manner the subtree weights, multiplying them times 100 and adding them together, starting from the heaviest ones, until a values greater than or equal to C is reached.

- **Applying XPT with a fixed functional coverage and number of instances:** in this case the above two strategies are combined. XPT first selects the proper substructures useful for reaching a certain percentage of functional coverage (as described above). Then considers the subtree weights of these selected subschemas and normalizes them so that their sum is still equal to 1. The new derived subtree weights are finally used for distributing among the selected substructures the fixed number of instances to be automatically derived.

5   The TAXI Tool

In this section we briefly describe the architecture of the TAXI tool, which implements the XPT strategy. The current version of TAXI can manage almost all elements of the XML Schema elements providing the set of required XML instances, even if some improvements are currently under implementation, such as the possibility of supporting namespaces or the usage of ontology for values assignment. TAXI will be released as open source code as soon as the development of the new added functionalities will terminate. Nevertheless in its current version it has been used as a proof-of-concept tool for verifying the efficiency and the applicability of the XPT methodology, providing encouraging results. TAXI takes an XML schema as input and parses it by using the W3C Document Object Model(DOM) [17]. It is mainly divided into five components (see Figure 3): User Interface, TSS, Preprocessor, SIP (Skeleton of Instances Producer), FIP (Final Instance Producer), and VP (Values Provider).

Specifically the User Interface manages the interaction with the user, who can influence and control the instance generation process accordingly with his/her specific requirements. By means of this components TAXI acquires the input to start the generation of the test case set. One of the tasks required to the user is therefore the selection of the XML Schema from which he/she wants to derive the valid instances and from this point ahead the generation proceeds automatically. User also needs to set the weights of the schema elements, and to select the test strategy. The weights as described in the previous section are used to represent the amount of test cases from different subtrees. Using weight and test strategy together TAXI can generate the proper amount of test cases from each subtree. The XML Schema is then passed to the Preprocessor component, which implements the preprocessor activities described in the previous subsection. The scope of this component is solving the tags `group`, `attributeGroup`, `ref`, `type`, `restriction`, `extension` and `all`. After this preprocessing stage, the input file is not a well-formed schema anymore, because the elements in the schema are not unique. In this so called "schema" there remain `sequence`,

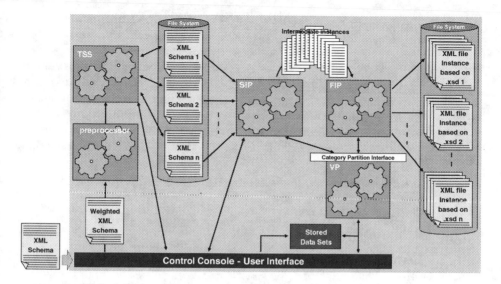

Fig. 3. Architecture of the tool TAXI

choice and simpleType elements. Then TAXI passes this "schema" to Test Strategy Selector. As seen, the first step of this component is choice solver, which produces multiple sub-schemas depending on the number of the choice constructs. At this point the component SIP (Skeleton of Instances Producer) retrieves and analyses each sub-schema, extracting from each element only the necessary information useful for the construction of the final instances. Meanwhile the weight of the child elements will be passed by the interface, and be attached to the sub-schema. Combining the weights with the test strategy, the total test cases can be calculated by TAXI automatically. In particular, when the condition $minOccurrences < maxOccurrences$ holds, collaborating with the component VP (Values Provider), it establishes the exact number of occurrences of each element. By using the collected data, the SIP component develops a set of skeleton files. These are mainly modified tree representations of the various sub-schemas in which special tags and instructions are introduced to make the final instances derivation easier. Specifically the number of skeletons to be produced results from the all possible combinations of the established occurrence values assigned to each element. Reflecting the activities described in the previous section the skeletons of instances so produced are finally analyzed by the FIP (Final Instance Producer) component. It uses the instructions provided by the SIP component in the skeleton, and collaborates with the VP component for receiving the correct values to be associated to each element. The final result is a set of instances, which are by construction conforming to the original schema and classified by sub-schemas. The VP (Values Provider) component has the task of providing the established occurrence of each element and the values to be assigned to each elements during the final instances derivation.

6   Considerations on Applicability of the Approach

The IMS Content Packaging Specification provides the functionality to describe and package learning materials, such as an individual course or a collection of courses, into interoperable, distributable packages. Content Packaging addresses the description, structure, and location of online learning materials and the definition of some particular content types.

As stated above the TAXI tool is still undergoing implementation, however in this section we provide a sample of its functionality, discussing its application within the e-Learning domain. In this domain, our purpose is to reduce the probability of having incorrect interactions among cooperating e-Learning tools: if the test cases are selected appropriately, the tools that pass all of them should be able to interoperate with the other tools that have been submitted to the same test campaign. Of course, in many cases the generation of all the possible instances could not be feasible given that the number could not be finite (consider for instance when an element has an unbounded *maxOccurences* attribute).

Learner Information Package is a IMS standard collection of information about a Learner (individual or group learners) or a Producer of learning content (creators, providers or vendors). As described in the IMS web site[4] the IMS Learner Information Package (IMS LIP) specification [18] addresses:

> "...the interoperability of internet-based Learner Information systems with other systems that support an Internet based learning environment. The intent of the specification is to define a set of packages that can be used to import data into and extract data from an IMS compliant Learner Information server, i.e. servers that in a eLearning environment collects data concerning pupils and/or eLearning content providers. A Learner Information server may exchange data with Learner Delivery systems or with other Learner Information servers. It is the responsibility of the Learner Information server to allow the owner of the learner information to define what part of the learner information can be shared with other systems. The core structures of the IMS LIP are based upon: accessibilities; activities; affiliations; competencies; goals; identifications; interests; qualifications, certifications and licences; relationship; security keys; and transcripts".

It is not difficult to understand the importance of conformance testing when such kind of open specifications are considered. The prefigured scenario is that different stakeholders will independently develop complex software systems that should all be able to take as input or generate in output conforming documents. The tacit assumption is that having considered an agreed specification they would be able to interoperate. Clearly this is far from being completely true. Even a simple XML based specification gives raise to infinite different XML instances. In particular it is possible to specify the same thing in many different ways but it is not difficult to find different parsers that will disagree on the

---

[4] http://www.imsglobal.org

conformance of an XML instance when the original specification imports many nested name spaces or complex tree structure.

In the next subsection we first analyse the dimensions of the feasible legal instances, for a given schema.

6.1   Number of Conforming Instances

Two different factors influence the variability of legal instances: instances can have different values for the same element (Data variability); or, instances can have different structures, i.e., they could contain different elements or different occurrences for the same element (Structural variability). For the case of structural variability three main reasons can be identified:

- the order of the elements in the instances (for instance the tag <all> leads to such kind of variability)
- the presence or otherwise of elements and/or attributes in the instances (for instance the tags <choice> or <use> lead to this situation)
- the number of possible occurrences of an element in the instances (due to the presence of attributes $minOccurrences$ and $maxOccurences$)

Starting from these considerations and only focusing on structural variability, the number of correct instances foreseen by a certain XML Schema (represented as a tree structure), can be derived using the following formulas:

$$ChoiceNode = 2^{\sharp\{OptionalAttributes\}} \sum_{i=1}^{n} Subtree_i \qquad (1)$$

$$AllNode = 2^{\sharp\{OptionalAttributes\}} n! \prod_{i=1}^{n} Subtree_i \qquad (2)$$

$$SequenceNode = \prod_{i=1}^{n} Subtree_i \qquad (3)$$

$$minMaxOccurNode = 2^{\sharp\{OptionalAttributes\}} \sum_{i=minOccur}^{maxOccur} (\prod_{j=1}^{n} Subtree_j)^i \qquad (4)$$

$$LeafNode = 2^{\sharp\{OptionalAttributes\}} (maxOccur - minOccur) \qquad (5)$$

In the formulas above, the variable n indicates the number of different subtrees of a given node. The name of the left member of a formula indicates when to apply it. For instance if the node contains a <choice> tag the formula to apply will be the first. In order to calculate the number of possible instances a simple visit of the XML Schema tree is sufficient. However in the general case this number cannot be calculated when there are unbounded occurrences of an element or loops in the structure of a subtree: for example, a complexType that in one of the corresponding subtrees contains an element of the same type.

Just to give a flavor we calculated the number of possible structurally different instances that can be generated starting from the LIP XML Schema [18]. According to the formula, under the restrictive assumption that no *maxOccurrences* attribute can assume values greater than three, from the schema [18] we calculate that there are 78912 valid instances that can be generated from the main element "product". To reduce the number of equivalent instances, we use boundary conditions strategy: when the minOccurences < maxOccurences, we use only the minimum value and maximum value to do the combination. With this simplified method, 35200 valid instances are obtained from the given schema.

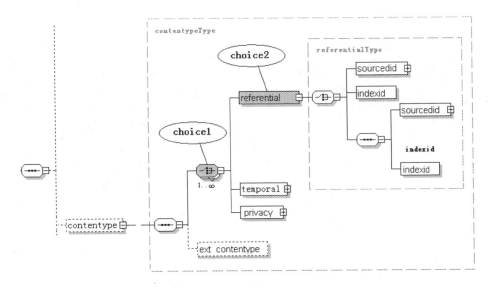

Fig. 4. Partial schema tree

This simple result can probably provide the most intuitive reason to suggest the use of a systematic approach to the generation of XML instances for testing purpose. Given that only a small part of the instances can be used for testing purpose it is absolutely necessary to apply a systematic strategy for the derivation of the test cases. The strategy should permit to focus on conditions that the tester could judge particularly critical in a specific setting. For instance for a particular application the tester could judge the variability on the number of occurrences more important than the order of the elements. Considering the schema that was presented in Fig 4, there are two `choice` elements: "choice1" is the child element of `contentype`, "choice2" is element "referential", which is a child element of "choice1". We set the weight for "choice1" first. There are three child elements in this complexType, we set the weight of "referential" as 0.5, the weight of "temporal" and "privacy" are 0.3 and 0.2. Then consider the weight for another choice element "referential" which has three child elements as well. We set the weight of "sourceid" as 0.3, "indexid" as 0.2, and the other one as 0.5. After solving `choice` 5 subtrees are derived. TAXI can calculate the weights for each subtree automatically according to the weights of choice nodes. The weights of these five sub-schemas are given below.

- The weight of subtree that includes "soureid" is 0.15
- The weight of subtree that includes "indexid" is 0.10
- The weight of subtree that includes "soureid" and "indexid" is 0.25
- The weight of subtree that includes "temporal" is 0.3
- The weight of subtree that includes "privacy" is 0.2

6.2   XPT vs. Random Generation

The possibility of automatically deriving instances from a XML Schema is an emerging problem in many fields of application. As mentioned in Section 2 some tools have been implemented to this purpose. However all of them rely on the random generation of instances, and do not implement any systematic and specific testing strategies. In this section we want to compare the performance of such a kind of existing tools with our tool TAXI. Specifically we select XMLSpy [11], which is an industrial standard XML development environment for modeling, editing, debugging, and transforming all XML technologies. For generating the instances, XMLSpy asks the user to perform some preliminary configuration settings, including: filling elements and attributes with data, whether generating the non-mandatory elements and attributes, generating a priori selection of mandatory `choice` element or not, and how many elements should be generated when *maxOccurrences* is more than one. Thus XMLSpy is different from TAXI both in the strategy implemented and in the typology of instances obtained. We list the mains aspects that characterize the two tools in the following.

1. The amount of instances: XMLSpy generates several configurations, but from each of them only one instance can be derived. TAXI has the capability of deriving large quantity of instances covering systematically all the aspects of a specific XML schema.
2. The value of elements: XMLSpy always gives a same fixed value for each data type. For instance the `<date>` type is fixed to "1967-08-13", and `<string>` type to "string". TAXI has the possibility of declaring a specific set of values for each data type or randomly generating as many values as required.
3. The solution of `<all>` elements: XMLSpy does not make difference in deriving instances when there is a `<all>` or `<sequence>` element, i.e. in the two cases the derived instances will have the same structure. TAXI generates all the possible combinations of the `<all>` children element, and then randomly selects one from them.
4. The solution of `<choice>` elements: In presence of a specific request from the user, XMLSpy can get instances with the first child element of `<choice>` element, otherwise XMLSpy leaves the content of choice element as empty. TAXI derives diverse instances for each of the `<choice>`'s children elements, covering in this manner all the possibilities.

5. The solution of occurrences: in XMLSpy all the values of occurrences must be fixed between 1 to 99. TAXI leaves the user both the possibility of declaring the values of occurrences or using the boundary values. In case of unbounded occurrences, if the user does not set a preference value, TAXI adopts a prefixed bound. The occurrences values are then combined to get instances with variation structures.

Considering a complex schema, TAXI nearly generates all possible combinations of complex elements and occurrences, and each instance has different values inside, while the instances from XMLSpy vary only in the amount of repeated elements. Concluding despite the good performance of XMLSpy, for the instance generation this tool applies a quite simple algorithm, which gives only few flexibility to the user and does not attempt to cover all the input domain. From the tester's point of view the derived instance cannot cover all the declared schema elements and consequently the functionalities of the application to be tested. Thus it could be claimed that TAXI is able to provide a test strategy, which is more comprehensive and covers all weaknesses of XMLSpy.

7   Conclusions

We have introduced the XPT approach for the systematic derivation of XML Instances from a XML Schema. XPT applies to the XML notation a well-known method for software black-box testing. Given the pervasiveness of XML in web-based and distributed applications, we are convinced that the proposed method can be very useful to check the quality of applications via a rigorous test campaign. In generak, we are interested in generating both valid and invalid instances (the latter for robustness test). On the tester's side, XPT targets the long-standing dream of automating the generation of test cases for black-box testing, which is routinely done by expert testers that analyse specifications of the input domain written in natural or semiformal language. If the input is formalized into XML Schema, then XPT can provide a much more systematic and cheaper strategy. The work we have described is still undergoing implementation. We will continue investigating the applicability to real-world case studies, in particular within the e-Learning domain. The most challenging issue that comes out from the investigation in this paper is the infeasibly high number of test instances that would be generated, therefore the identification and implementation of sensible heuristic to reduce the generated instances is compelling.

References

1. W3CXML: W3cxml. http://www.w3.org/XML/ (1996)
2. W3CXMLSchema: W3c xmlschema. http://www.w3.org/XML/Schema (1998)
3. XMLTestSuite: Extensible markup language (xml) conformance test suites. http://www.w3.org/XML/Test/ (2005)
4. NIST: Software diagnostics&conformance testing division: Web technologies. http://xw2k.sdct.itl.nist.gov/brady/xml/index.asp (2003)

5. RTTS: Rtts: Proven xml testing strategy. http://www.rttsweb.com/services/index.cfm (nd)
6. SQC: Xml schema quality checker. http://www.alphaworks.ibm.com/tech/xmlsqc (2001)
7. W3CXMLValidator: W3c validator for xml schema. http://www.w3.org/2001/03/webdata/xsv (2001)
8. XMLJudge: Xml judge. http://www.topologi.com/products/utilities/xmljudge.html (nd)
9. EasyCheXML: Easychexml. http://www.stonebroom.com/xmlcheck.htm (nd)
10. Li, J.B., Miller, J. In: Testing the Semantics of W3C XML Schema. COMPSAC 2005 (2005) 443 – 448
11. XMLSpy: Xml spy. http://www.altova.com/products_ide.html (2005)
12. Toxgene: Toxgene. http://www.cs.toronto.edu/tox/toxgene/ (2005)
13. SunXMLInstanceGenerator: Sun xml instance generator. http://wwws.sun.com/software/xml/developers/instancegenerator/index.html (2003)
14. Ostrand, T., Balcer, M.: The category-partition method for specifying and generating functional tests. Communications of ACM **31**(6) (1988)
15. Basanieri, F., Bertolino, A., Marchetti, E.: The cow_suite approach to planning and deriving test suites in uml projects. In: Proc. Fifth International Conference on the Unified Modeling Language UML 2002, LNCS 2460, Dresden, Germany (2002) 383–397
16. Bertolino, A., Gao, J., Marchetti, E., Polini, A.: Partition testing from xml schema. Technical report ISTI-45/2005 (2005)
17. DocumentObjectModel: Document object model.   http://www.w3.org/DOM/ (2005)
18. AAVV: IMS learning information package v.1.0.1. On-line at: http://www.imsglobal.org/content/packaging/cpv1p2pd/imscp_oviewv1p2pd.html (2005)

Transformations of UML 2 Models Using Concrete Syntax Patterns*

Markus Schmidt

Real-Time Systems Lab
Darmstadt University of Technology
D-64283 Darmstadt, Germany
markus.schmidt@es.tu-darmstadt.de

Abstract. Model transformations are an important part of the MDA approach. The process of converting a PIM into a PSM should be done by certain model transformations. While there are many transformation languages for UML available they all share the discrepancy between the syntax of the transformation specification language and the visual UML syntax. Today model transformations are defined either in a textual manner or in a language that uses constructs from the underlying metamodel. This paper presents a novel approach to specify model transformations as patterns in the concrete syntax of UML 2. These patterns are easier to read than usual transformation specifications and use only standard UML 2 constructs. This is achieved using the built-in extension mechanism of UML 2 - the Profiles. Besides the specification, these profiles offer the application of patterns within any UML 2 compliant modeling tool. As such, these patterns can be seen as a front-end for model transformation.

Keywords: Model Transformations, Patterns, UML 2 Profiles.

1 Introduction

Patterns and model transformations are closely related in model-driven software engineering. While patterns specify source and target model the execution of model transformations creates the target model. Transformations between models is a key activity within the MDA [1] framework. The importance of model transformation is stressed by Sendall and Kozaczynski [2] as they describe it as "The heart and soul of model-driven software development".

Such transformations can be defined to cross different modeling languages or to change models within the same language. Graph based transformations is the most popular way to express model transformations. This seems to be a natural choice since most modeling language are also graph based. An overview of graph transformation in the context of model-driven engineering is given by Grunske et.al [3]. They propose some requirements a good transformation language should

---

* Work supported in part by the European Community's Human Potential Programme under contract HPRN-CT-2002-00275, SegraVis.

N. Guelfi and D. Buchs (Eds.): RISE 2006, LNCS 4401, pp. 130–143, 2007.

hold. One of these requirements states that "transformation rules should be easy to understand". While it is necessary to use transformation rules that are understandable by themselves, it is also important that there is a certain kind of similarity between the transformation rules and the models to transform.

One common way to describe transformation rules for a modeling language (e.g. UML) is to use the abstract syntax of this language (e.g. metamodel of UML). One major drawback of this method is the discrepancy between abstract and concrete syntax. Transformation rules in abstract syntax can easily become complex and hard to read. For the case of UML the user must also know the metamodel. As UML is a very extensive language this is a very challenging task for most users. As an example of a transformation rule based on a metamodel we will present a simple transformation within a UML statemachine. Figure 1 shows the insertion of a transition **beta** between the state **A** and state **C**.

Fig. 1. informal description of a transformation that adds a transition

We use QVT [4] an an example of a transformation language that is based on a metamodel. The QVT rule for the transformation in figure 1 is shown in figure 2. The transformation rule itself is understandable but there is little relation between the statemachine and the transformation rule. Only a single transition must be inserted but the rule contains many more elements.

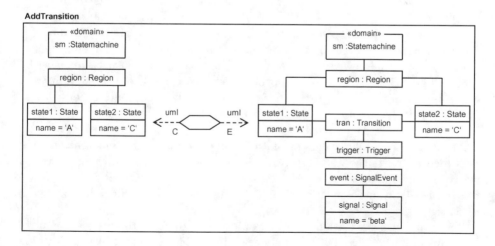

Fig. 2. QVT transformation to add a transition between two states

Another drawback is the different notation of the model element. States and transitions have their special notation in a statemachine diagram. But as the transformation language is based on the metamodel all elements have the same rectangle notation.

What we are looking for is a methodology that gives the user the ability to specify model transformations in the same visual language as he develops his models. As our focus lies on UML 2.0 [5], that means specifying transformations with standard constructs of UML 2.0. If this would be possible, it has two important advantages for the user

- it is not necessary to learn another language
- it can be done with any UML 2.0 modeling tool

Before we describe our approach in the remainder of this paper we compare our intention with related work in the next section. Section 3 exemplifies the fundamentals of our work - the UML 2.0 Profiles. Some motivating examples of pattern specification with profiles are given in section 4. Section 5 describes our approach as a front-end for model transformation. A classification as a general model transformation approach is shown in section 6. Section 7 concludes the paper with a discussion of further directions.

2 Related Work

Patterns and especially their relationship to model transformation have been subject of research before. This section outlines different transformation languages that are able to transform UML models. We will pay special attention to their transformation syntax and universal applicability.

Story diagrams [6] are a graph rewrite language that is heart of the open source modeling tool Fujaba [7]. Story diagrams adopt some UML 1.x diagrams. Class diagrams are used for the specification of graph schemes, activity diagrams for the graphical representation of control structures and collaboration diagrams as a notation for graph rewrite rules. A major disadvantage is that patterns must be specified in the abstract syntax. Another drawback comes from the tool Fujaba, which is the only tool that uses story diagrams. Fujaba can only generate code for Java, so anyone who uses story diagrams is bound to Java code.

Architecture Stratification [8] is an approach that connects multiple views on a single system with refinement translation. There exists an implementation SPin [9] which supports the automatic transformation of models into more detailed versions and thus represents basic support for Architecture Stratification. Since this implementation is a plugin for Fujaba it has the same benefits and drawbacks as Story diagrams.

The model transformation framework Mercator [10] uses stereotypes to control the transformation. It is designed to be used in the MDA context by transforming a PIM into a PSM. Only UML class diagrams are supported and the current prototype supports basic UML-to-Java transformations.

A graphical transformation language for UML is UMLX [11]. UMLX uses standard UML class diagrams to define information schema and their instances, and extends the class diagrams to define inter-schema transformations. A transformation diagram uses special visual elements and as such can not be used with standard UML editors. Transformations are metamodel-based and as such not very readable if other diagram types than class diagrams are used.

The upcoming standard language QVT [4] from the object management group seems to be a natural choice for specifying pattern for UML 2.0 models since QVT and UML 2.0 are both based upon MOF [12]. Transformations are written in a relational language either in a textual notation or in a graphical notation. Graphical transformations are expressed using extended UML object diagrams. So a transformation rule for statecharts contains only the rectangles of the meta-classes for state and transition and not the typical round boxes for states or the transition arrows.

Baar and Whittle [13] proposed the pattern language PICS (patterns in concrete syntax) as a more readable notation for transformation rules. They modify the language of the underlying metamodel with some information from the syntax of the concrete model to generate PICS. While the resulting transformation rules are more readable than QVT transformations, it is necessary to create a new PICS metamodel for every model the patterns should work on. So one PICS metamodel to transform class diagrams and one to transform statecharts. Furthermore, a special tool is necessary to create these transformations.

3   UML 2.0 Profiles

This section gives a short introduction in the foundation of our work - the UML 2.0 profiles. Some interesting changes were made in the transition from UML 1.x to UML 2.0 which are important for this work.

Since version 2.0 the profiles are a separated package of the UML metamodel defined in the Superstructure document [5]. This package is shown in figure 3.

A profile is now a specific kind of a package and contains some restrictions on the possible extensions of a reference metamodel (e.g UML and CWM). We will not discuss these restrictions in this paper and refer the reader to the specification document [5].

The primary extension construct is the stereotype, which is a limited kind of metaclass. A stereotype must always be used in combination with a metaclass that it extends. The notation for an extension is an arrow pointing from a stereotype to the extended metaclass.

Two stereotypes are defined in figure 4. The stereotype Clock extends the metaclasses Component and Class and contains an attribute resolution. The stereotype Creator extends only the metaclasses Class and has two attributes. The additional constraint required states that every UML 2.0 class must be annotated with this stereotype. As you can see it is possible for a stereotype to extend more than one metaclass and vice versa a metaclass can be extended by more than one stereotype.

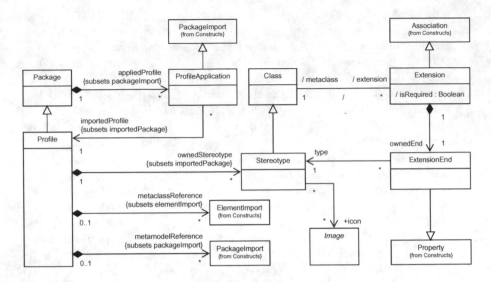

Fig. 3. Profiles package from UML 2.0 Superstructure [5]

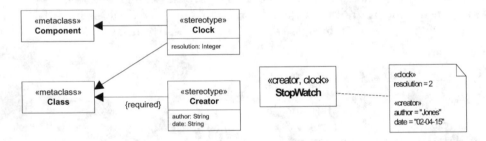

Fig. 4. Stereotypes extend metaclasses   **Fig. 5.** Application of stereotypes with parameters

The assignment of values to attributes of a stereotype is done using a UML comment. The body of this comment holds the assignments in form of name-value pairs. This is shown in figure 5 where the UML 2.0 class StopWatch is annotated with stereotypes from figure 4.

The profiles of UML 2.0 offer two important features. First, the ability to use a profile as a package and as such to import other profiles and package to provide a hierarchy of profiles. Second, to restrict the application of a stereotype to model elements that are instances of the correct metamodel element.

4   Using Profiles to Specify Transformations

This section shows some motivating example on how UML 2.0 Profiles can be used to specify pattern in the concrete syntax of UML 2.0 models.

4.1   Singleton

Our first attempt is to specify a very basic pattern - the singleton. Even though it is a very simple example, it is rich enough to explain the basic idea of our approach.

Figure 6 shows the class Demo in two different ways. On the left hand side with an annotated stereotype singleton that indicates that this class is (or should be) a singleton class. The class on the other side has all the elements (attribute, constructor, method) that makes a class to a singleton class.

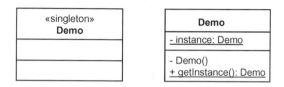

Fig. 6. class with singleton stereotype and class with singleton elements

The left hand side shows the application (via annotated stereotype) of the singleton pattern and the right hand side the expanded pattern. So the classes can be seen as the source and the target of this pattern. What is missing is a way to describe the transition from source to target model with standard constructs of UML 2.0.

The first step is to define a profile that allows the annotation of a stereotype to a class. Figure 7 shows this profile and the application of this stereotype. Now the model is well-formed since we have a profile defining the used stereotype and this stereotype is annotated to a UML class. But this model gives no hints about the necessary transformations to expand the singleton pattern.

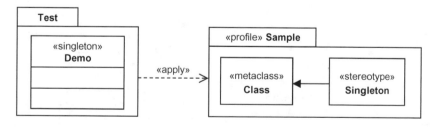

Fig. 7. Profile for singleton and application of this profile

The idea to specify these transformations is to use the expanded singleton class from Figure 6 and annotate all elements that must be added. This kind of annotations can be realized with stereotypes, whereas these stereotypes represent model modifications.

Figure 8 shows a UML 2.0 model that uses a certain profile, whereas all stereotypes extend the topmost metamodel element *Element*. Therefore, every model element of UML 2.0 can be annotated with these stereotypes. Stereotype New stands for the addition of a new model element and This specifies the reference element of the pattern. Package Singleton contains the expanded class with annotated stereotypes to describe the role of model elements in the pattern. The reference element is the class itself and the other three elements must be added if the pattern is expanded.

The package Singleton can be seen as a specification of the singleton pattern since both the structure and the behavior of the pattern are specified. It is interesting that the profile from Figure 7 can be extracted from this package. Since the reference element is a class and the name of the package is Singleton we can automatically generated the profile shown in Figure 7.

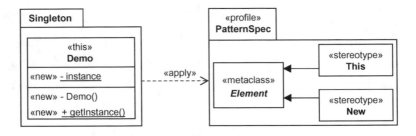

Fig. 8. Profile for pattern specification and application as a singleton definition

Moreover, we can automatically extract the transformation rules from the package. For every element that is annotated with New we create a transformation rule that adds the element to the model. These two steps, creation of the profile and creation of the transformation rules, can be done by a program. Figure 9 shows the two types of data that such a program produce.

Fig. 9. generated profile and transformations

On the left hand side the profile that contains the stereotype for the application of the pattern. Note that the extension of the metaclass Class restricts the application of the stereotype to UML classes. So the profile offers a simple kind of validation. The transformations are shown on the right hand side. The presentation is very informal and only given for completeness. An implementation will create the transformation rules with respect to the used transformation engine.

One major drawback of the specified pattern is the static nature. This pattern has no parameters and can only be applied to a class called Demo.

4.2   Patterns with Parameters

This section shows how parameters can be specified within our approach. The ability to use parameters is based on attributes of a stereotype and on a special syntax for element names. As described in section 3 a stereotype can have an attribute that can be assigned with a value via a UML comment. This gives us the ability to set the value if the pattern is applied to a model element. What is missing is the ability to define an element name, or parts of a name, as a parameter. But this is already defined in the context of the UML 2.0 template mechanism. The UML 2.0 template package contains string expressions that defines a syntax for strings with parameters. String expressions appears between $ signs, where parameters are shown between angle brackets.

An application of these string expressions is shown in Figure 10. Two states are shown, whereas the Timeout state has a constant name and the other name is a parameter. As this state is also the reference element of this pattern, the pattern can be applied to any state and the parameter $name$ holds the actual name. Other parameters are the time inside the event of the transition and the event that specifies the liveness of the reference state. As a whole this pattern specifies the verification of a liveness event of a single state. A transition to a timeout state is performed if this event is not received within a certain period.

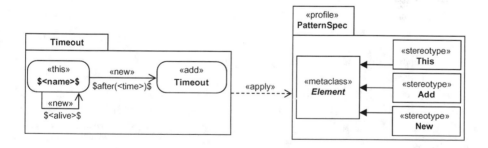

Fig. 10. Profile for a state with timeout

The two types of data that can be generated from the specification of the timeout pattern is shown in Figure 11. The profile shows the stereotype Timeout that extends the metaclass State. Two parameters of the pattern are defined as attributes of the stereotype. The name parameter is implicit, because this assignment is automatically done if the pattern is applied to a state.

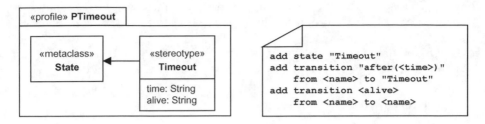

Fig. 11. Generated profile and transformations

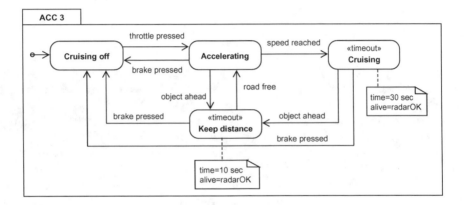

Fig. 12. Application of the timeout pattern

An application of this pattern is shown within a simplified statechart of an adaptive cruise control in Figure 12. The timeout pattern is applied to two states with different values for the parameters.

5   Realization of Our Approach

As we arrogated in the introduction, is should be possible to integrate our approach easily in any UML modeling tools. While we currently working on an integration in the modeling tool Together Architect [14], we present only the ideas in this section.

First, we present an overview of the development process within a single modeling tool. After this, we present the fundamental profile in more detail.

5.1   Development Process

The whole process of specification, application and expansion of model transformations can be done with a single modeling tool. Figure 13 shows this process in an abstract manner.

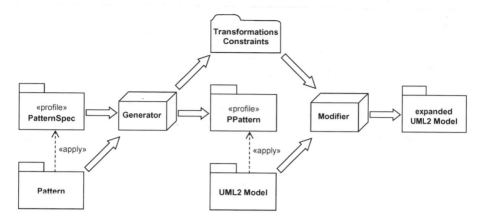

Fig. 13. Process within a single modeling tool

The only models that a user must create are the two packages (Pattern and UML2 Model) at the bottom of this figure. The Pattern package contains transformation specification (pattern). The Generator uses this pattern and creates a profile for the application of the pattern and some data containing transformation and constraints for the expansion of the pattern. The created profile must be used to apply the pattern to the model. The expansion is performed by the modifier who takes the transformations and constraints to generate an expanded model. The most abstract parts of the process are Generator and Modifier. The implementation of these parts depends on the used modeling tool since it is necessary to read and write models. So for most tools, Generator and Modifier will be realized as plugins that use the tool API to access the models. Another way is the realization as textual QVT scripts. So any modeling tool that supports QVT will be able to execute the Generator and Modifier.

5.2 Profile to Specify Transformations

In order to be able to specify transformations a fundamental profile must be given that must be applied to transformation specifications. This profile **PatternSpec** is shown in figure 14 and contains stereotypes for basic transformation operations and notational purposes. We use some abstract stereotypes for structural purposes and to apply some constraints.

We omitted some constraints to reduce the complexity of the figure. The real profile contains more constraints that prevents invalid combinations (e.g. **This** and **New**).

If a model element as part of a transformation specification is annotated with a stereotype the meaning of this element is as follows:

- **This** element is reference point of the pattern
- **New** element will be added

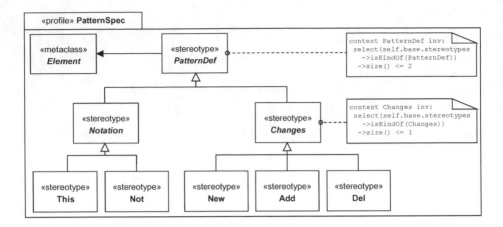

Fig. 14. Profile for the specification of patterns

- **Add** element will be added only if it is not available
- **Del** element must be available and will be deleted
- **Not** element must not be available

6   Classification as a Model Transformation Approach

The presented approach can be seen as a front-end for a graph based model transformation approach.

We will give a short classification of our approach in relation to the classification scheme proposed by Czarnecki and Helsen [15]. They present the result of their domain analysis as a set of feature diagrams. For lack of space we focus only on the features of transformation rules.

Figure 15 shows the feature diagram for transformation rules form Czarnecki and Helsen [15]. Features of our approach are marked with bold rectangle and bold typeface.

As source and target model are represented within a single UML 2.0 diagram a transformation rule is specified in a combined LHS/RHS form. Variables of or transformation rules are meta-attributes of stereotypes. As an assignment of such meta-attributes can only be done with UML 2.0 comments, all variables are untyped. This is a weakness of our approach but unavoidable if we use the concrete syntax of UML 2.0. It is also possible to add some logic in form of OCL-Constraints, even though we didn't use constraints in previous examples.

Patterns are specified as parts of UML 2.0 diagram and as such in graphical form with the concrete syntax of the model to transform. Every pattern is syntactically typed because of the relationship between a stereotype and the extended metaclass. So it is an easy task for a modeling tool to validate the application of a pattern.

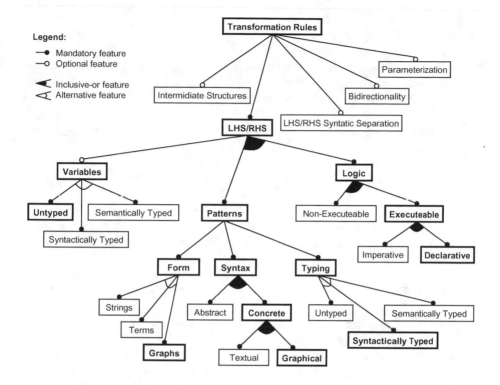

Fig. 15. Features of transformation rules

7   Conclusions and Outlook

The challenge of this paper was the development of a method to specify model transformations for any UML 2.0 diagram in the same concrete visual syntax and with no other than the standard constructs of UML 2.0.

Since transformations are not supported directly (only as limited patterns in collaboration diagrams) in UML 2.0 it was reasonable to make use of the extension mechanism of UML 2.0 - the profiles. First the extension mechanism was used to provide a profile to specify transformations with the contained stereotype. A usual UML 2.0 diagram became a transformation specification simply through the annotation with a stereotype form this profile.

After that we realized that such a transformation specification contains enough information for the application and expansion of itself. Information from a transformation specification can be used to generate two different types of data

- a profile describing the application and containing information for syntactically validation
- a transformation with constraints to perform the expansion

The first type of data can be used immediately within a UML 2.0 modeling tool to use the specified transformation in some diagrams. Since this data is given in the form of a profile, the user has a simple kind of syntactically validation.

The other type of data can not be used directly since UML 2.0 doesn't provide any kind of model transformation. The generation and the application of these data depends on the used modeling tool.

This approach turns out to be a front-end for graph-based model transformation of any UML 2.0 diagram. The transformation rules are specified as pattern in the concrete visual syntax of UML 2.0. This is an important benefit compared to other model transformation languages. On the other side this is not a first-class model transformation approach. One limitation is that source and target model are instances of the same metamodel. It is a desired feature since we only want to work with UML 2.0.

A real limitation is the restricted expressive power of transformations using our approach. One simple example is a transformation rule that renames the name of any classifier. This transformation can be specified easily in QVT, but not with our approach. This comes form the fact that the model element classifier is not a UML 2.0 model element and as such not visible at level M1. So this approach is not able to replace metamodel based transformation languages, but this is not the intention. The intention is the definition of high level transformations for any kind of UML 2.0 model.

This paper covers only the ground potential that UML 2.0 Profiles offer for MDA. The ability to place models from different diagram types into a single profile can be used to specify patterns over more than one diagram type. So it could be possible to specify a pattern that contains structural information (e.g. classes) and information about the behavior (e.g. statemachines).

References

1. OMG: MDA Guide Version 1.0.1. OMG. (2003) http://www.omg.org/docs/omg/03-06-01.pdf.
2. Sendall, S., Kozaczynski, W.: Model transformation: The heart and soul of model-driven software development. IEEE Softw. **20**(5) (2003) 42–45
3. Grunske, L., Geiger, L., Zündorf, A., van Eetvelde, N., van Gorp, P., Varró, D.: Using graph transformation for practical model driven software engineering. In Beydeda, S., Book, M., Gruhn, V., eds.: Model-Driven Software Development. Volume II. Springer Verlag (2005) 91–119
4. OMG: MOF 2.0 Query/View/Transformation Final Adopted Specification (ptc/2005-11-01). (2005) http://www.omg.org/cgi-bin/doc?ptc/2005-11-01.
5. OMG: UML 2.0 Superstructure Specification formal/05-07-04. OMG. (2005) http://www.omg.org/docs/formal/05-07-04.pdf.
6. Fischer, T., Niere, J., Torunski, L., Zündorf, A.: Story diagrams: A new graph rewrite language based on the unified modeling language and java. In: TAGT'98: Selected papers from the 6th International Workshop on Theory and Application of Graph Transformations, London, UK, Springer-Verlag (2000) 296–309
7. Fujaba Development Group: Fujaba Tool Suite. (2006) http://www.fujaba.de.

8. Atkinson, C., Kühne, T.: Aspect-Oriented Development with Stratified Frameworks (2003)
9. Klar, F., Kühne, T., Girschick, M.: SPin - a Fujaba Plugin for Architecture Stratification. In: 3rd Int. Fujaba Days 2005: "MDD in Practice". (2005) 17–23
10. Witthawaskul, W., Johnson, R.: An object oriented model transformer framework based on stereotypes. In: 3rd Workshop in Software Model Engineering at The Seventh International Conference on the Unified Modeling Language. (2004)
11. Willink, E.: UMLX: A graphical transformation language for MDA. In Rensink, A., ed.: Model Driven Architecture: Foundations and Applications, University of Twente, the Netherlands (2003) CTIT Technical report TR-CTIT-03-27.
12. OMG: Meta Object Facility(MOF) 2.0 Core Specification. OMG. (2003) http://www.omg.org/docs/ptc/03-10-04.pdf.
13. Baar, T., Whittle, J.: On the usage of concrete syntax in model transformation rules. Technical Report 2006-002, École Polytechnique Fédérale de Lausanne (EPFL) (2006)
14. Borland Software Corporation: Together Architect 2006. (2006) http://www.borland.com.
15. Czarnecki, K., Helsen, S.: Classification of model transformation approaches. In: 2nd OOPSLA03 Workshop on Generative Techniques in the Context of MDA. (2003)

Towards a Formal, Model-Based Framework for Control Systems Interaction Prototyping

Matteo Risoldi[1] and Vasco Amaral[2]

[1] Université de Genève
24, Rue Général-Dufour
CH 1211 Geneva 4
matteo.risoldi@cui.unige.ch
[2] Universidade Nova de Lisboa
Quinta da Torre
P 2829-516 Caparica
vasco.amaral@di.fct.unl.pt

Abstract. This paper provides an overview of a starting project called BATIC^{3}S (Building Adaptive Three-dimensional Interfaces for Critical Complex Control Systems). This project aims to bring a more viable approach in the fields of Graphical User Interfaces (GUI), software modeling and verification, automatic code generation, and adaptivity. The goal is to build a comprehensive methodology for semi-automated, formal model-based generation of effective, reliable and adaptive 3D GUIs for diagnosing control systems. This can be used to assist in GUI development for very complex systems, like industrial systems, high energy physics experiments and similar.

1 Introduction

Developing Graphical User Interfaces (GUIs) for complex control systems is costly, difficult and error prone. Large hardware systems as you can find in industries, physics research centers or transportation (airplanes) have a high complexity coming from the number of components, their hierarchical interaction and the large number of parameters to be monitored at once. This poses challenges in particular concerning the correctness of the control, the navigation issues and the paradigm for human interaction. Therefore, it is of first importance to systematize the specification and modeling of systems, to find new ways of interaction and to minimize the development cost of GUI production in order to be able to test interfaces from a usability point of view.

In this paper we will present a work in progress, stating our views on how various software engineering techniques and aspects can be integrated and coordinated in a methodology to standardize and assist the development of such interfaces. We will speak through examples about what technologies we are using for it. Finally we will briefly illustrate two case studies that are currently guiding our work. A survey on related work, with analysis and a comparative study of previous approaches in the field of user interface prototyping for control systems, has been done in [4].

N. Guelfi and D. Buchs (Eds.): RISE 2006, LNCS 4401, pp. 144–159, 2007.

2   The General Approach

2.1   Definition of a Control System

Control systems (CS) can be defined as mechanisms that provide output variables of a system by manipulating the inputs (from sensors). The field of CS is wide, and ranges from the very simple to the very complex. To avoid a lack of applicability, we had to reduce the field to systems with some specific features. The definition of a CS we use (and a very widely accepted one) is a system which has a hierarchical organization, in which every elementary object can be grouped with others, and composite objects (groups) can be grouped as well, forming a hierarchical tree in which the root represents the whole system and the leaves are the actual devices that form it. Typically this grouping will reflect a physical container-contained composition (but it could follow other relations as well). Elementary and composite objects can receive commands and communicate states and alarms. Figure 1 shows a partial example of such a system, a simple drink vending machine (DVM). We will use it also in following examples.

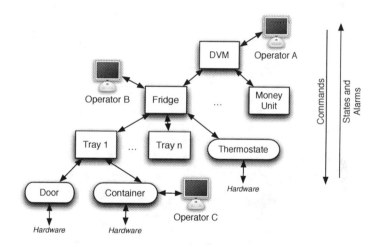

Fig. 1. An example of hierarchical control system: drink vending machine

We can see basic, low level components: the *Door*, the *Container* and the *Thermostate*. These get input directly from the hardware (through sensors, for example), and have simple states which depend on this input (e.g. the Thermostate might have states *TempOk*, *TempWarning* and *TempError*, depending on a temperature sensor). These basic components are grouped in various ways - Door and Container are grouped in a *Tray*, which is a composite object; several trays and a Thermostate are grouped in a *Fridge*. The latter, and another composite *Money Unit*, are in turn grouped into the top object, *DVM*. We see that the operators might have access to the system at various levels, either at a higher level or only to a part of it, according to their needs or their profile.

In such a system, commands should be able to be passed down in the hierarchy, so that for example Operator A is able to send commands not only to DVM, but also to Tray1. States and alarms, instead, should flow up, meaning that an object that fails should notify its state to its ancestor objects, which might in turn decide to update their states depending on this information. This is essential for diagnosing faults even at the highest levels.

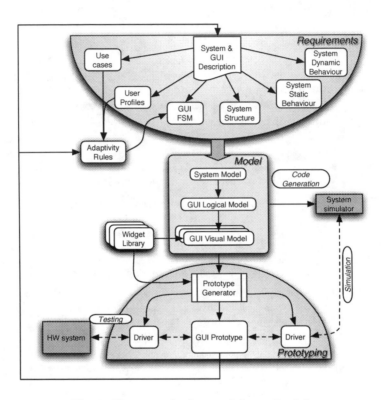

Fig. 2. The general schema of the methodology

2.2 The Methodology

Figure 2 shows how we defined the methodology for GUI building. There is an initial phase where the requirements and specifications for the system and GUI are gathered (top semicircle). From this information, a model is built semi-automatically (central square). Finally, a prototype is generated from the model (bottom semicircle). In the following sections we will analyze these three phases, explain some technological choices that have been made for their application, and discuss the advantages that we find.

3   Gathering Requirements

We start with the requirements of the System and the GUI, which should be provided by the system engineers/technicians/users, what we call System Experts in general. These should include:

- A description of the system structure, in its hierarchical aspects (as i Figure 1) as well as in its geometrical properties (shape, location, dimensions of every component of the system that we shall represent in the GUI);
- The system behaviour, as in what commands objects can accept, and what values they may communicate; this is a concept akin to what we call *interface* for a Class in OO programming;
- The dynamic behaviours for all the objects of the system, and also how they compose (i.e. how an object can react, by changing its state, to a child object's state change);
- The FSM for the GUI, describing its initial and possible states (e.g. different levels of visualization, different operation modes) and how they might change in reaction to events;
- Use cases and user profiles, which are needed to establish adaptivity rules.

Adaptivity rules describe how the interface should react to a number of factors[19], including user knowledge, both static (profile) and dynamic (training), events in the system (faults, alarms) or particular actions. Adaptation is a complex and vast topic which would require an article on its own, and we will not treat it here.

3.1   Formalizing Requirements

A problem that most developers meet at some point is that there is usually an impedence problem between the way of thinking of software developers and system experts. Software developers have their mind focused on getting requirements for building an interface, often ignoring or simply not understanding some of the requests coming from the system experts. System experts, on the other hand, might have a faint idea of what rigour is needed to express requirements for developers, but have a very deep knowledge of the information to provide, and it is only they who can say if a software meets the requirements or not. This risks causing production of poor software which only partially meets the requests and is a challenge to modify and maintain.

Previous research in the field [7] has shown with experimental data that efforts to provide a more understandable specification can greatly help in reducing error rates and increasing comprehension. Other works [18] have shown that one important factor to reduce ambiguity and complexity of specifications is to define a precise domain to work with, although the conclusions point out that this is not enough and that no unique technique can ensure an all-purpose solution even for a specific domain. As we found in more research [10,14,3], there are however some clear advances whenever the field has some standardized ways of specifying it. If one can rely on having certain information under a certain form, there are stronger assumptions that can be done on the efficiency of a proposed solution.

We are trying to express the system features by defining a domain specific framework which is at the same time simple enough for system experts to use and formal enough for developers to work on. Also, we want this to be usable in practice, not only in theory. To achieve this, first of all we concentrated on a very specific domain, as we discussed when giving a definition of control systems. Then, we adopted a base for the framework which is in fact a composition of several approaches:

- we use a domain specific language (DSL), suitable to express hierarchical and functional characteristics of objects.
- for storing this data we use a database (according to a very well-established schema for control systems[1]) containing the system composition, geometry and dataflow. Often this kind of database generally will already exist, because it's used in the system engineering phase, for construction and testing. In other cases still it should not be difficult to build, because of its modularity and the fact that the information it asks for has normally been defined anyway.
- we are deriving a dynamic state-machine language from State Manager Language (SML) [9]; this solution also presents an advantage in which SML is a widely used language as it is integrated in one of the major monitoring and supervision softwares, PVSS II [8].

An example of specification is the following. Let's consider a part of the hierarchy of the DVM of Figure 1: a fridge containing a tray and a thermostate, with the tray containing a door and a container for drinks. In Listing 1.1 the Container class is defined.

Listing 1.1. Definition of a Container

```
class:  Container;
type:  A;
geomshape:  Box;
dimensions:  100*100*900;
coordinates:  10*2*10;
property drinkNumber:  integer;
method  refill(p1:  integer);
    drinkNumber=drinkNumber+p1;
end  method;
method buy();
    if(state!=Empty)  then
        drinkNumber=drinkNumber-1;
    else  exception;
end  method;
state:  Empty / INITIAL_STATE;
```

```
       when  refill(p1)  do  refilled;
   action:  refilled;
   if  (post(drinkNumber)>5)then  terminate_action/state=OK;
   else  if  (post(drinkNumber) <= 5 && post(drinkNumber)>0)
   then  terminate_action/state=LowNumber;
   end  action;
 end  state;
 state:  LowNumber;
  when  buy()  do  bought;
  when  refill(p1)  do  refilled;
  action:  bought;
       if  (post(drinkNumber)=0)
       then  terminate_action  /  state=Empty;
       else  terminate_action  /  state=LowNumber;
   end  action;
   action:  refilled;
       ...
   end  action;
 end  state;
   ...  \\  more  states  definitions...
 end  class;
```

We can see the description of the base features of the object class - its name, type, and the geometrical features. The type is useful if we want to define features at a sub-class level: there might be different types of containers, and in each type we might have specific features, but still have a container. This can help in large scale systems, where the number of types is generally much more limited than the number of objects.

The functional features (properties and methods) are then listed. For each property we have its type; for each method we define the types of the parameters and an implementation. Note that in this phase the specification should abstract objects to focus on the control aspects; we don't implement all the details of the buy method, but simply the fact that it takes one drink from the container.

Finally, there is the definition of the state machine. States are listed one after the other, and the initial state (here Empty) is indicated. For each state, where relevant, the possible events are listed, and the actions triggered by the event are written. Here, in the state Empty, whenever there is a refill event, the new value of drinkNumber is checked; if it is more than fine, the object goes to state OK; if it is more than 0 but less or equal to 5, it goes to state LowNumber. Note the post statement, which expresses the value of a property *after* the event; this allows us to distinguish between pre- and post-conditions of events.

An interesting case to see is the definition of the state machine for a composite object, a Tray. In Listing 1.2 we can see how a state change can be triggered by the state change of a child object. The event here is the state change of a child object, `container1`. Complex events can be envisaged when there are several children objects, for example establishing a majority rule where the state turns to `Faulty` only if the majority of children are `Faulty`.

Listing 1.2. State change trigger   **Listing 1.3.** Instantiating a class

```
class: Tray;
...
state: OK;
    when container1
    in_state Empty
    do GOFAULTY;
    action: GOFAULTY
        terminate_action
        / state=Faulty;
    end action;
end state;
...
end class;
```

```
object: container1;
    class: Container;
    type: A;
    parent: tray1;
end object;
```

We then have to declare the instances of the classes, as in Listing 1.3. We are saying here that there is an object `container1` which belongs to the previously declared class `Container`, and that it is a child of Tray. We can declare as many objects of this class as we want, and build complex hierarchies in a very simple recurring way (we will declare a Tray object to have a Fridge parent, we will declare a Fridge object to have a DVM parent...).

Since we can't foresee system experts writing directly into a DSL or a database, unless we fall again in the difficulty problems approached by [7], we have to develop tools based on wizards which help them provide the requirements, and which represent the organization of the system in a comprehensible way. Not only this, but also allow a partial specification of a system when the requirements are not complete (a common guideline in rapid software development).

4   Modeling

We want a model that expresses hierarchy. We need to model elementary and composite objects, with dynamic states that as we saw can be composite as well. We want to be able to interact with objects at various levels of the hierarchy (as in Figure 1). Another very relevant feature is concurrency: in any given real-world system, more events can occur at the same time, and they could trigger state changes or communications which are concurrent. In order to avoid the nightmare of having to model every single execution case, we needed a modeling language that already takes into account concurrency via its semantics.

The choice was the Concurrent Object-Oriented Petri Nets (CO-OPN) language [6,5], a formalism based on Petri Nets with abstract algebraic data types. A strong motivation for the choice is that CO-OPN allows for mathematical verification of formal model properties (thanks to its strictly formal semantics) and for automated test generation and selection. Related work has been published on the subject ([13,11]).

It is supported by a tool, CoopnBuilder, which allows Java code generation from the model. This can be used to generate and run tests on the model even before passing to the implementation phase [2,12]. Finally, it has a coordination model, based on *Contexts*[6], which goes further than typical Petri Nets strategies for hierarchy based on substitution of nets with transitions (see the remarks on limits of subnet substitutions with transitions in [16] and several papers by P. Palanque and R. Bastide, which can be found in [15]) and can efficiently scale for large systems thanks to its modularity.

4.1 Transforming Requirements to a Model Using Meta-modeling

By specifying the system as in the previous section, we have enough information to produce two outcomes. The first is to construct a model of *the system itself*. This will be important with respect to testing the developed interfaces prior to implementing them. The second thing is to deduce *elements of the GUI* from the features of the system. There are two sources of information for this task: the nature of the data exchange with the object (what methods and parameters it has, if they are in input or output) and the type of paradigm of interaction (like 2D windows and buttons, 3D, textual...). These factors are processed according to tables of rules (similar to [18]) which establish a "best guess" of what should be used to represent the object, eventually offering alternatives. The developer can still adapt this choice according to specific requirements. For example, the `Container` object has a `refill` method with an integer parameter. Rules could say that in this case a suitable 2D representation is a textfield (for the integer parameter) and a button (to send the command). The developer could choose to use a combobox instead of a textfield. This will be done using a transformation engine (called *Model Transformer*) with a graphical interface resuming relevant features for every object (and letting the developer make modifications to single objects or to whole classes).

To produce these outcomes, the completed specification, expressed in our DSL, is transformed automatically by the Model Transformer to a formal model of both the system and the GUI using the CO-OPN language. This is possible thanks to having both the meta-models of CO-OPN and of our DSL, and to meta-model based transformations which are defined between the two. The transformation technique from other languages to CO-OPN is a vast subject, for which related work has been published [17]. The structure of the resulting model is the subject of the following subsections.

4.2   A Structured Model

The model we use is structured in a way that separates functionality and visualization, in a way very much inspired to the Model-View-Controller pattern. With the information we gathered in the initial phase (and that we refined through the model transformer) we can produce three different models. The first, called System Model, represents the physical system. It models all its objects in their hierarchy and inter-communication aspects, by using CO-OPN contexts and synchronization between objects. It can be built using the information about the hierarchy of the system (for structuring the model), the data flow of every object (for defining every object's methods/gates), and the dynamic behaviour of the system (for defining the internal state machine of every object as well as the synchronization axioms between objects). The second model, called GUI Logical Model, is a model of the GUI in its behavioural aspects. We don't have its actual visual representation here, but only its abstraction in terms of interaction - what objects make it up, what are their structural parameters, what they accept and return, and how they interface with the objects of the system in terms of commands and values. The third and last, called GUI Visual Model, models the visual aspects of the GUI and the associated semantics. Models communicate with each other just like the interface communicates with the system (see Figure 3).

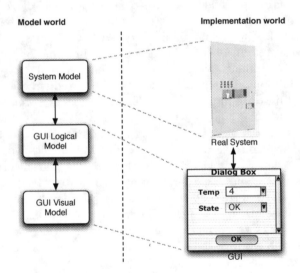

Fig. 3. The structure of the model

4.3   The System Model

As an example of the system model we can build one for our example specification of the DVM. A part of the System model is shown in Figure 4(a), using CO-OPN graphical notation. As a quick reference, large white squares are context, grey squares are objects; small black rectangles are methods, and small

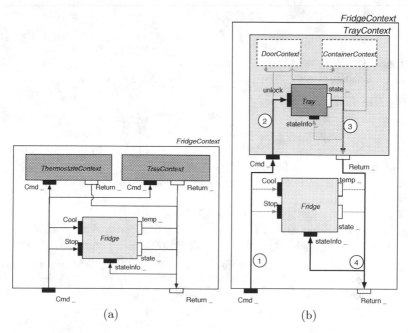

Fig. 4. Part of the System model and hierarchical communication

white rectangles are gates (events). Arrows represent axioms of synchronization between gates and methods. The underscore near some methods and gates represents its parameter, which is an algebraic data type (ADT) token.

The hierarchy is obtained by having CO-OPN contexts for each object; the context of a child object is contained in the context of the parent object (see TrayContext which is contained in FridgeContext). The functional aspects of objects are expressed with a CO-OPN object associated with each context (see the Fridge object, associated with FridgeContext), that presents methods and events of the object, and that keeps state information. The object also models the implementation of methods via its internal Petri Net.

To model vertical communication in the hierarchy, every context has a Cmd method and a Return gate. These two have axioms that allow the routing of commands and messages in the hierarchy to the right objects. The Cmd method takes as parameters the name of the target object, the name of the method to call and its parameters. The Return gate gives back the name of the object sending the message, the name of the message and its parameters. Let's see this with an example. In Figure 4(b) we are highlighting the sequence of synchronizations using thicker arrows, numbered 1-4 in sequence (the numbers in circles are only for illustration purposes, and not part of the CO-OPN formalism). We are calling the unlock method of the Tray object. To do so we call Cmd Tray unlock [] on the outmost context (in this case FridgeContext). The Cmd method has 3 possible synchronizations: calling the Cool or Stop methods of Fridge, or passing the call to the child context. Axiom 1 in the FridgeContext will say that if the object name in the `Cmd` call is not `Fridge`, the right synchronization is with the child context's `Cmd` (arrow 1):

$$(o = Fridge) = false =>$$
$$Cmd\ In\ FridgeContext\ obj\ met\ With\ Cmd\ In\ TrayContext\ obj\ met; \quad (1)$$

Similarly, the axioms in `TrayContext` will make so that the call is passed to the `unlock` method of the `Tray` object (arrow 2).

A very similar strategy is used for sending up messages using the `Return` gate. In arrow 3 a state change of `Tray` is sent out through the `Return` gate, in a form like `Return Tray state OK`. When passing into `FridgeContext` (arrows 4), not only the message is passed on to the upper `Return` gate, but the state change of the child is notified to the `Fridge` object, which will eventually decide whether to change state (according to its state machine).

In other words, the outmost context will act as an interface to the model, taking inputs and giving outputs. This, in addition to giving an elegant abstraction, allows us to have a single entry/exit point, which in the implementation phase is an advantage (we can substitute the outmost context of the model with a communication driver). Since this pattern is repetitive and all the information needed to build it is already in the specification, it can be easily generated by the model transformer, and regenerated with the model as the specification changes.

Thanks to CO-OPN transactional semantics, we can also automatically manage the case of a wrong method call (non existing method or object or wrong parameters) without adding mechanisms to manage it. When a command is passed down, it will not succeed until all the synchronisations called by it succeed. For a wrong call all the possible synchronisation sequences will fail at some point, and the fail will be propagated to the caller.

4.4   The GUI Logical Model

This model is built mainly from the analysis of the objects in the system, in terms of what interaction they require. This is part of the information in the Model Transformer tool, notably the part that says what kind of data is input/output. According to the choices made in the transformer tool, and by using a library of corresponding model patterns, we can build a model which represents the flow of info between the GUI and the system. A similar approach had been used by [18]: for example, if we know that an object has a command which accepts no parameters and returns an integer, we can abstract its GUI behaviour with a model providing a method with no parameters and a gate with an integer parameter. Continuing our example of the DVM, Figure 5 shows the logical model for the control of the Tray object from Figure 4(b), and its communication with the System model.

The GUI object is represented by a CO-OPN object and context, and for each method we want to control from the GUI there is a method on the model (e.g. the `unlock` method here). Calls on these methods are sent (together with

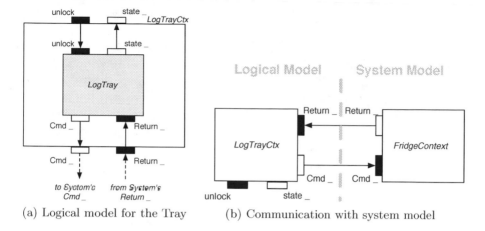

(a) Logical model for the Tray   (b) Communication with system model

Fig. 5. The GUI Logical Model

the object's name) to the System model's Cmd method. Messages coming from the System's Return gate are received and eventually sent to the GUI through gates (e.g. the state gate here).

This model does not worry about calculating states; in principle, the GUI should only reflect the state of the system. No state is changed unless the system communicates so.

4.5 The GUI Visual Model

Finally, we shall model the actual visual aspect of the GUI. This model, called GUI Visual Model is modular; we build it using components taken from a library of "model widgets", in fact pieces of CO-OPN models representing basic controls; these widgets can be assembled and composed to build more complex objects with elaborate behaviour. These objects will be mapped to objects in the GUI logical model. The decision about what widget to use comes from the choices made in the Model Transformer, where the developer decided that for a particular object, say, a text field and a red/green led were needed.

To finish our example, let's see the visual model for the Tray object. The model transformer will have shown us that there is an unparametrized input (unlock has no parameters) and that there is an enumerator output (the state, which can be {OK, Faulty}). Let's suppose that we chose a 2D windows and buttons paradigm, and that for the unlock command we accepted the default suggestion, a button (perfect to send a command without having parameters). For the state feedback, the default suggestion was a combo box, but we rather decided for a coloured led, mapping different colours to different values of the enumerator (green=OK, red=locked). Based on these choices, the model in Figure 6 can be built using widgets for SimpleButton and ColourLed.

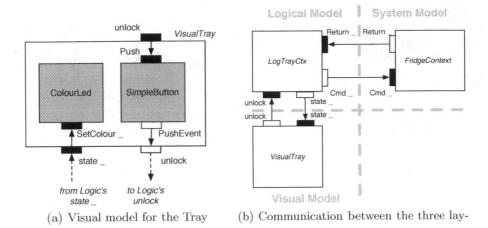

(a) Visual model for the Tray   (b) Communication between the three layers

Fig. 6. The GUI Visual Model

Using multiple paradigms. One aspect deriving from the use of widgets libraries and by the separation between logical and visual model is that we might as well have multiple paradigms used for the interface. Already at the Model Transformer level we should be able to choose what kind of interaction paradigm we want (a 2D windows and buttons GUI, a graph, a text console, a 3D stereo immersive GUI), and this would have a consequence on the kind of suggestions we get (and choices we can make) in the model transformer. Also, it is easy to realize that while the visual aspect of the components will change (along with the GUI Visual Model), the data flow remains the same (along with the GUI Logical Model) . In fact, a redefinition of the paradigm should only affect the GUI Visual Model, allowing us to have a stable behaviour model for the GUI.

5   Generating a GUI Prototype

The third phase of the methodology is the prototype generation. The information to be used for building an actual prototype is first of all the GUI Logical and Visual models. This gives us the input/outputs and coordination of the GUI objects (logical) and what objects have to be used (visual). Then, since we want to have an actual implementation of the GUI, we have to establish a correspondence between the widgets of the visual model and actual code widgets, e.g. translate a pushbutton model into real code for a pushbutton.

However, there are some aspects to a GUI which are not pertinent to the objects contained in it, but rather to the specific implementation of the GUI itself. The requirements might have included details about the language to use for the GUI, the interaction/navigation method, the screen estate used, and so on. It is easy to realize that some of these requirements can only be formalized if strong restrictions are made to what can be specified. On the one hand we can do this, by foreseeing only a limited amount of possible paradigms, languages, interaction modes and so on; on the other hand, this implies a loss of flexibility that might be too much for certain cases.

5.1   Communication

In addition to generating an executable GUI, the prototype generator must take into account the need for this prototype to communicate with the system. As Figure 2 shows, the prototype can be tested against the "code-generated" simulator (*simulation* branch in the Figure) or against the real control system (*testing* branch), or any other simulator which uses the same communication model. This requires appropriate *drivers* to ensure communication. Since the same model was used to generate the prototype and the simulator, and since the generated simulator is structured with a standardized Javabeans architecture, it is possible to generate automatically a driver to connect the two. For the communication with the real system, there are however aspects which are specific to the particular case. The most common cases are accepting commands via a bus, or via SOAP messages. The prototype must then provide a communication driver at least for these two cases, that has to be parametrized to match the real system.

6   Case Studies

One large case study which we are following in collaboration with CERN[1] is the control system for the Silicon Strip Tracker of the CMS experiment[2], a detector of particles for a high energy physics experiment in the Large Hadron Collider at CERN. This system, composed of several thousands objects and with a very complex hierarchy, has very strict requirements in terms of reliability of the GUI, and makes a good case study. Over a period of one year, we have been analyzing the system to make sure we fully understand all the aspects of complexity of such a system (avoiding the risk of oversimplifying our approach). After this initial study phase, we defined the DVM case study. What we have seen in Figure 1 is a part of this actual specification; the complete one has hot and cold drinks, completely defined FSMs and can be controlled and diagnosed through an advanced interface. The DVM has the same complexity issues of the CMS Tracker but on a minor scale: hierarchical structure; several objects of the same classes; interdependent state changes for the objects; possibility of having different user profiles/levels of access. This allows for a lightweight work even in the initial phase where all the tools are not yet implemented, without oversimplifying the problem. The system description as well as the system model have been defined. We are currently in the process of formalizing the transformation from the specification to the system model, identifying the necessary steps that have to be fixed and automated.

---

[1] http://www.cern.ch
[2] http://cmsdoc.cern.ch

In a second phase, we will apply the results of our studies to the CMS experiment and get results for a larger scale case study. We are confident in the scalability of the model, due to the fact that the complexity is efficiently approached by CO-OPN's coordination model. In fact from our preliminary models what turns out is that, as long as the communication is vertical in the hierarchy (a reasonable constraint to pose for control systems), no further complexity is added when the object hierarchy gets higher than 2 (also because the model does not need to be done by hand). The major difficulty for scalability could come from the human interaction needed in the earlier phases of the methodology. To help solve this we can make use of a feature of control systems: whenever there is a very large number of components in a system, it is also true that it will generally be possible to group them in large sets which have some (or even all) features equal (for example: all 10 drink containers in a DVM; all 37000 silicon detectors in the CMS tracker). Thanks to this we can provide the tools with the ability of easily defining sets of objects, and specifying properties at the level of classes of objects. This could be more easily done thanks to the type identifier we presented in section 3.1.

7   Conclusions and Future Work

We presented a methodology which allows for semi-automatic GUI generation for complex control systems. The methodology is centered on a domain specific language and meta-model based transformations into a formally-defined language, and allows for automated software verification and testing. This, and the domain specific assumptions, can be used to build a framework to greatly facilitate the task of specifying a system.

For the immediate future, after the definition of the language and framework has been completed, we will concentrate on the automatization aspects and the building of tools. After the case study of the drink vending machine has been done, we will apply the methodology to the larger case study, to verify scalability and refine furtherly the process.

An aspect which still has to be thoroughly studied is what is needed at the GUI Logical level to express the behaviour of the GUI itself, i.e. the internal coordination between objects. We are identifying what are the requirements to gather in this respect; once this has been done, we will investigate how to express them and what techniques to use to model them.

Acknowledgements

The project, started in October 2005, is a collaboration between the University of Geneva (CH), Universities of Applied Sciences: Engineering School of Geneva and Haute Ecole Valaisanne (CH), Universidade Nova de Lisboa (P), and CERN (CH). The project is funded by the Hasler Foundation (http:// www.haslerstiftung.ch).

References

1. A. Aerts, F. Glege, and M. Liendl. A Database perspective on CMS Detector Data. In *Proceedings of CHEP04 conference*, 2004.
2. S. Barbey, D. Buchs, and C. Péraire. A theory of specification-based testing for object-oriented software. In *EDCC*, pages 303–320, 1996.
3. P. J. Barclay, T. Griffiths, J. McKirdy, J. Kennedy, R. Cooper, N. W. Paton, and P. Gray. Teallach – a flexible user-interface development environment for object database applications. *Journal of Visual Languages & Computing*, 14(1):47–77, February 2003.
4. B. Barroca and V. Amaral. Rapid prototyping of user interfaces for control systems: A survey. Technical report, SMV Group, University of Geneva, 2006.
5. O. Biberstein, D. Buchs, and N. Guelfi. Object-Oriented Nets with Algebraic Specifications: The CO-OPN/2 Formalism. In *Concurrent Object-Oriented Programming and Petri Nets*, pages 73–130, 2001.
6. D. Buchs and N. Guelfi. A formal specification framework for object-oriented distributed systems. *IEEE Trans. Software Eng.*, 26(7):635–652, 2000.
7. D. Carr. Interaction object graphs: an executable graphical notation for specifying user interfaces. In P. Palanque and F. Paternò, editors, *Formal methods in Human-Computer Interaction*, pages 141–155. Springer-Verlag, 1997.
8. ETM. ETM professional control - PVSS II. URL: http://www.pvss.com.
9. B. Franek and C. Gaspar. SMI++ - State Management Interface. URL: http://cern.ch/smi.
10. KGB. Team bibliography. URL: http://kgb.ijs.si/KGB/accomplishments.php.
11. L. Lúcio. Syntax and semantics of satel (semi automatic testing language). Technical report, SMV Group, University of Geneva, 2006.
12. L. Lucio, L. Pedro, and D. Buchs. A Test Language for CO-OPN Specifications. In *RSP '05: Proceedings of the 16th IEEE International Workshop on Rapid System Prototyping (RSP'05)*, pages 195–201, Washington, DC, USA, 2005. IEEE Computer Society.
13. L. Lucio, L. Pedro, and D. Buchs. A test selection language for co-opn specifications. In *IEEE International Workshop on Rapid System Prototyping*, pages 195–201, 2005.
14. F. Moussa, C. Kolski, and M. Riahi. A model based approach to semi-automated user interface generation for process control interactive applications. *Interacting with Computers*, 12(3):245–279, January 2000.
15. P. Palanque. Publications. URL: http://liihs.irit.fr/palanque/publications.html.
16. P. Palanque and R. Bastide. Petri net based design of user-driven interfaces using the interactive cooperative objects formalism. In *Proceedings of EUROGRAPHICS workshop on "design, specification and verification of Interactive systems"*, 1994.
17. L. Pedro, L. Lucio, and D. Buchs. Principles for system prototype and verification using metamodel based transformations (accepted for publication). In *Proceedings of RSP 2006 conference*, 2006.
18. J. Vanderdonckt. Knowledge-Based Systems for Automated User Interface Generation: the TRIDENT Expierence. In *Proceedings of the CHI 95 workshop on Knowledge Based Support for the User Interface Design Process*, 1995.
19. G. Viano, A. Parodi, J. Alty, C. Khalil, I. Angulo, D. Biglino, M. Crampes, C. Vaudry, V. Daurensan, and P. Lachaud. Adaptive user interface for process control based on multi-agent approach. In *AVI '00: Proceedings of the working conference on Advanced visual interfaces*, pages 201–204, New York, NY, USA, 2000. ACM Press.

SketchiXML: A Design Tool for
Informal User Interface Rapid Prototyping

Adrien Coyette, Jean Vanderdonckt, and Quentin Limbourg

Belgian Lab. of Computer-Human Interaction (BCHI), Information Systems Unit (ISYS)
Louvain School of Management (LSM), Université catholique de Louvain (UCL),
Place des Doyens 1, B–1348 Louvain-la-Neuve (Belgium)
{coyette,vanderdonckt,limbourg}@isys.ucl.ac.be
http://www.isys.ucl.ac.be/bchi

Abstract. Sketching consists of a widely practiced activity during early design phases of product in general and for user interface development in particular in order to convey informal specifications of the interface before actually implementing it. It is quite interesting to observe that designers as well as end users have abilities to sketch parts or whole of the final user interface they want, while discussing the advantages and shortcomings. SketchiXML consists of a multi-platform multi-agent interactive application that enables designers, developers, or even end users to sketch user interfaces with different levels of details and support for different contexts of use. The results of the sketching are then analyzed to produce interface specifications independently of any context, including user and platform. These specifications are exploited to progressively produce one or several interfaces, for one or many users, platforms, and environments.

1 Introduction

Designing the right User Interface (UI) the first time is very unlikely to occur. Instead, UI design is recognized as a process that is intrinsically open (new considerations may appear at any time), iterative (several cycles are needed to reach an acceptable result), and incomplete (not all required considerations are available at design time). Consequently, means to support early UI design has been extensively researched [12] to identify appropriate techniques such as paper sketching, prototypes, mock-ups, diagrams, etc. Most designers consider hand sketches on paper as one of the most effective ways to represent the first drafts of a future UI [4,7,12, 15,16,17]. Indeed, this kind of unconstrained approach presents many advantages: sketches can be drawn during any design stage, it is fast to learn and quick to produce, it lets the sketcher focus on basic structural issues instead of unimportant details (e.g., exact alignment, typography, and colors), it is very appropriate to convey ongoing, unfinished designs, and it encourages creativity, sketches can be performed collaboratively between designers and end-users. Furthermore, the end user may herself produce some sketches to initiate the development process and when the sketch is close enough to the expected UI, an agreement can be signed between the designer and the end user, thus facilitating the contract and validation. Van Duyne et al. [20] reported

N. Guelfi and D. Buchs (Eds.): RISE 2006, LNCS 4401, pp. 160–176, 2007.

that creating a low-fidelity UI prototype (such as UI sketches) is at least 10 to 20 times easier and faster than its equivalent with a high-fidelity prototype (such as produced in UI builders). The idea of developing a computer-based tool for sketching UIs naturally emerged from these observations [12,17]. Such tools would extend the advantages provided by sketching techniques by: easily creating, deleting, updating or moving UI elements, thus encouraging typical activities in the design process [3] such as model-checking and revision. Some research was carried out in order to propose a hybrid approach, combining the best of the hand-sketching and computer assisted interface design, but this marriage highlights five shortcomings:

1. Some tools only support sketching activities, without producing any output: when the designer and the end user agreed upon a sketch, a contract can be signed between them and the development phase can start from the early design phase, but when the sketch is not transformed, the effort is lost.
2. Sketching tools that recognize the drawing do produce some output, but not in a reusable format: the design output is not necessarily in a format that is directly reusable as development input, thus preventing reusability.
3. Sketching tools are bound to a particular programming language, a particular UI type, a particular computing platform or operating system: when an output is produced, it is usually bound to one particular environment, therefore preventing developers from re-using sketches in new contexts, such as for various platforms.
4. Sketching tools do not take into account the sketcher's preferences: as they impose the same sketching scheme, the same gestures for all types of sketchers, a learning curve may prevent these users from learning the tool and efficiently using it.
5. Sketching tools do not allow a lot of flexibility in the sketch recognition: the user cannot choose when recognition will occur, degrading openness and when this occurs, it is difficult to return to a previous state.

In the remainder of this paper, Section 2 demonstrates that state-of-the-art UI sketching tools all suffer from some of the above shortcomings. Section 3 provides an overview of the Concrete User Interface (CUI) used in the sketching process, which results from widget abstraction. In Section 4, these widgets are recognized on demand. The multi-agent architecture of SketchiXML is outlined to support various scenarios in different contexts of use with examples. Section 5 concludes the paper.

2 Related Work

UI prototypes usually fall into three categories depending on their degree of fideity, which is the precision to which they reproduce the reality of the desired UI.

The *high-fidelity* (Hi-Fi) prototyping tools support building a UI that looks complete, and might be usable. Moreover, this kind of software is equipped with a wide range of editing functions for all UI widgets: erase, undo, move, specify physical attributes, etc... This software lets designers build a complete GUI, from which is produced an accurate image (e.g., Adobe Photoshop, PowerPoint) or code in a determined programming language (e.g., Visual Basic, DreamWeaver). Even if the final result is not executable, it can still be considered as a high fidelity tool given that the result provided looks complete.

The *medium-fidelity* (Me-Fi) approach builds UI mock-ups giving importance to content, but keeping secondary all information regarding typography, color scheme or others minor details. A typical example is Microsoft Visio, where only the type, the size and the contents of UI widgets can be specified graphically.

Low-fidelity (Lo-Fi) drafting tools are used to capture the general information needed to obtain a global comprehension of what is desired, keeping all the unnecessary details out of the process. The most standard approaches for Lo-Fi prototyping are the "paper and pencil technique", the "whiteboard/blackboard and post-it approach" [16]. Such approaches provide access to all the components, and prevent the designer from being distracted from the primary task of design. Research shows that designers who work out conceptual ideas on paper tend to iterate more and explore the design space more broadly, whereas designers using computer-based tools tend to take only one idea and work it out in detail [20]. Many designers have reported that the quality of the discussion when people are presented with a Hi-Fi prototype was different than when they are presented with a Lo-Fi mock up. When using Lo-Fi prototyping, the users tend to focus on the interaction or on the overall site structure rather than on the color scheme or others details irrelevant at this level.

Consequently, Lo-Fi prototyping offers a clear set of advantages compared to the Hi-Fi perspective, but at the same time suffers from a lack of assistance. For instance, if several screens have a lot in common, it could be profitable to use copy and paste instead of rewriting the whole screen each time. A combination of these approaches appears to make sense, as long as the Lo-Fi advantages are maintained. This consideration results two families of software tools which support UI sketching and representing the scenarios between them, one with and one without code generation.

DENIM [15] helps web site designers during early design by sketching information at different refinement levels, such as site map, story board and individual page, and unifies the levels through zooming views. DENIM uses pen input as a natural way to sketch on screen, but do not produce any final code or other output.

In contrast, SILK [12], JavaSketchIt [4] and Freeform [16,17] are major applications for pen-input based interface design supporting code generation. SILK uses pen input to draw GUIs and produce code for OpenLook operating system. JavaSketchIt proceeds in a slightly different way than Freeform, as it displays the shapes recognized in real time, and generates Java UI code. JavaSketchIt uses the CALI library [4] for the shape recognition, and widgets are formed on basis of a combination of vectorial shapes. The recognition rate of the CALI library is very high and thus makes JavaSketchIt easy to use, even for a novice user. Freeform only displays the shapes recognized once the design of the whole interface is completed, and produces Visual Basic 6 code. The technique used to identify the widgets is the same than JavaSketchIt, but with a slightly lower recognition rate. Freeform also supports scenario management thanks to a basic storyboard view similar to that provided in DENIM.

To enable sketching of widgets which are traditionally found in window managers, there is a need to have an internal representation of the UI being built, in terms of those widgets. Therefore, the next section introduces a means for specifying such a UI in terms of concrete interaction objects, instead of widgets.

3 The Concrete User Interface in UsiXML

The need for abstracting widgets existing in various toolkits, window managers, or Integrated Development Environments (IDEs) has appeared since the early nineties. At that time, the main goal for introducing an abstraction for widgets was the desire to specify them independently of any underlying technology, mainly the different operating systems and the different window managers working with the same operating system. For this purpose, the notion of Abstract Interaction Object (AIO) has been introduced to provide an abstraction of the same widget across those different toolkits, window managers, and operating systems so as to manipulate one single specification of this widget [18]. Another goal was the desire to entirely specify the presentation and the behavior of the widget [6,8].

Since that time, much progress has been accomplished towards improving the expressiveness of these abstractions, to the ultimate point of having extensive specifications of an entire UI in a User Interface Description Language (UIDL). The most representative examples are XML-compliant UIDLs such as UIML [1], UsiXML [13,14], and XIML [9]. A noticeable example is also the effort of specifying domain-oriented widgets such as those covered by the ARINC 661 Specifications in the domain of widgets for automated cockpits [2,3]. In order to be rigorous for the abstraction with respect to which the specification needs to be expressed, a reference framework is first introduced.

3.1 A Reference Framework for User Interfaces in Multiple Contexts

The foundation of the approach adopted here is to rely constantly on the same User Interface Description Language (UIDL) throughout the development life cycle. This UIDL is UsiXML (User Interface eXtensible Markup Language – http://www.usixml. org) which is characterized by the following principles [13,14]:

- *Expressiveness of UI*: any UI is expressed depending on the context of use thanks to a suite of models that are analyzable, editable, and manipulable by a software agent.
- *Central storage of models*: each model is stored in a model repository where all UI models are expressed similarly.
- *Transformational approach*: each model stored in the model repository may be subject to one or many transformations supporting various development steps. Each transformation is itself specified thanks to UsiXML [14].

Contrarily to other UIDLs such as UIML and XIML, UsiXML [12] enables specifying various levels of information and details until a final UI is obtained and depending on the project. It is not necessary to specify all models at all levels involved in the UI development life cycle. For this purpose, UsiXML is structured according to four basic levels of abstractions defined by the Cameleon reference framework [5] (Figure 1) established during the European project Cameleon.

At the top level is the ***Task & Concepts*** level that describes the various interactive tasks to be carried out by the end user and the domain objects that are manipulated by these tasks. These objects are considered as instances of classes representing the concepts.

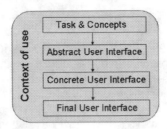

Fig. 1. The four levels of the Cameleon reference framework (source: [5])

An **Abstract UI** (AUI) provides a UI definition that is independent of any modality of interaction (e.g., graphical interaction, vocal interaction, 3D interaction etc.). An AUI is populated by *Abstract Containers* (ACs), *Abstract Individual Components* (AICs) and abstract relationships between. AICs represent basic system interactive functions, which are referred to as *facets* (i.e., input, output, navigation, and control). In this sense, AICs are an abstraction of widgets found in graphical toolkits (like windows, buttons) and in vocal toolkits (like vocal input and output widgets in the vocal interface). Two AUI relationships that can be defined between AICs:

1. *Dialog transition*: specifies a navigation transition within a abstract container or across several abstract containers.
2. *Spatio-temporal relationship*: characterizes the physical constraints between AICs as they are presented in time and space.

As an AUI does not refer to any particular modality, we do not know yet how this abstract description will be concretized: graphical, vocal or multimodal. This is achieved in the next level.

The **Concrete UI** (CUI) concretizes an AUI for a given context of use into *Concrete Interaction Objects* (CIOs) so as to define layout and/or interface navigation of 2D graphical widgets and/or vocal widgets. Any CUI is composed of CIOs, which realize an abstraction of widgets sets found in popular graphical and vocal toolkits (e.g., Java AWT/Swing, HTML 4.0, Flash DRK6, VoiceXML, and VoxML). A CIO is defined as an entity that users can perceive and/or manipulate (e.g., push button, text field, check box, vocal output, vocal input, vocal menu). The CUI abstracts a Final UI in a way that is independent of any toolkit peculiarities.

The **Final UI** (FUI) is the operational UI, i.e. any UI running on a particular computing platform either by interpretation (e.g., through a Web browser) or by execution (e.g., after the compilation of code in an interactive development environment). The **Context of use** describes all the entities that may influence how the user's task is carrying out with the future UI. It takes into account three relevant aspects, each aspect having its own associated attributes contained in a separate model: *user type* (e.g., system experience, task experience, task motivation), *computing platform type* (e.g., mobile platform vs. stationary), and *physical environment type* (e.g., office conditions, outdoor conditions). These attributes initiate transformations that are applicable depending on the current context of use. In order to map different elements belonging to the models described above, UsiXML provides the designer with a set of pre-defined *mappings* [14]:

- *Manipulates*: maps a task onto a domain concept.
- *Updates*: maps an interaction object and a domain model concept (specifically, an attribute).
- *Triggers*: maps an interaction object and a domain model concept (specifically an operation).
- *Is Executed In*: maps a task onto an AUI or CUI element.
- *Is Reified By*: maps an abstract object into a concrete one through an abstraction transformation.

3.2   The Concrete User Interface in UsiXML

The semantics of the UsiXML are defined in a UML class diagram (Fig. 2 is illustrating a portion of this metamodel). Each class, attribute or relation of this class diagram is transformed into a XML Schema defining the concrete syntax of the UsiXML language in general. All other levels of the reference framework depicted in Figure 1 are equally expressed in UsiXML to support seamless transition between any levels of abstraction to any other one. A CUI is assumed to be expressed without any reference to any particular computing platform or toolkit of that platform. A CUI model consists of a hierarchical decomposition of CIOs (any UI entity that users can perceive such as text, image, animation and/or manipulate such as a push button, a list box, or a check box) that are linked together with *cuiRelationships* between. A CIO is characterized by [14]:

- *id*: an internally attributed identifier of a CIO;
- *name*: a name given to the CIO to reflect its function, purpose;
- *icon*: a reference to an icon attached to the CIO, if any;
- *content*: a reference to the textual contents of a CIO, if any;
- *defaultContent*: the default value of its textual contents, if any;
- *defaultIcon*: the default icon of this CIO, if any;
- *defaultHelp*: the default text for helping the user on this CIO;
- *help*: the extended help system for helping the user on this CIO;
- *currentValue*: the current value of the CIO at run-time, if any.

At the second level, each CIO is sub-typed into sub-CIOs depending on the interaction modality chosen: *graphicalCIO* for GUIs, *auditoryCIO* for vocal interfaces, etc. Each *graphicalCIO* inherits from the above properties of the CIO. Specific attributes include, but are not limited to:

- *isVisible*: is set to true if a graphicalCio is visible;
- *isEnabled*: is set to true if a graphicalCIO is enabled;
- *fgColor* and *bgColor*: are the foreground and background colors;
- *toolTipDefaultContent*: for the default content of the tooltip;
- *toolTipContent*: the contents of the tooltip depending on the context of use, which may vary from one user to another;
- *transparencyRate*: for supporting translucid interfaces;

Each *graphicalCIO* can then belong to one category: *graphicalContainer* for all widgets containing other widgets such as window, frame, dialog box, table, box and their related decomposition or *graphicalIndividualComponent* for all other traditional widgets that are typically found. UsiXML supports (Figure 2) *textComponent, videoComponent, imageComponent, imageZone, radioButton, toggleButton, icon, checkbox, item, comboBox, button, tree, menu, menuItem, drawingCanvas, colorPicker, hourPicker, datePicker, filePicker, progressionBar, slider,* and *cursor.*

Thanks to this progressive inheritance mechanism, every final elements of the CUI inherits from the upper properties depending on the category they belong to. The properties that have been chosen in UsiXML have been decided because they belong to the intersection of property sets of major toolkits and window managers, such as Windows GDI, Java AWT and Swing, HTML. Of course, only properties of high common interest were kept. In this way, a CIO can be specified independently from the fact that it will be further rendered in HTML, VRML or Java. This quality is often referred to as the property of **platform independence.** Therefore, the CIOs defined at the CUI level remain independent of any computing platform (and thus of any underlying toolkit) since the same CUI could be specified in principle for different computing platforms and devices.

In the next section, we will see how this Concrete User Interface can be sketched in SketchiXML and stored internally in terms of UsiXML tags.

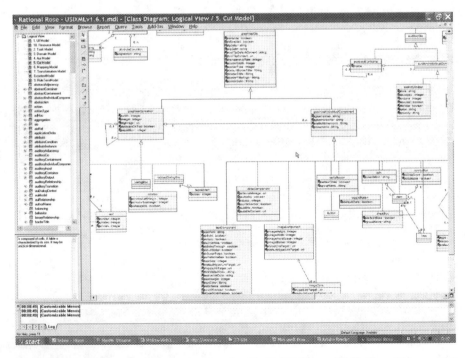

Fig. 2. The Concrete User Interface level defined in UsiXML as a UML Class Diagram [14]

4 SketchiXML Development

The main requirements to address are the following: to support shape recognition, to provide spatial shape interpretation, to provide usability advice at design time, to handle several kinds of input, to generate UsiXML specifications at design-time, and to operate in a flexible way. To address these requirements, a BDI (*Belief-Desire-Intention*) agent-oriented architecture [7] was considered appropriate: such architecture allows building robust and flexible applications by distributing the responsibilities among autonomous and cooperating agents. Each agent is in charge of a specific part of the process, and co-operates with the others in order to provide the service required according to the designer's preferences. This kind of approach has the advantage of being more flexible, modular and robust than traditional architecture including object-oriented ones [7].

4.1 SketchiXML Architecture

The application was built using the SKwyRL-framework (its usage is summarized in [7]), a framework aimed at defining, formalizing and applying socially based catalogues of styles and patterns to construct agent and multi-agent architectures. The joint-venture organizational style pattern was applied to design the agent-architecture of SketchiXML. It was chosen on basis of non-functional requirements Ri, as among all organizational styles defined in the SKwyRL framework, the joint venture clearly matches the aforementioned requirements as the most open and distributed organizational style.

The architecture (Fig. 3) is structured using $i*$ [7], a graph where each node represents an *actor* (or system component) and each link between two actors indicates that one actor depends on the other for some goal to be attained. A dependency describes an "agreement" (called *dependum*) between two actors: the *depender* and the *dependee*. The *depender* is the depending actor, and the *dependee*, the actor who is depended upon. The type of the dependency describes the nature of the agreement. *Goal* dependencies represent delegation of responsibility for fulfilling a goal; *softgoal* dependencies are similar to goal dependencies, but their fulfillment cannot be defined precisely; task dependencies are used in situations where the dependee is required.

When a user wishes to create a new SketchiXML project, she contacts the *Broker* agent, which serves as an intermediary between the external actor and the organizational system. The *Broker* queries the user for all the relevant information needed for the process, such as the target platform, the input type, the intervention strategy of the *Adviser* agent,... According to the criteria entered, the coordinator chooses the most suitable handling and coordinates all the agents participating in the process in order to meet the objectives determined by the user. For clearness, the following section only considers a situation where the user has selected real time recognition, and pen-input device as input. So, the *Data Editor* agent then displays a white board allowing the user to draw his hand-sketch interface. All the strokes are collected and then transmitted to the *Shape Recognizer* agent for recognition. The recognition engine of this agent is based on the CALI library [4], a recognition engine able to identify shapes of different sizes, rotated at arbitrary angles, drawn with dashed, continuous strokes or overlapping lines.

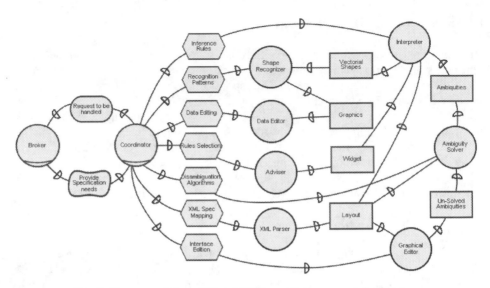

Fig. 3. i* representation of SketchiXML architecture as a Joint-Venture

Subsequently, the *Shape Recognizer* agent provides all the vectorial shapes identified with relevant information such as location, dimension or degree of certainty associated to the *Interpreter* agent. Based on these shape sets, the *Interpreter* agent attempts to create a component layout. The technique used for the creation of this layout takes advantage of the knowledge capacity of agents. The agent stores all the shapes identified as his belief, and each time a new shape is received all the potential candidates for association are extracted. Using its set of patterns the agent then evaluates if shape pairs form a widget or a sub-widget. The conditions to be tested are based on a set of fuzzy spatial relations allowing to deal with imprecise spatial combinations of geometric shapes and to fluctuate with user preferences. Based on the widgets identified by the *Interpreter*, the *Adviser* agent assists the designer with the conception of the UIs in two different ways.

Firstly, by providing real-time assistance to the designer by attempting to detect UI patterns in the current sketch in order to complete the sketch automatically. Secondly in a post operational mode, the usability adviser provides usability advice on the interface sketched. If the *Interpreter* fails to identify all the components or to apply all the usability rules, then the *Ambiguity Solver* agent is invoked. This agent evaluates how to solve the problem according to the initial parameters entered by the user.

The agent can either attempt to solve the ambiguity itself by using its set of disambiguation algorithms, or to delegate it to a third agent, the *Graphical Editor* agent. The *Graphical Editor* displays all the widget recognized at this point, as classical element-based software, and highlights all the components with a low degree of certainty for confirmation. Once one of these last three agents evoked has sufficient certainty about the overall widget layout, the UI is sent to the *XML Parser* agent for UsiXML generation.

4.2 Low-Fidelity Prototyping with SketchiXML

The first step in SketchiXML consists of specifying parameters that will drive the low-fidelity prototyping process (Fig. 4): the project name, the input type (i.e. on-line sketching or off-line drawing that is scanned and processed in one step-Fig. 5), the computing platform for which the UI is prototyped (a predefined platform can be selected such as mobile phone, PDA, TabletPC, kiosk, ScreenPhone, laptop, desktop, wall screen, or a custom one can be defined in terms of platform model [10]), the output folder, the time when the recognition process is initiated (ranging from on-demand manual to fully automatic each time a new widget can be detected- this flexibility is vital according to experiments), the intervention mode of the usability advisor (manual, mixed-initiative, automatic), and the output quality stating the response time vs. quality of results of the recognition and usability advisor processes. In Fig. 7, the UsiXML parsing is set on fully manual mode, and the output quality is set on medium quality. The quality level affects the way the agents consider a widget layout to be acceptable, or the constraints used for the pattern matching between vectorial shapes. The sketching phase in that situation is thus very similar to the sketching process of an application such as FreeForms [17]. Of course, the designer is always free to change these parameters while the process is running.

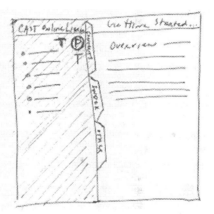

Fig. 4. Creating a new SketchiXML prototype   **Fig. 5.** Scanned UI sketching

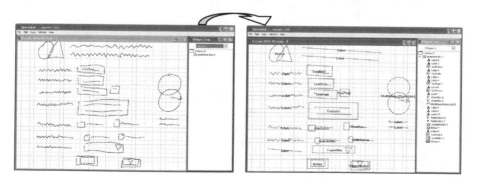

Fig. 6. SketchiXML workspace

Fig. 6 illustrates the SketchiXML workspace configured for designing a UI for a standard personal computer. On the left part we can observe that shape recognition is disabled as none of the sketches is interpreted, and the widget layout generated by the *Interpreter* agent remains empty. The right part represents the same UI with shape recognition and interpretation. Fig. 7 depicts SketchiXML parameterized for a Pock-etPC platform and its results imported in GrafiXML, a UsiXML-compliant graphical UI editor that can generate code for HTML, XHTML, and Java (http://www.usixml. org/index.php?view=page&idpage=10).

When shape recognition is activated, each time a new widget is identified the color of the shapes turns to green, and the widget tree generated by the *Interpreter* is up-dated. Changing the context has a deep impact on the way the system operates. As an example, when a user builds a user interface for one platform or another, adaptations need to be based on the design knowledge that will be used for evaluation, by select-ing and prioritizing rule sets, and on the set of available widgets. As the size of the drawing area is changing, the set of constraints used for the interpretation needs to be tailored too, indeed if the average size of the strokes drawn is much smaller than on a standard display, the imprecision associated with each stroke follows the same trend. We can thus strengthen the constraints to avoid any confusion.

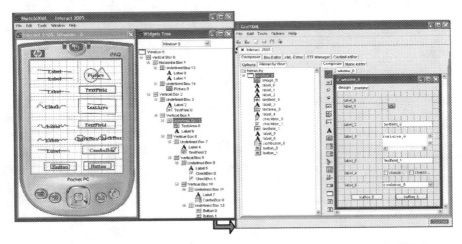

Fig. 7. SketchiXML workspace configured for a PDA and its import in GrafiXML

Once the design phase is complete, SketchiXML parses the informal design to pro-duce UsiXML specifications. Fig. 8 gives an overview of the UsiXML specifications generated from UI drawn in Fig. 7. Each widget is represented with standard values for each attribute, as SketchiXML is only aimed at capturing the UI core properties. In addition, the UsiXML specifications integrate all the information related to the context of use as specified in the wizard depicted on Fig. 7: information for the user model, the platform model, and the environment model [10]. As UsiXML allows de-fining a set of transformation rules for switching from one of the UsiXML models to another, or to adapt a model for another context, such information is thus required. Fig. 7 illustrates the SketchiXML output imported in GrafiXML, a high fidelity UI graphical editor. On basis of the informal design provided during the early design, a programmer can re-use the output without any loss of time to provide a revised version of the UI with all the characteristics that can and should not be defined during the early design phase. This contrasts with a traditional approach, where a programmer had to implement user interfaces on basis of a set of blackboard photographs or sheets of paper, and thus start the implementation process from the beginning.

```xml
<?xml version="1.0" encoding="UTF-8"?>
<uiModel id="Interact_2005" name="Interact 2005"
    creationDate="2005-01-06T14:51:31.656+01:00" schemaVersion="1.6.1"
    xmlns="http://www.usixml.org">
    <version modifDate="2005-01-06T14:51:31.656+01:00" xmlns="">1</version>
    <authorName xmlns="">SketchiXML</authorName>
    <cuiModel id="Interact_2005_6-cui" name="Interact 2005-cui">
        <window id="window_0" name="window_0" isVisible="true"
            isEnabled="true" fgColor="#000000" bgColor="#ece9d8" borderWidth="0" width="400"
            height="350"
            isAlwaysOnTop="false" windowLeftMargin="0" windowTopMargin="0" isResizable="true">
            <box id="box_0" name="box_0" isVisible="false"
                isEnabled="true" width="400" height="350" type="horizontal" isFlow="false"
                isFill="false"
                isScrollable="false" isSplitable="false" isDetachable="false"
                isResizableVertical="false"
                isResizableHorizontal="false" relativeMinWidth="0" relativeMinHeight="0"
                isBalanced="false"
                relativeWidth="0" relativeHeight="0">...
                <textComponent id="label_0" name="label_0"
                    isVisible="true" isEnabled="true" fgColor="#000000" bgColor="#ece9d8"
                    visitedLinkColor="#000000"
                    activeLinkColor="#000000" isBold="true" isItalic="false" isUnderline="false"
                    isStrikethrough="false" isSubscript="false" isSuperscript="false"
                    isPreformatted="false"
                    textColor="#000000" textSize="12" textFont="Dialog" textMargin="0"
                    textVerticalAlign="middle"
                    textHorizontalAlign="left" scrollStyle="scroll" scrollDirection="left"/>...
                <imageComponent id="image_0" name="image_0" isVisible="true" isEnabled="true"
                    defaultHyperLinkTarget=""/>...
                <button id="button_1" name="button_1" isVisible="true" isEnabled="true"
                    fgColor="#000000" bgColor="#ece9d8"/>...
            </box> </window>
    </cuiModel>
    <contextModel id="interact_2005-contextModel_0" name="interact_2005-contextModel_pda">
        <context id="interact_2005-context_0" name="interact_2005-context_pda">
            <userStereotype id="interact_2005-user_US_0" language="en_US"
                stereotypeName="interact_2005-user_US"
                taskExperience="1" systemExperience="1" deviceExperience="1" taskMotivation="1"/>
            <platform id="windows_mobile_2003" name="windows_mobile_2003">
                <softwarePlatform OSName="Windows" OSVersion="2003" OSVendor="Microsoft Corp."/>
                <hardwarePlatform screenSize="240x320" />
            </platform></context></contextModel>
    <resourceModel id="Interact 2005_6" name="Interact 2005"/>
</uiModel>
```

Fig. 8. Excerpt of the UsiXML specifications generated by SketchiXML

As the Usability Advisor intervention time has been specified as "automatic" (Fig. 4), each time a usability deviation is detected with respect to usability guidelines, a tool tip message is produced in context, attached to the widget on concern. For this purpose, a set of form-based usability guidelines have been encoded in GDL (Guideline Definition Language), a XML-compliant description of guidelines that can be directly related to UsiXML widgets.

SketchiXML is able to capture any type of sketching, only some of them are recognized as widgets and then turned into corresponding UsiXML specifications. If a UI sketch does incorporate other types of contents, such as illustrations, graphs, decorations,

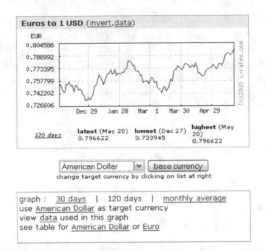

Fig. 9. Example of a UI containing native widgets and custom widgets

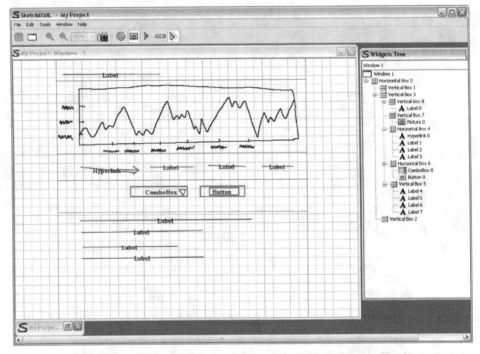

Fig. 10. The UI sketching corresponding to the UI depicted in Fig. 9

manual sketches (e.g. as in Fig. 9), all of them will be incorporated and saved in the corresponding files. Unrecognized elements will be simply stored as images along with their contents. Custom widgets are defined similarly: their graphical representation is sketched and saved as an image. At any time, the designer may ask to show the graphical representation of the UI with or without the part which has been recognized

(Fig. 10). In this way, the designer is not distracted from native widgets which are recognized and custom widgets which are not recognized (Fig. 10).

Finally, it is possible to request a UI preview at any time by sending the corresponding UsiXML file to GrafiXML, the high-fidelity editor (which can be freely downloaded from http://www.usixml.org/index.php?view=page&idpage=10). Fig. 11 reproduces a simple UI sketched for a PocketPC (specified in the profile), which is therefore restricted to the widgets that are only available on this platform (e.g., J2ME edition). Fig. 12 shows the related rendering for this environment.

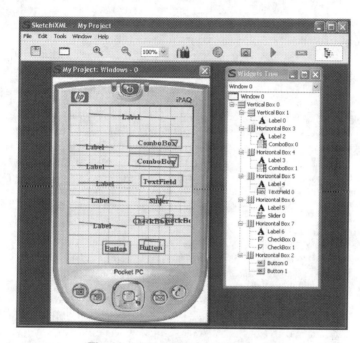

Fig. 11. A UI sketched for a Pocket PC

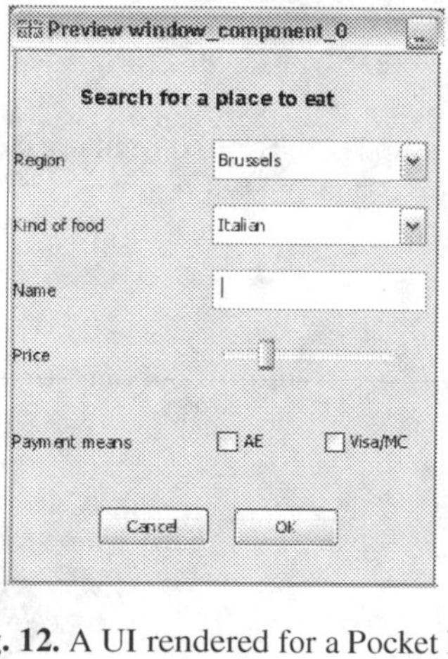

Fig. 12. A UI rendered for a Pocket PC

5 Conclusion

The main difference between SketchiXML considered here as a tool for sketching the UI during the prototyping phase is that the effort done during this phase is not lost: it is automatically transformed into specifications written in UsiXML in order to pass them to other software which communicate by exchanging UsiXML files. It could be in particular a high-fidelity UI editor such as GrafiXML (as illustrated in Fig. 7) or any other UsiXML-compliant editor. Elements of the sketch which are not recognized are simply saved as images which are then reproduced at any time. Therefore, the current level of fidelity of the prototyped UIs may be increased by recuperating these specifications into another editor and continuing to refine their specifications until a final UI is reached. From this moment, any UsiXML-compliant rendering engine (such as a code generator or interpreter) could render the UI at run-time, even if this is during the prototyping phase [11,19].

It is obvious that at the beginning of the UI development life cycle, the UI requirements are not yet well done, especially if the UI concerns a new domain of activity, where little or no previous experience or history exists. For those cases where a substantive experience already exists, this prototyping phase may be reduced to reopening previously existing UI specifications and tailoring them to the new project. In both cases, the sketching tool is able to support designers, developers, or even end-users to refine their ideas until a final UI is obtained with consensus between the stakeholders.

Acknowledgments

We gratefully thank the support from of the Request research project under the umbrella of the WIST (Wallonie Information Société Technologies) program under convention n°031/5592 RW REQUEST) and from the SIMILAR network of excellence (The European research taskforce creating human-machine interfaces SIMILAR to human-human communication), supported by the 6th Framework Program of the European Commission, under contract FP6-IST1-2003-507609 (http://www.similar. cc). We warmly thank J.A. Jorge, F.M.G. Pereira and A. Caetano for allowing us to use JavaSketchIt and the CALI library in our research. Preliminary work on UsiXML has been achieved under the umbrella of the Cameleon European project: the authors also want to warmly thank the partners of this project for their fruitful discussion. UsiXML is now available as a Consortium whose affiliation is free: to register as a member, go to http://www.usixml.org/index.php?view=register&start=47. Finally, the authors want to thank the RUIPIACS workshop organizers who allowed us to present this work.

References

1. Ali M.F., Pérez-Quiñones M.A., Abrams M.: *Building Multi-Platform User Interfaces with UIML.* In: Seffah, A., Javahery, H. (eds.): Multiple User Interfaces: Engineering and Application Framework. John Wiley, Chichester (2004) 95–118.
2. Barboni, E., Navarre, D., Palanque, Ph., Basnyat, S.: *Model-Based Engineering of Widgets, User Applications and Servers Compliant with ARINC 661 Specification.* In: Proceedings of the 13th Conference on Design, Specification, and Verification of Interactive Systems DSV-IS'2006 (Dublin, July 26-28, 2006). Lecture Notes in Computer Science, Springer Verlag, Berlin (2006).

3. Bastide, R., Navarre, D., Palanque, P.A.: *A Tool-supported Design Framework for Safety Critical Interactive Systems.* Interacting with Computers **15**,3 (2003) 309–328.
4. Caetano, A., Goulart, N., Fonseca, M., Jorge, J.: *JavaSketchIt: Issues in Sketching the Look of User Interfaces.* In: Proc. of the 2002 AAAI Spring Symposium - Sketch Understanding (Palo Alto, March 2002). AAAI Press, Menlo Park (2002) 9–14.
5. Calvary, G., Coutaz, J., Thevenin, D., Limbourg, Q., Bouillon, L., Vanderdonckt, J.: *A Unifying Reference Framework for Multi-Target User Interfaces.* Interacting with Computer **15**,3 (2003) 289–308.
6. Carr, D.A., *Specification of Interface Interaction Objects.* In: Proc. of ACM Conf. on Human Aspects in Computing Systems CHI'94 (Boston, April 24-28, 1994). Vol. 2, ACM Press, New York (1994) p. 226.
7. Coyette, A., Vanderdonckt, J.: *A Sketching Tool for Designing Anyuser, Anyplatform, Anywhere User Interfaces.* In: Proc. of 10ᵗʰ IFIP TC 13 Int. Conf. on Human-Computer Interaction INTERACT'2005 (Rome, 12-16 September 2005), Lecture Notes in Computer Science, Vol. 3585, Springer-Verlag, Berlin, 2005, 550–564.
8. Duke, D.J., Harrison, M.D.: *Abstract Interaction Objects.* Computer Graphics Forum **12**,3 (1993) 25–36.
9. Eisenstein, J., Vanderdonckt, J., Puerta, A.: *Model-Based User-Interface Development Techniques for Mobile Computing.* In: Lester J. (ed.): Proc. of 5ᵗʰ ACM Int. Conf. on Intelligent User Interfaces IUI'2001 (Santa Fe, January 14-17, 2001). ACM Press, New York (2001) 69–76.
10. Florins, M., Vanderdonckt, J.: *Graceful Degradation of User Interfaces as a Design Method for Multiplatform Systems.* In: Proc. of Int. Conf. on Intelligent User Interfaces IUI'04 (Funchal, January 13-16, 2004). ACM Press, New York (2004) 140–147.
11. Grolaux, D., Vanderdonckt, J., Van Roy, P.: *Attach me, Detach me, Assemble me like You Work.* In: Proc. of 10ᵗʰ IFIP TC 13 Int. Conf. on Human-Computer Interaction INTERACT'2005 (Rome, September 12-16, 2005), Lecture Notes in Computer Science, Vol. 3585, Springer-Verlag, Berlin (2005) 198–212.
12. Landay, J., Myers, B.A.: *Sketching Interfaces: Toward More Human Interface Design.* IEEE Computer 34, 3 (March 2001) 56–64.
13. Limbourg, Q., Vanderdonckt, J., Michotte, B., Bouillon, L., Lopez, V.: *UsiXML: a Language Supporting Multi-Path Development of User Interfaces.* In: Proc. of 9ᵗʰ IFIP Working Conf. on Engineering for Human-Computer Interaction jointly with 11ᵗʰ Int. Workshop on Design, Specification, and Verification of Interactive Systems EHCI-DSVIS'2004 (Hamburg, July 11-13, 2004). Lecture Notes in Computer Science, Vol. 3425. Springer-Verlag, Berlin (2005) 200–220.
14. Limbourg, Q., *Multi-path Development of User Interfaces*, Ph.D. thesis, Université catholique de Louvain, Louvain-la-Neuve, November 2004.
15. Newman, M.W., Lin, J., Hong, J.I., Landay, J.A.: *DENIM: An Informal Web Site Design Tool Inspired by Observations of Practice.* Human-Computer Interaction 18 (2003) 259–324.
16. Plimmer, B.E., Apperley, M.: *Software for Students to Sketch Interface Designs.* In: Proc. of 9ᵗʰ IFIP TC 13 Int. Conf. on Human-Computer Interaction INTERACT'2003 (Zurich, 1-5 September 2003). IOS Press, Amsterdam (2003) 73–80.
17. Plimmer, B.E., Apperley, M.: *Interacting with Sketched Interface Designs: An Evaluation Study.* In: Proc. of ACM Conf. on Human Aspects in Computing Systems CHI'04 (Vienna, April 24-29, 2004). ACM Press, New York (2004) 1337–1340.

18. Vanderdonckt, J., Bodart, F.: *Encapsulating Knowledge for Intelligent Automatic Interaction Objects Selection*. In: Proc. of the ACM Conf. on Human Factors in Computing Systems INTERCHI'93 (Amsterdam, April 24-29, 1993). ACM Press, New York (1993) 424–429.
19. Vanderdonckt, J.: *A MDA-Compliant Environment for Developing User Interfaces of Information Systems*. In: Pastor, O. & Falcão e Cunha, J. (eds.), Proc. of 17th Conf. on Advanced Information Systems Engineering CAiSE'05 (Porto, 13-17 June 2005). Lecture Notes in Computer Science, Vol. 3520. Springer-Verlag, Berlin (2005) 16–31.
20. van Duyne, D.K., Landay, J.A., Hong, J.I..: *The Design of Sites: Patterns, Principles, and Processes for Crafting a Customer-Centered Web Experience*. Addison-Wesley, Reading (2002).

Author Index

Lecture Notes in Computer Science

For information about Vols. 1–4349

please contact your bookseller or Springer

Vol. 4399: T. Kovacs, X. Llorà, K. Takadama, P.L. Lanzi, W. Stolzmann, S.W. Wilson (Eds.), Learning Classifier Systems. XII, 345 pages. 2007. (Sublibrary LNAI).

Vol. 4398: S. Marchand-Maillet, E. Bruno, A. Nürnberger, M. Detyniecki (Eds.), Adaptive Multimedia Retrieval: User, Context, and Feedback. XI, 269 pages. 2007.

Vol. 4397: C. Stephanidis, M. Pieper (Eds.), Universal Access in Ambient Intelligence Environments. XV, 467 pages. 2007.

Vol. 4396: J. García-Vidal, L. Cerdà-Alabern (Eds.), Wireless Systems and Mobility in Next Generation Internet. IX, 271 pages. 2007.

Vol. 4395: M. Daydé, J.M.L.M. Palma, Á.L.G.A. Coutinho, E. Pacitti, J.C. Lopes (Eds.), High Performance Computing for Computational Science - VECPAR 2006. XXIV, 721 pages. 2007.

Vol. 4394: A. Gelbukh (Ed.), Computational Linguistics and Intelligent Text Processing. XVI, 648 pages. 2007.

Vol. 4393: W. Thomas, P. Weil (Eds.), STACS 2007. XVIII, 708 pages. 2007.

Vol. 4392: S.P. Vadhan (Ed.), Theory of Cryptography. XI, 595 pages. 2007.

Vol. 4391: Y. Stylianou, M. Faundez-Zanuy, A. Esposito (Eds.), Progress in Nonlinear Speech Processing. XII, 269 pages. 2007.

Vol. 4390: S.O. Kuznetsov, S. Schmidt (Eds.), Formal Concept Analysis. X, 329 pages. 2007. (Sublibrary LNAI).

Vol. 4389: D. Weyns, H.V.D. Parunak, F. Michel (Eds.), Environments for Multi-Agent Systems III. X, 273 pages. 2007. (Sublibrary LNAI).

Vol. 4385: K. Coninx, K. Luyten, K.A. Schneider (Eds.), Task Models and Diagrams for Users Interface Design. XI, 355 pages. 2007.

Vol. 4384: T. Washio, K. Satoh, H. Takeda, A. Inokuchi (Eds.), New Frontiers in Artificial Intelligence. IX, 401 pages. 2007. (Sublibrary LNAI).

Vol. 4383: E. Bin, A. Ziv, S. Ur (Eds.), Hardware and Software, Verification and Testing. XII, 235 pages. 2007.

Vol. 4381: J. Akiyama, W.Y.C. Chen, M. Kano, X. Li, Q. Yu (Eds.), Discrete Geometry, Combinatorics and Graph Theory. XI, 289 pages. 2007.

Vol. 4380: S. Spaccapietra, P. Atzeni, F. Fages, M.-S. Hacid, M. Kifer, J. Mylopoulos, B. Pernici, P. Shvaiko, J. Trujillo, I. Zaihrayeu (Eds.), Journal on Data Semantics VIII. XV, 219 pages. 2007.

Vol. 4379: M. Südholt, C. Consel (Eds.), Object-Oriented Technology. VIII, 157 pages. 2007.

Vol. 4378: I. Virbitskaite, A. Voronkov (Eds.), Perspectives of Systems Informatics. XIV, 496 pages. 2007.

Vol. 4377: M. Abe (Ed.), Topics in Cryptology – CT-RSA 2007. XI, 403 pages. 2006.

Vol. 4376: E. Frachtenberg, U. Schwiegelshohn (Eds.), Job Scheduling Strategies for Parallel Processing. VII, 257 pages. 2007.

Vol. 4374: J.F. Peters, A. Skowron, I. Düntsch, J. Grzymała-Busse, E. Orłowska, L. Polkowski (Eds.), Transactions on Rough Sets VI, Part I. XII, 499 pages. 2007.

Vol. 4373: K. Langendoen, T. Voigt (Eds.), Wireless Sensor Networks. XIII, 358 pages. 2007.

Vol. 4372: M. Kaufmann, D. Wagner (Eds.), Graph Drawing. XIV, 454 pages. 2007.

Vol. 4371: K. Inoue, K. Satoh, F. Toni (Eds.), Computational Logic in Multi-Agent Systems. X, 315 pages. 2007. (Sublibrary LNAI).

Vol. 4370: P.P Lévy, B. Le Grand, F. Poulet, M. Soto, L. Darago, L. Toubiana, J.-F. Vibert (Eds.), Pixelization Paradigm. XV, 279 pages. 2007.

Vol. 4369: M. Umeda, A. Wolf, O. Bartenstein, U. Geske, D. Seipel, O. Takata (Eds.), Declarative Programming for Knowledge Management. X, 229 pages. 2006. (Sublibrary LNAI).

Vol. 4368: T. Erlebach, C. Kaklamanis (Eds.), Approximation and Online Algorithms. X, 345 pages. 2007.

Vol. 4367: K. De Bosschere, D. Kaeli, P. Stenström, D. Whalley, T. Ungerer (Eds.), High Performance Embedded Architectures and Compilers. XI, 307 pages. 2007.

Vol. 4366: K. Tuyls, R. Westra, Y. Saeys, A. Nowé (Eds.), Knowledge Discovery and Emergent Complexity in Bioinformatics. IX, 183 pages. 2007. (Sublibrary LNBI).

Vol. 4364: T. Kühne (Ed.), Models in Software Engineering. XI, 332 pages. 2007.

Vol. 4362: J. van Leeuwen, G.F. Italiano, W. van der Hoek, C. Meinel, H. Sack, F. Plášil (Eds.), SOFSEM 2007: Theory and Practice of Computer Science. XXI, 937 pages. 2007.

Vol. 4361: H.J. Hoogeboom, G. Păun, G. Rozenberg, A. Salomaa (Eds.), Membrane Computing. IX, 555 pages. 2006.

Vol. 4360: W. Dubitzky, A. Schuster, P.M.A. Sloot, M. Schroeder, M. Romberg (Eds.), Distributed, High-Performance and Grid Computing in Computational Biology. X, 192 pages. 2007. (Sublibrary LNBI).

Vol. 4358: R. Vidal, A. Heyden, Y. Ma (Eds.), Dynamical Vision. IX, 329 pages. 2007.

Vol. 4357: L. Buttyán, V. Gligor, D. Westhoff (Eds.), Security and Privacy in Ad-Hoc and Sensor Networks. X, 193 pages. 2006.

Vol. 4355: J. Julliand, O. Kouchnarenko (Eds.), B 2007: Formal Specification and Development in B. XIII, 293 pages. 2006.

Vol. 4354: M. Hanus (Ed.), Practical Aspects of Declarative Languages. X, 335 pages. 2006.

Vol. 4353: T. Schwentick, D. Suciu (Eds.), Database Theory – ICDT 2007. XI, 419 pages. 2006.

Vol. 4352: T.-J. Cham, J. Cai, C. Dorai, D. Rajan, T.-S. Chua, L.-T. Chia (Eds.), Advances in Multimedia Modeling, Part II. XVIII, 743 pages. 2006.

Vol. 4351: T.-J. Cham, J. Cai, C. Dorai, D. Rajan, T.-S. Chua, L.-T. Chia (Eds.), Advances in Multimedia Modeling, Part I. XIX, 797 pages. 2006.